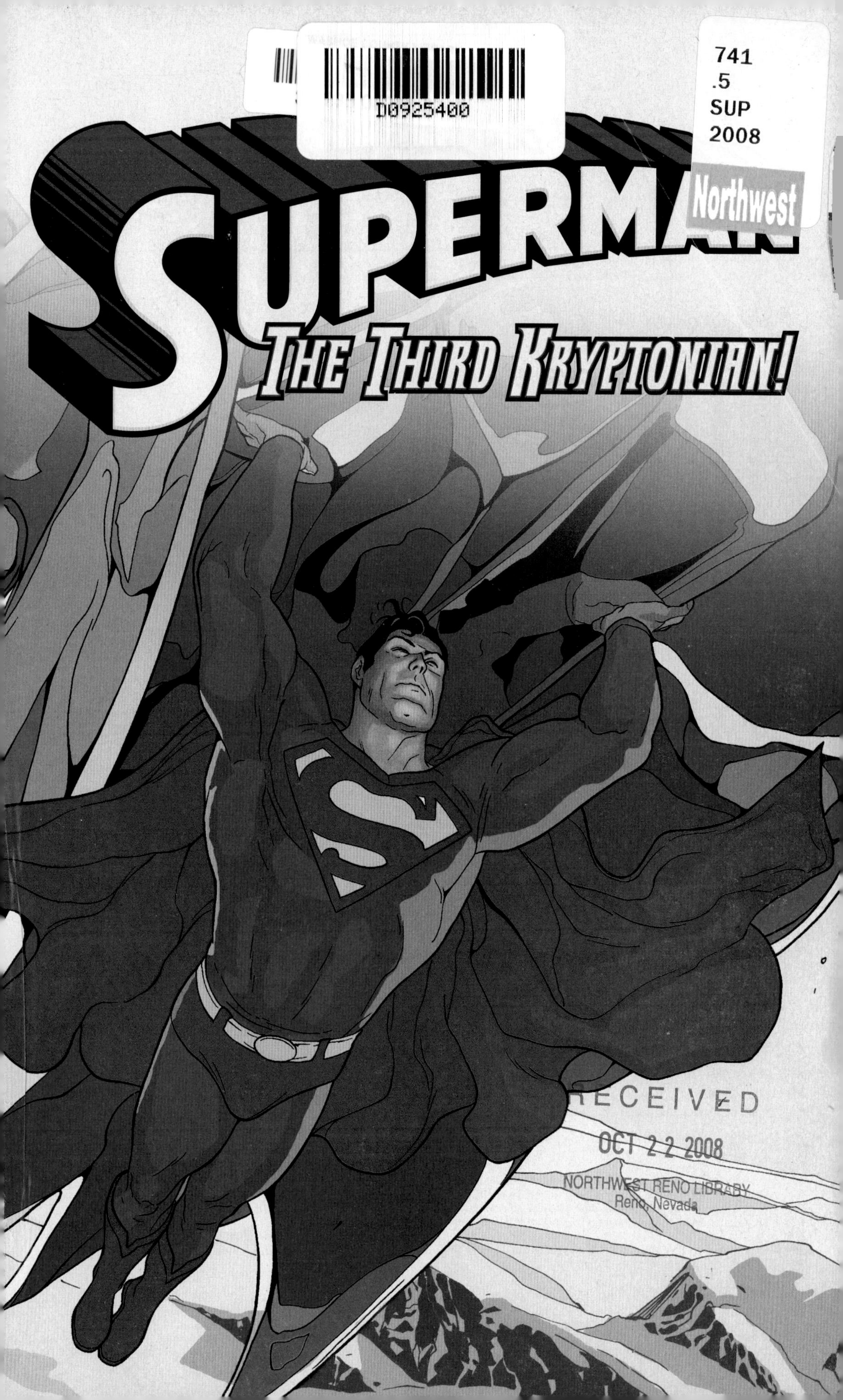
SUPERMAN
THE THIRD KRYPTONIAN!

Dan DiDio *Senior VP-Executive Editor*

Matt Idelson *Editor-original series*

Nachie Castro *Associate Editor-original series*

Bob Harras *Editor-collected edition*

Robbin Brosterman *Senior Art Director*

Paul Levitz *President & Publisher*

Georg Brewer *VP-Design & DC Direct Creative*

Richard Bruning *Senior VP-Creative Director*

Patrick Caldon *Executive VP-Finance & Operations*

Chris Caramalis *VP-Finance*

John Cunningham *VP-Marketing*

Terri Cunningham *VP-Managing Editor*

Alison Gill *VP-Manufacturing*

David Hyde *VP-Publicity*

Hank Kanalz *VP-General Manager, WildStorm*

Jim Lee *Editorial Director-WildStorm*

Paula Lowitt *Senior VP-Business & Legal Affairs*

MaryEllen McLaughlin *VP-Advertising & Custom Publishing*

John Nee *Senior VP-Business Development*

Gregory Noveck *Senior VP-Creative Affairs*

Sue Pohja *VP-Book Trade Sales*

Steve Rotterdam *Senior VP-Sales & Marketing*

Cheryl Rubin *Senior VP-Brand Management*

Jeff Trojan *VP-Business Development, DC Direct*

Bob Wayne *VP-Sales*

Cover by Renato Guedes
Publication design by Joseph DiStefano

SUPERMAN: THE THIRD KRYPTONIAN

Published by DC Comics. Cover and compilation Copyright © 2008 DC Comics. All Rights Reserved.

Originally published in single magazine form in ACTION COMICS 847, SUPERMAN 668-670, and SUPERMAN ANNUAL 13. Copyright © 2007, 2008 DC Comics. All Rights Reserved. All characters, their distinctive likenesses and related elements featured in this publication are trademarks of DC Comics. The stories, characters and incidents featured in this publication are entirely fictional. DC Comics does not read or accept unsolicited submissions of ideas, stories or artwork.

DC Comics, 1700 Broadway, New York, NY 10019
A Warner Bros. Entertainment Company
Printed in Canada. First Printing.
ISBN: 978-1-4012-1987-1

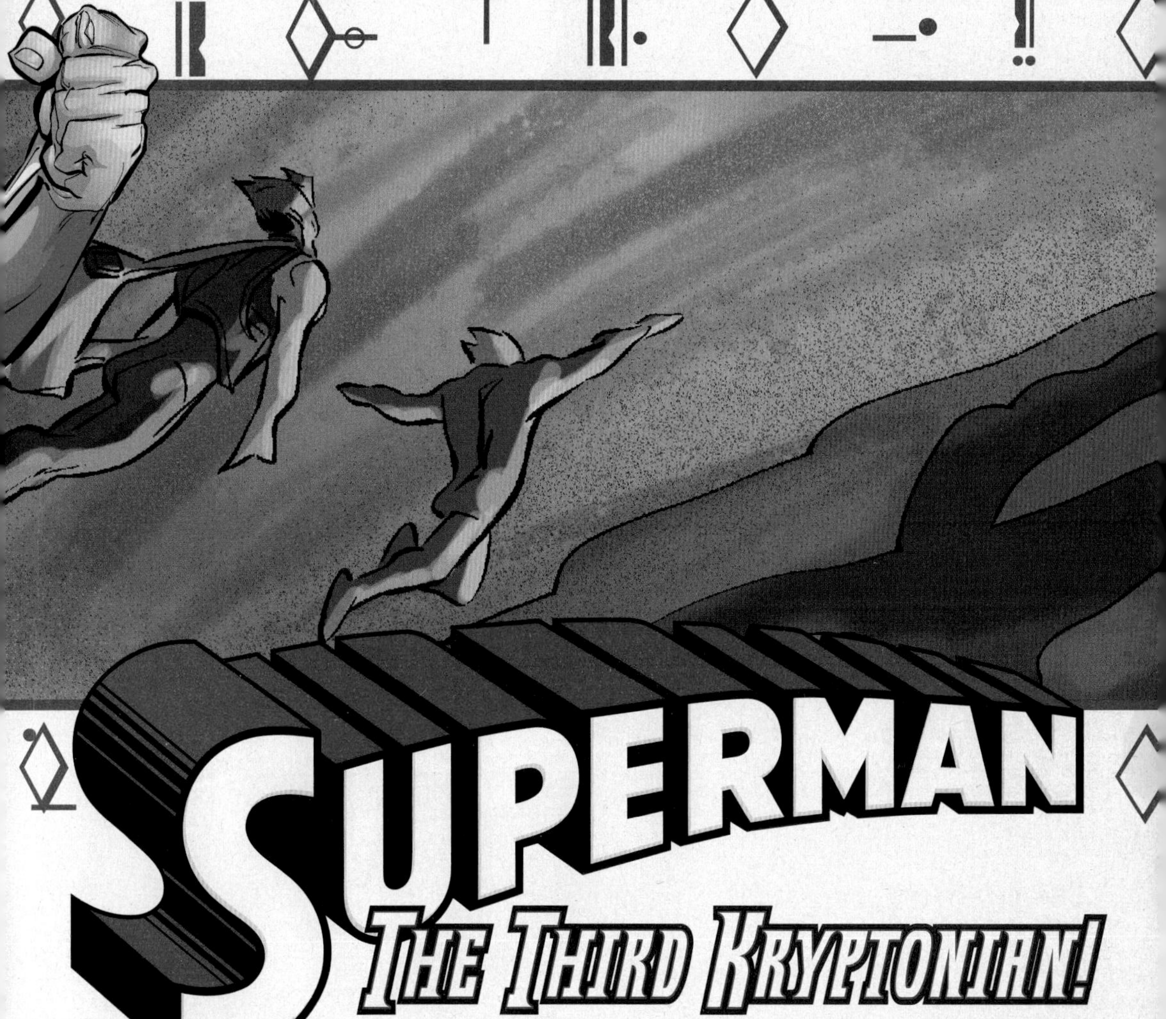

SUPERMAN
THE THIRD KRYPTONIAN!

THE THIRD KRYPTONIAN

KURT BUSIEK writer

RICK LEONARDI penciller

DAN GREEN
with **RICK LEONARDI** inkers

COMICRAFT lettering

ALEX SINCLAIR
PETE PANTAZIS colors

THE BEST DAY

KURT BUSIEK script & co-plot

FABIAN NICIEZA co-plot

RENATO GUEDES pencils & color

JOSÉ WILSON MAGALHÃES inker

PAT BROSSEAU lettering

INTERMEZZO

DWAYNE MCDUFFIE writer

RENATO GUEDES art & color

TRAVIS LANHAM lettering

Superman created by Jerry Siegel and Joe Shuster

Cover art by Renatos Guedes. Cover color by Brad Anderson.

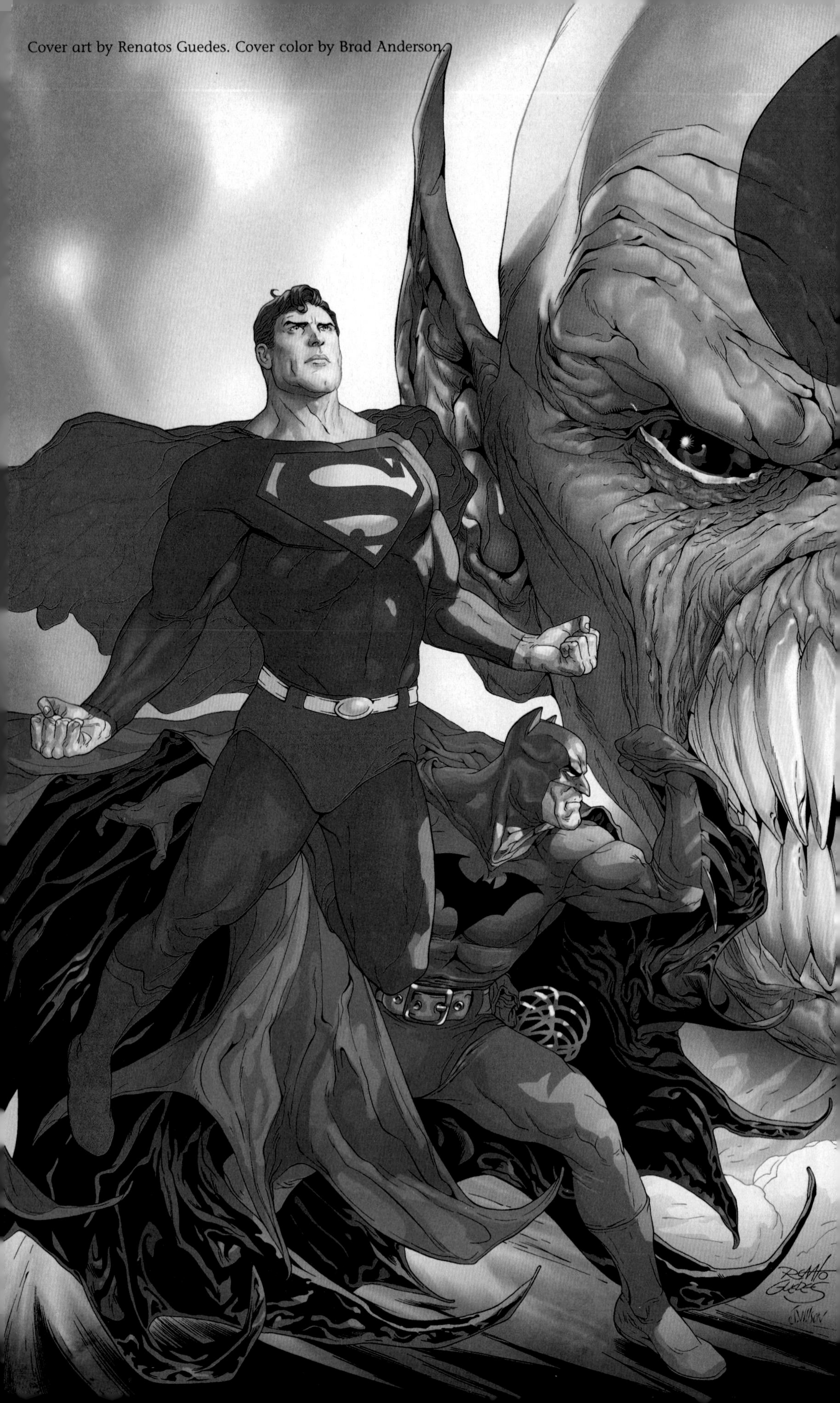

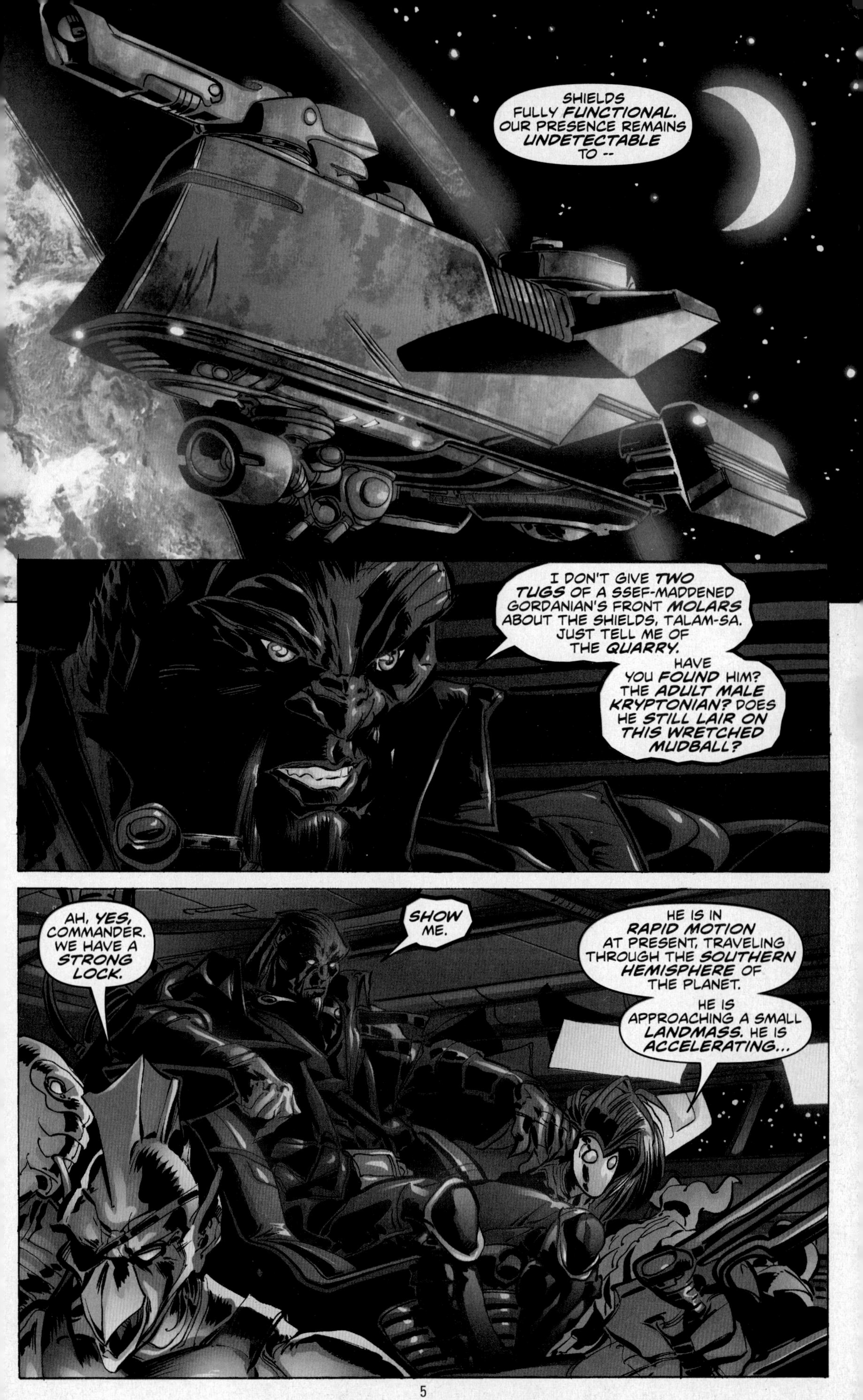
SHIELDS FULLY FUNCTIONAL. OUR PRESENCE REMAINS UNDETECTABLE TO --
I DON'T GIVE TWO TUGS OF A SSEF-MADDENED GORDANIAN'S FRONT MOLARS ABOUT THE SHIELDS, TALAM-SA. JUST TELL ME OF THE QUARRY.
HAVE YOU FOUND HIM? THE ADULT MALE KRYPTONIAN? DOES HE STILL LAIR ON THIS WRETCHED MUDBALL?
AH, YES, COMMANDER. WE HAVE A STRONG LOCK.
SHOW ME.
HE IS IN RAPID MOTION AT PRESENT, TRAVELING THROUGH THE SOUTHERN HEMISPHERE OF THE PLANET.
HE IS APPROACHING A SMALL LANDMASS. HE IS ACCELERATING...

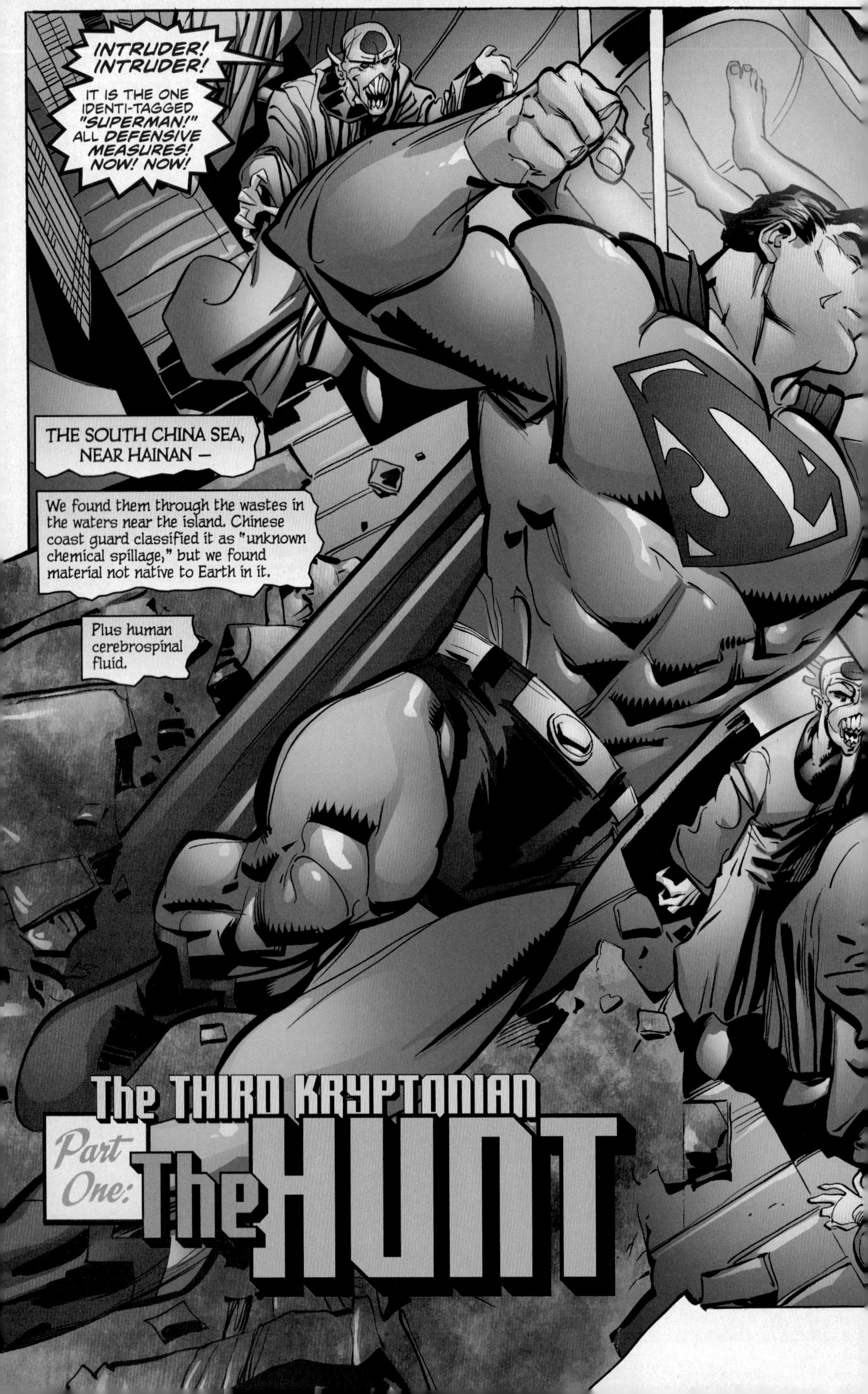
INTRUDER! INTRUDER!
IT IS THE ONE IDENTI-TAGGED "SUPERMAN!" ALL DEFENSIVE MEASURES! NOW! NOW!
THE SOUTH CHINA SEA, NEAR HAINAN —
We found them through the wastes in the waters near the island. Chinese coast guard classified it as "unknown chemical spillage," but we found material not native to Earth in it.
Plus human cerebrospinal fluid.
The THIRD KRYPTONIAN
Part One: The HUNT

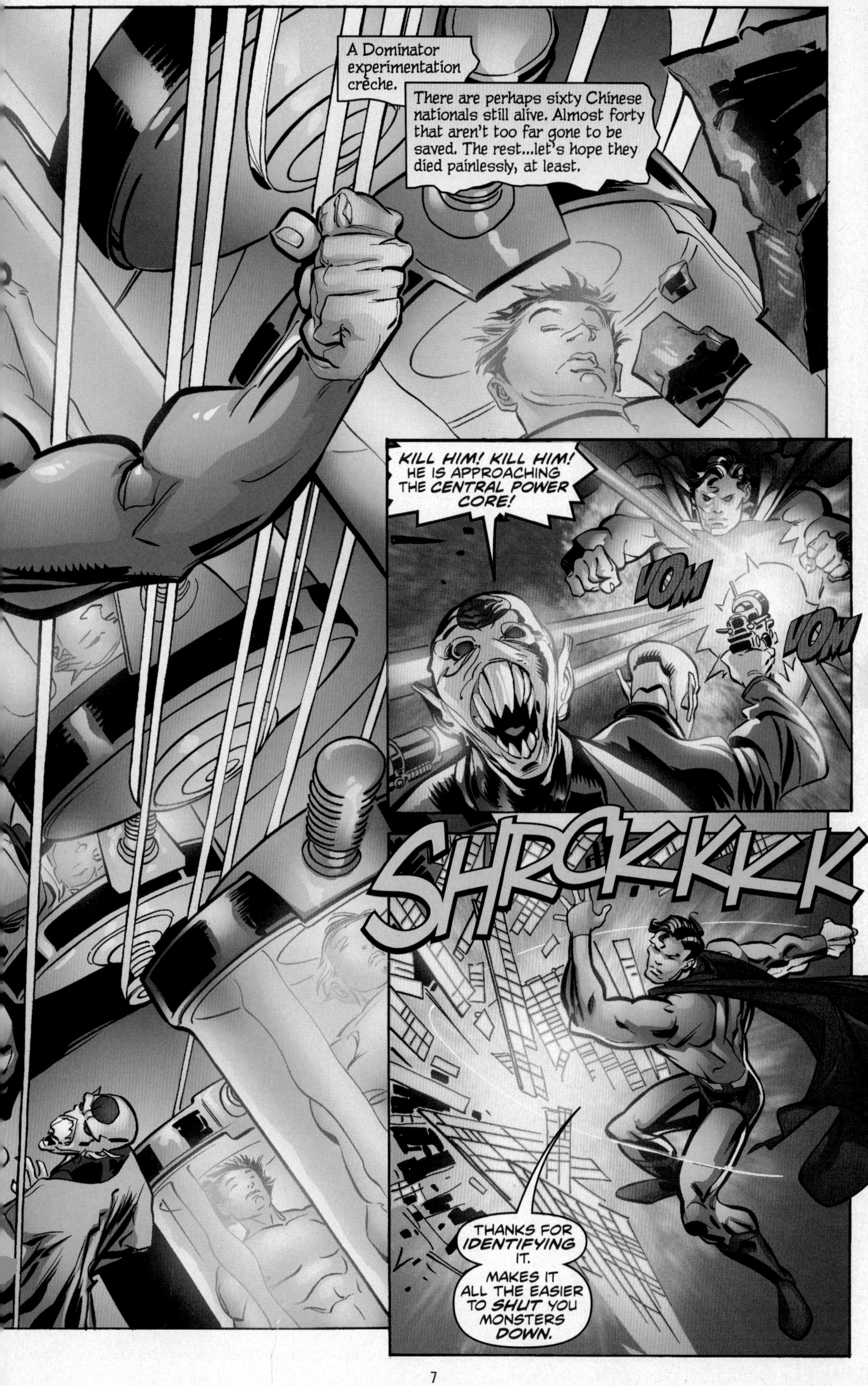
A Dominator experimentation crèche.
There are perhaps sixty Chinese nationals still alive. Almost forty that aren't too far gone to be saved. The rest...let's hope they died painlessly, at least.
KILL HIM! KILL HIM! HE IS APPROACHING THE CENTRAL POWER CORE!
VOM
VOM
SHRCKKKK
THANKS FOR IDENTIFYING IT.
MAKES IT ALL THE EASIER TO SHUT YOU MONSTERS DOWN.

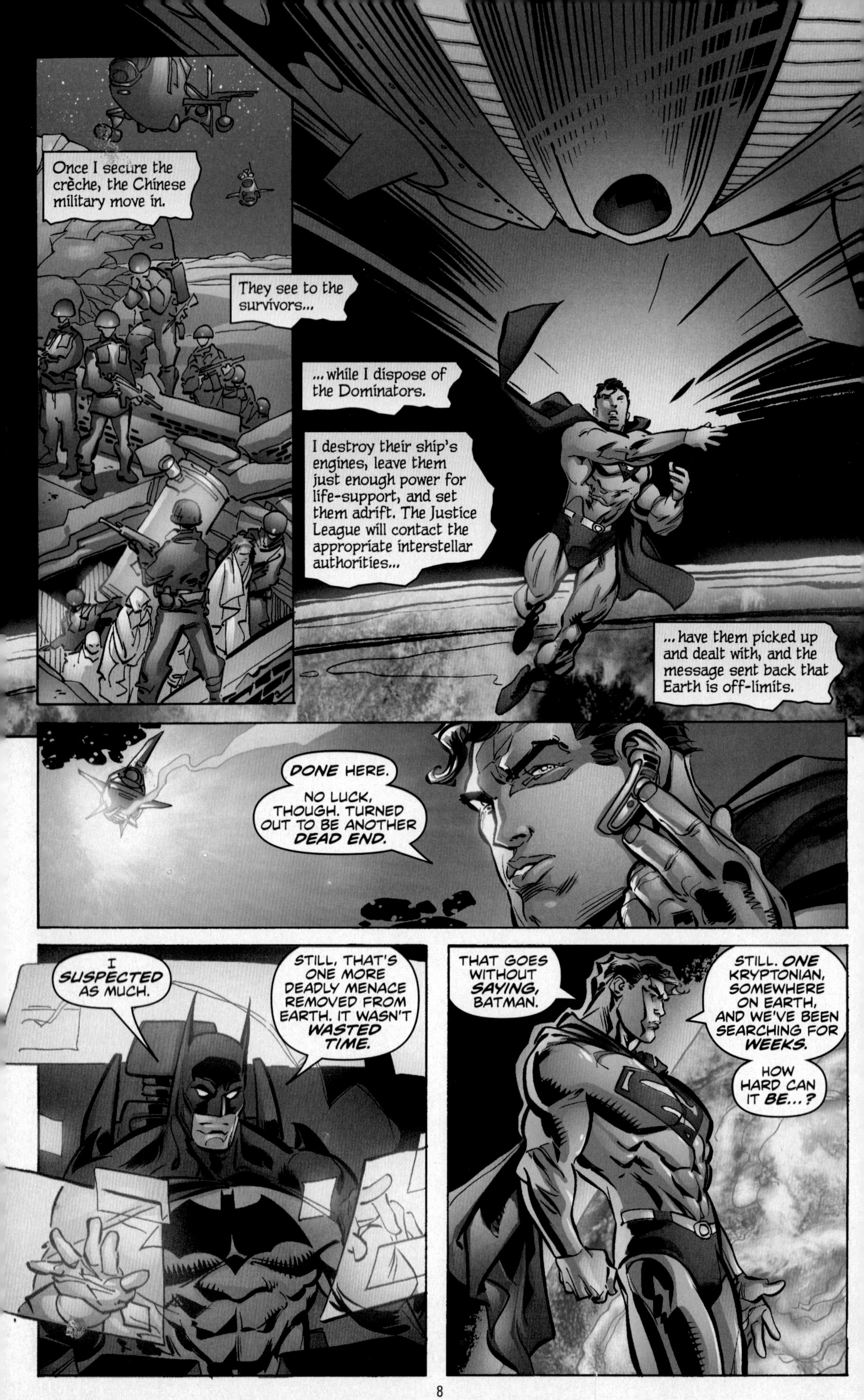
Once I secure the crèche, the Chinese military move in.
They see to the survivors...
...while I dispose of the Dominators.
I destroy their ship's engines, leave them just enough power for life-support, and set them adrift. The Justice League will contact the appropriate interstellar authorities...
...have them picked up and dealt with, and the message sent back that Earth is off-limits.
DONE HERE.
NO LUCK, THOUGH. TURNED OUT TO BE ANOTHER DEAD END.
I SUSPECTED AS MUCH.
STILL, THAT'S ONE MORE DEADLY MENACE REMOVED FROM EARTH. IT WASN'T WASTED TIME.
THAT GOES WITHOUT SAYING, BATMAN.
STILL. ONE KRYPTONIAN, SOMEWHERE ON EARTH, AND WE'VE BEEN SEARCHING FOR WEEKS.
HOW HARD CAN IT BE...?

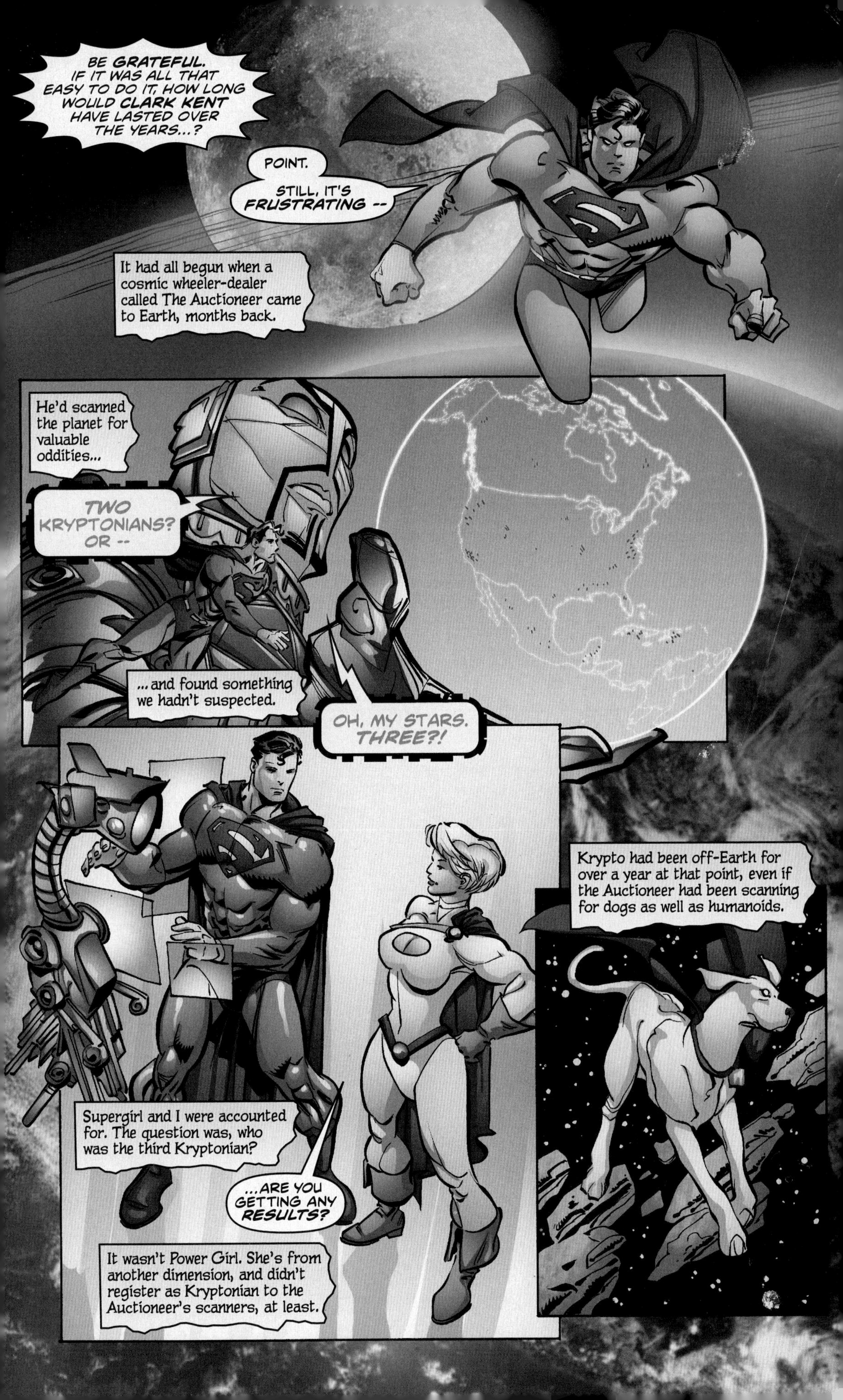
BE GRATEFUL. IF IT WAS ALL THAT EASY TO DO IT, HOW LONG WOULD CLARK KENT HAVE LASTED OVER THE YEARS...?
POINT.
STILL, IT'S FRUSTRATING --
It had all begun when a cosmic wheeler-dealer called The Auctioneer came to Earth, months back.
He'd scanned the planet for valuable oddities...
TWO KRYPTONIANS? OR --
...and found something we hadn't suspected.
OH, MY STARS. THREE?!
Supergirl and I were accounted for. The question was, who was the third Kryptonian?
...ARE YOU GETTING ANY RESULTS?
It wasn't Power Girl. She's from another dimension, and didn't register as Kryptonian to the Auctioneer's scanners, at least.
Krypto had been off-Earth for over a year at that point, even if the Auctioneer had been scanning for dogs as well as humanoids.

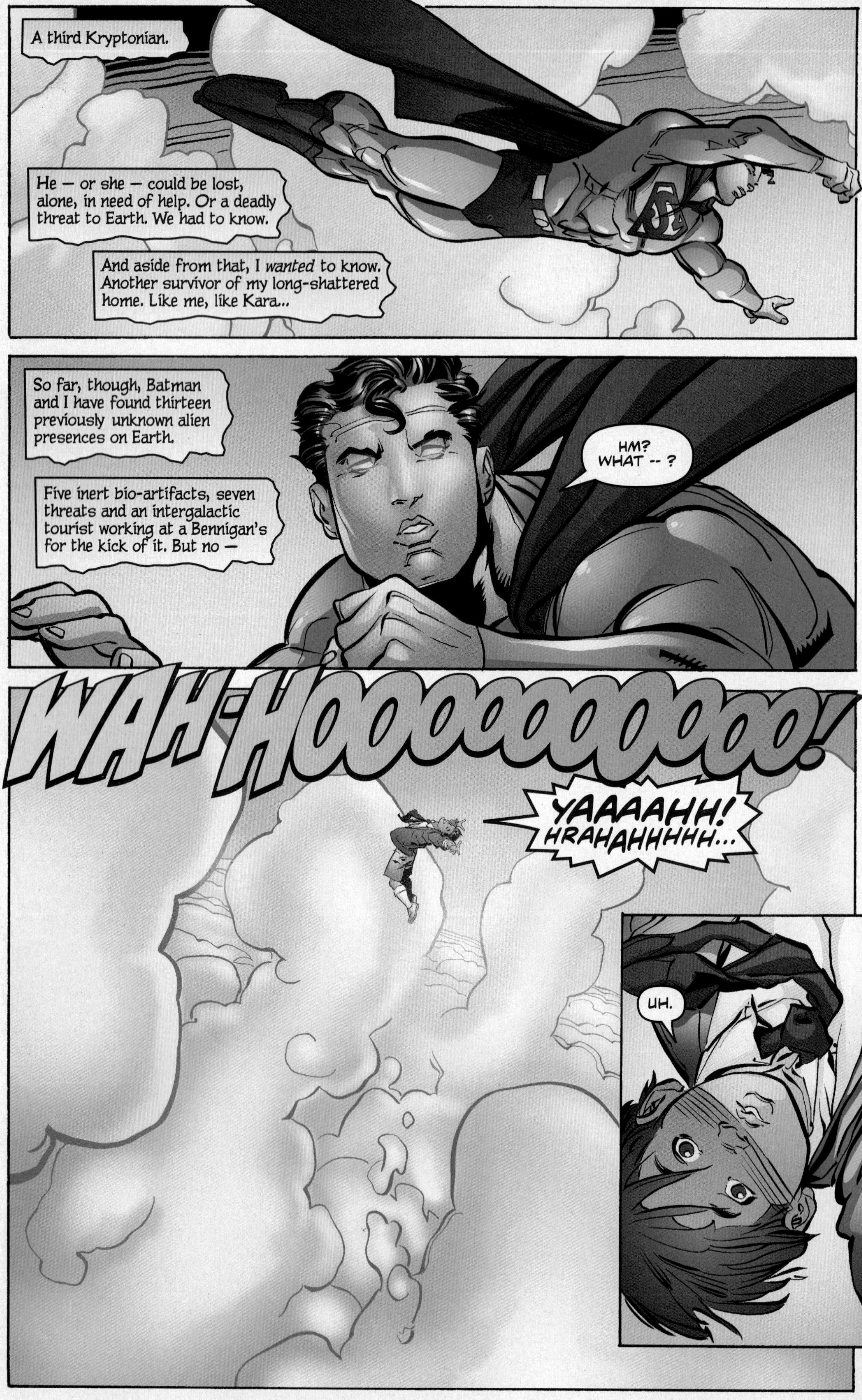
A third Kryptonian.
He — or she — could be lost, alone, in need of help. Or a deadly threat to Earth. We had to know.
And aside from that, I *wanted* to know. Another survivor of my long-shattered home. Like me, like Kara...
So far, though, Batman and I have found thirteen previously unknown alien presences on Earth.
Five inert bio-artifacts, seven threats and an intergalactic tourist working at a Bennigan's for the kick of it. But no —
HM? WHAT -- ?
WAH-HOOOOOOOOOO!
YAAAAHH! HRAHAHHHHH...
UH.

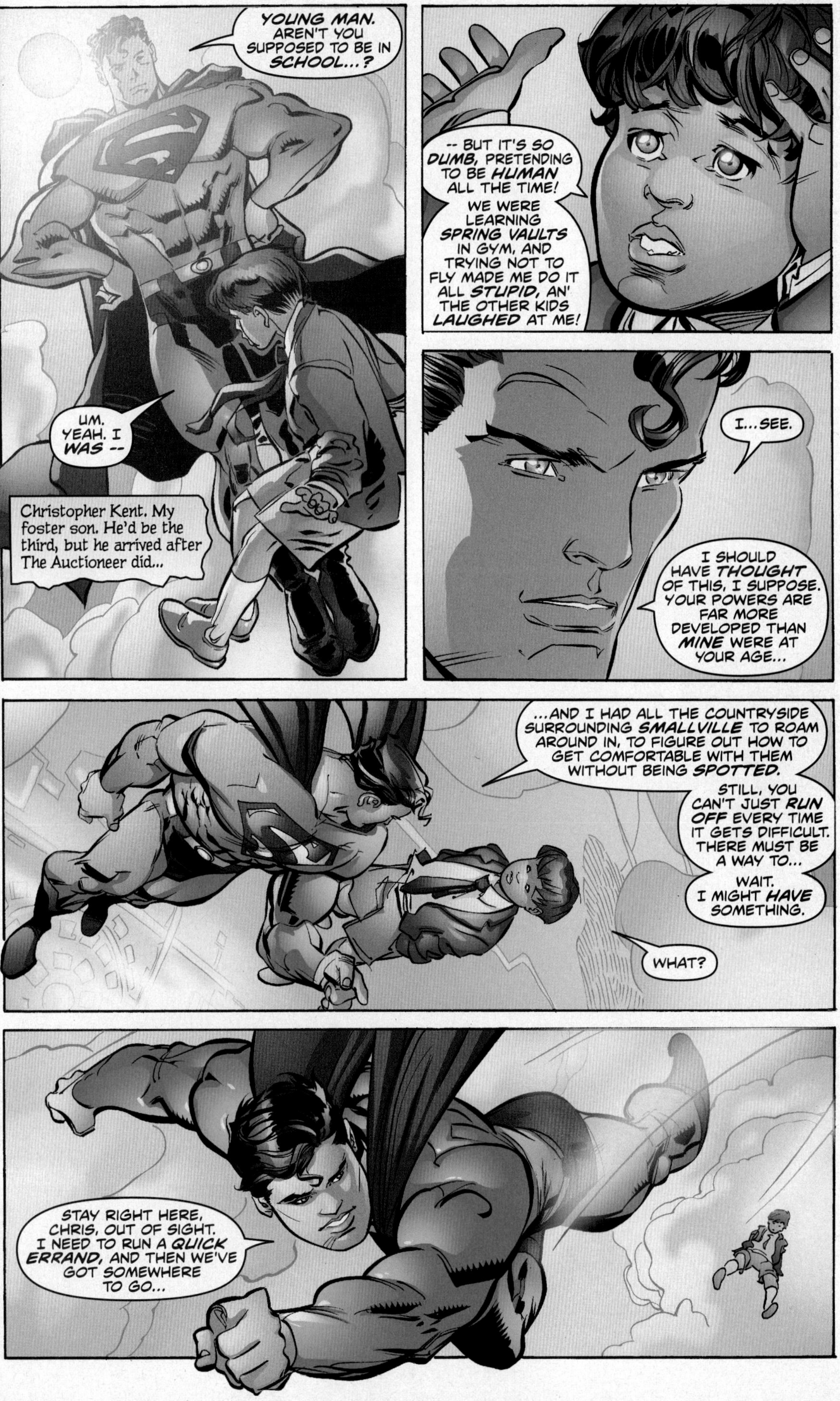
YOUNG MAN. AREN'T YOU SUPPOSED TO BE IN SCHOOL...?
UM. YEAH. I WAS --
Christopher Kent. My foster son. He'd be the third, but he arrived after The Auctioneer did...
-- BUT IT'S SO DUMB, PRETENDING TO BE HUMAN ALL THE TIME!
WE WERE LEARNING SPRING VAULTS IN GYM, AND TRYING NOT TO FLY MADE ME DO IT ALL STUPID, AN' THE OTHER KIDS LAUGHED AT ME!
I...SEE.
I SHOULD HAVE THOUGHT OF THIS, I SUPPOSE. YOUR POWERS ARE FAR MORE DEVELOPED THAN MINE WERE AT YOUR AGE...
...AND I HAD ALL THE COUNTRYSIDE SURROUNDING SMALLVILLE TO ROAM AROUND IN, TO FIGURE OUT HOW TO GET COMFORTABLE WITH THEM WITHOUT BEING SPOTTED.
STILL, YOU CAN'T JUST RUN OFF EVERY TIME IT GETS DIFFICULT. THERE MUST BE A WAY TO...
WAIT. I MIGHT HAVE SOMETHING.
WHAT?
STAY RIGHT HERE, CHRIS, OUT OF SIGHT. I NEED TO RUN A QUICK ERRAND, AND THEN WE'VE GOT SOMEWHERE TO GO...

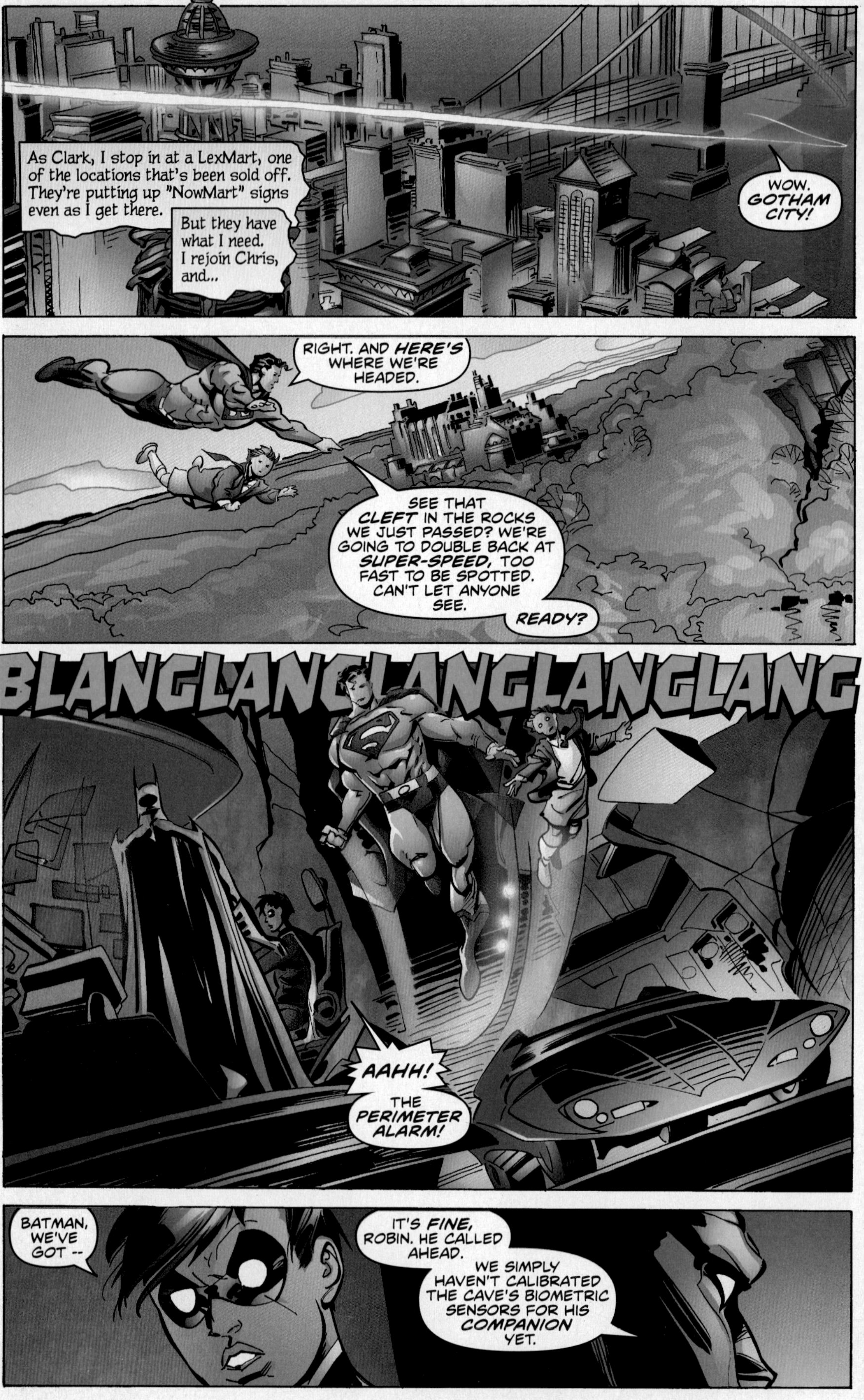
As Clark, I stop in at a LexMart, one of the locations that's been sold off. They're putting up "NowMart" signs even as I get there.
But they have what I need. I rejoin Chris, and...
WOW. GOTHAM CITY!
RIGHT. AND HERE'S WHERE WE'RE HEADED.
SEE THAT CLEFT IN THE ROCKS WE JUST PASSED? WE'RE GOING TO DOUBLE BACK AT SUPER-SPEED, TOO FAST TO BE SPOTTED. CAN'T LET ANYONE SEE.
READY?
BLANGLANGLANGLANGLANG
AAHH!
THE PERIMETER ALARM!
BATMAN, WE'VE GOT --
IT'S FINE, ROBIN. HE CALLED AHEAD.
WE SIMPLY HAVEN'T CALIBRATED THE CAVE'S BIOMETRIC SENSORS FOR HIS COMPANION YET.

WASHOE COUNTY
LIBRARY SYSTEM
www.washoecountylibrary.us

Sparks Library   1125 12th Street   352-3200
M,T,W,F 10-6, Th 10-7, Sat 10-5 CLOSED SUN

Items that you checked out

Title: Adventures of Superman.
ID: 31235037127797
Due: Saturday, May 25, 2019

Title: Adventures of Superman.
ID: 31235037343600
Due: Saturday, May 25, 2019

Title: Batman Li'l Gotham.
ID: 31235036925688
Due: Saturday, May 25, 2019

Title: Batman Li'l Gotham.
ID: 31235037199937
Due: Saturday, May 25, 2019

Title: Superman :
ID: 31235036294242
Due: Saturday, May 25, 2019

Title: The third Kryptonian! /
ID: 31235033133740
Due: Saturday, May 25, 2019

Total items: 6
Account balance: $0.00
5/4/2019 2:05 PM
Checked out: 21
Overdue: 0
Hold requests: 0
Ready for pickup: 0

SPRING BREAK BOREDOM BUSTER
STUFFED ANIMAL SLEEPOVER
Friday, March 29 @ 5pm
Renew online @ washoecountylibrary.us

LIBRARY SYSTEM
www.washoecountylibrary.us

Sparks Library   1125 12th Street   352-3200
M T W Th 10-9 Fr 10-7 Sat 10-5 CLOSED SUN

Items that you checked out

Title: The Adventures of Superman
ID: 31230637127797
Due: Saturday, May 25, 2019

Title: The Adventures of Superman
ID: 31230637343800
Due: Saturday, May 25, 2019

Title: Batman Lil Gotham
ID: 31230502902686
Due: Saturday, May 25, 2019

Title: Batman Lil Gotham
ID: 31230637139937
Due: Saturday, May 25, 2019

Title: Superman
ID: 31230635454242
Due: Saturday, May 25, 2019

Title: The third (Kryptonian)
ID: 31230633133740
Due: Saturday, May 25, 2019

Total items: 6
Account balance: $0.00
5/4/2019 2:05 PM
Checked out: 21
Overdue: 0
Hold requests: 0
Ready for pickup: 0

SPRING BREAK BOREDOM BUSTER
STUFFED ANIMAL SLEEPOVER
Friday March 29 @ 5pm
Renew online @ washoecountylibrary.us

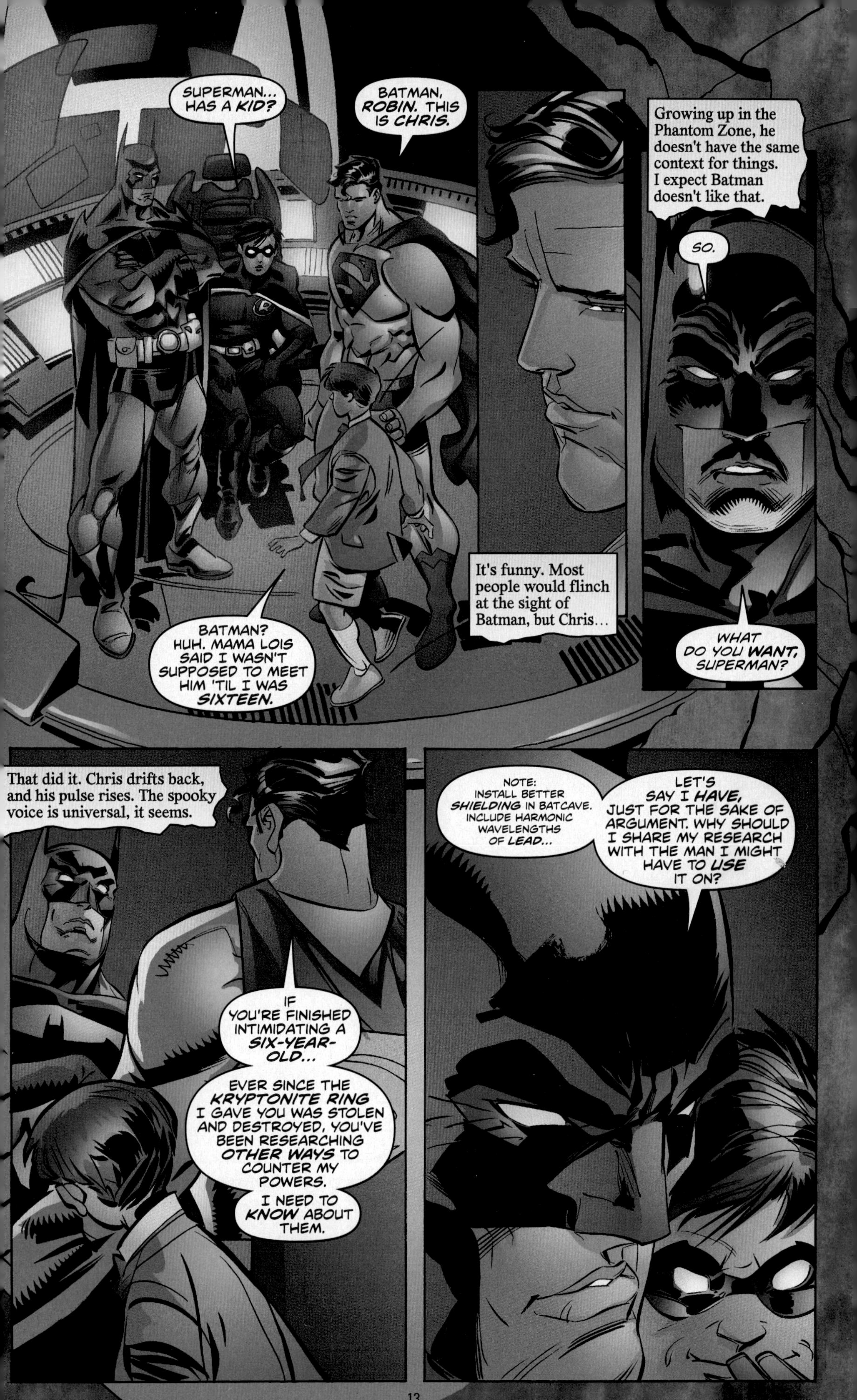
SUPERMAN... HAS A KID?
BATMAN, ROBIN. THIS IS CHRIS.
Growing up in the Phantom Zone, he doesn't have the same context for things. I expect Batman doesn't like that.
SO.
It's funny. Most people would flinch at the sight of Batman, but Chris...
BATMAN? HUH. MAMA LOIS SAID I WASN'T SUPPOSED TO MEET HIM 'TIL I WAS SIXTEEN.
WHAT DO YOU WANT, SUPERMAN?
That did it. Chris drifts back, and his pulse rises. The spooky voice is universal, it seems.
IF YOU'RE FINISHED INTIMIDATING A SIX-YEAR-OLD...
EVER SINCE THE KRYPTONITE RING I GAVE YOU WAS STOLEN AND DESTROYED, YOU'VE BEEN RESEARCHING OTHER WAYS TO COUNTER MY POWERS.
I NEED TO KNOW ABOUT THEM.
NOTE: INSTALL BETTER SHIELDING IN BATCAVE. INCLUDE HARMONIC WAVELENGTHS OF LEAD...
LET'S SAY I HAVE, JUST FOR THE SAKE OF ARGUMENT. WHY SHOULD I SHARE MY RESEARCH WITH THE MAN I MIGHT HAVE TO USE IT ON?

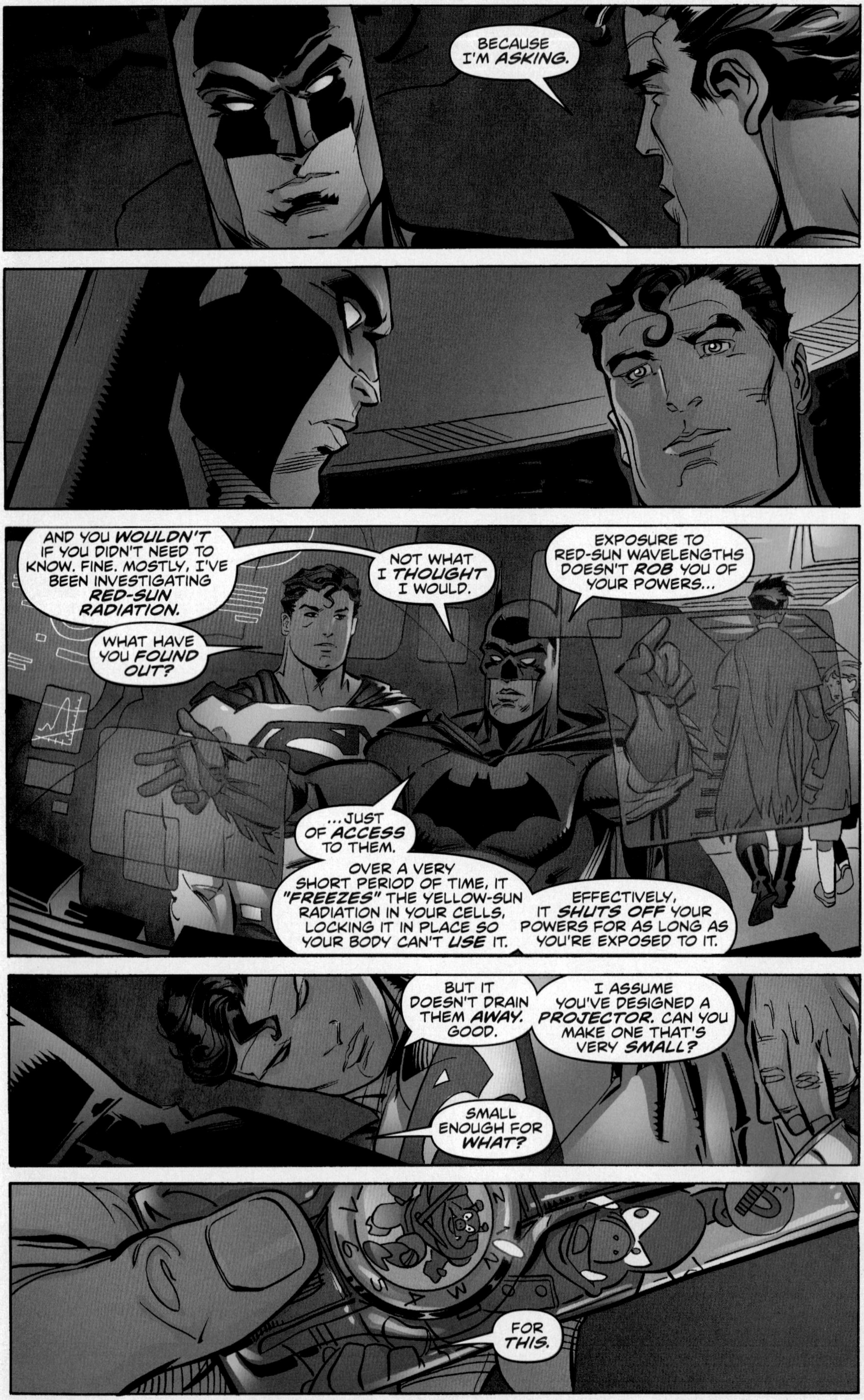
BECAUSE I'M ASKING.
AND YOU WOULDN'T IF YOU DIDN'T NEED TO KNOW. FINE. MOSTLY, I'VE BEEN INVESTIGATING RED-SUN RADIATION.
WHAT HAVE YOU FOUND OUT?
NOT WHAT I THOUGHT I WOULD.
EXPOSURE TO RED-SUN WAVELENGTHS DOESN'T ROB YOU OF YOUR POWERS...
...JUST OF ACCESS TO THEM.
OVER A VERY SHORT PERIOD OF TIME, IT "FREEZES" THE YELLOW-SUN RADIATION IN YOUR CELLS, LOCKING IT IN PLACE SO YOUR BODY CAN'T USE IT.
EFFECTIVELY, IT SHUTS OFF YOUR POWERS FOR AS LONG AS YOU'RE EXPOSED TO IT.
BUT IT DOESN'T DRAIN THEM AWAY. GOOD.
I ASSUME YOU'VE DESIGNED A PROJECTOR. CAN YOU MAKE ONE THAT'S VERY SMALL?
SMALL ENOUGH FOR WHAT?
FOR THIS.

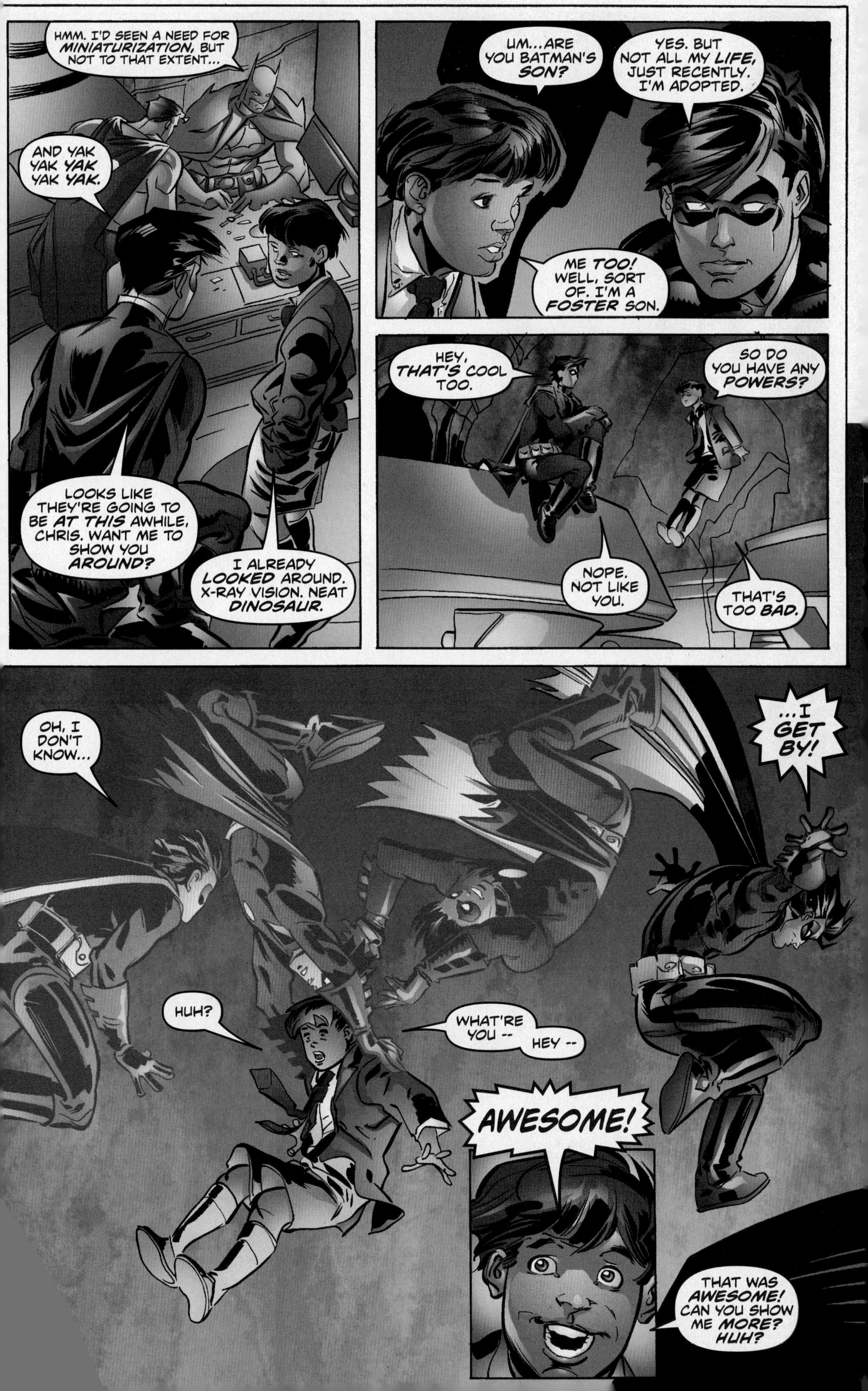
HMM. I'D SEEN A NEED FOR MINIATURIZATION, BUT NOT TO THAT EXTENT...
AND YAK YAK YAK YAK YAK.
LOOKS LIKE THEY'RE GOING TO BE AT THIS AWHILE, CHRIS. WANT ME TO SHOW YOU AROUND?
I ALREADY LOOKED AROUND. X-RAY VISION. NEAT DINOSAUR.
UM...ARE YOU BATMAN'S SON?
YES. BUT NOT ALL MY LIFE, JUST RECENTLY. I'M ADOPTED.
ME TOO! WELL, SORT OF. I'M A FOSTER SON.
HEY, THAT'S COOL TOO.
SO DO YOU HAVE ANY POWERS?
NOPE. NOT LIKE YOU.
THAT'S TOO BAD.
OH, I DON'T KNOW...
...I GET BY!
HUH?
WHAT'RE YOU --
HEY --
AWESOME!
THAT WAS AWESOME! CAN YOU SHOW ME MORE? HUH?

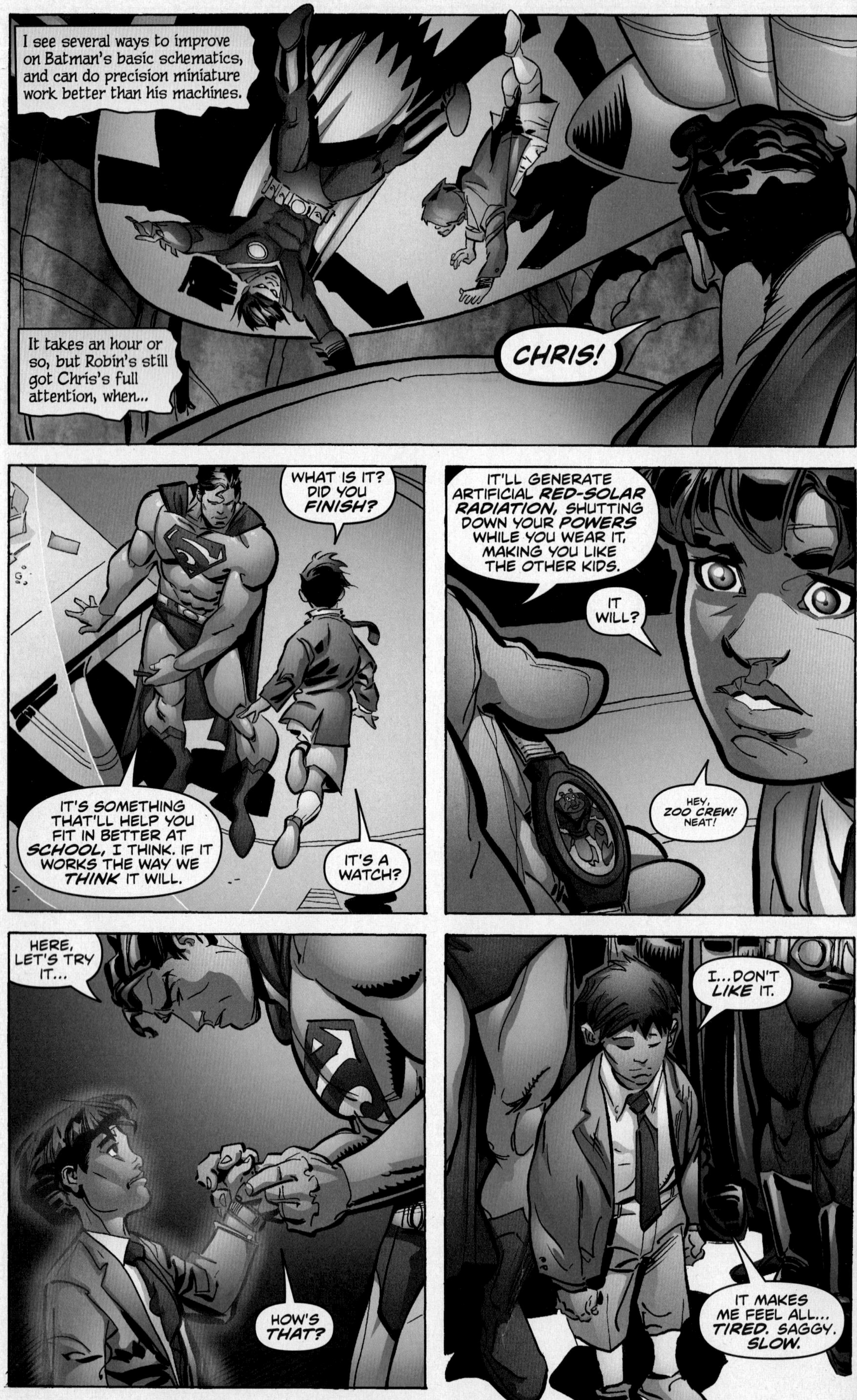
I see several ways to improve on Batman's basic schematics, and can do precision miniature work better than his machines.
It takes an hour or so, but Robin's still got Chris's full attention, when...
CHRIS!
WHAT IS IT? DID YOU FINISH?
IT'S SOMETHING THAT'LL HELP YOU FIT IN BETTER AT SCHOOL, I THINK. IF IT WORKS THE WAY WE THINK IT WILL.
IT'S A WATCH?
IT'LL GENERATE ARTIFICIAL RED-SOLAR RADIATION, SHUTTING DOWN YOUR POWERS WHILE YOU WEAR IT, MAKING YOU LIKE THE OTHER KIDS.
IT WILL?
HEY, ZOO CREW! NEAT!
HERE, LET'S TRY IT...
HOW'S THAT?
I...DON'T LIKE IT.
IT MAKES ME FEEL ALL... TIRED. SAGGY. SLOW.

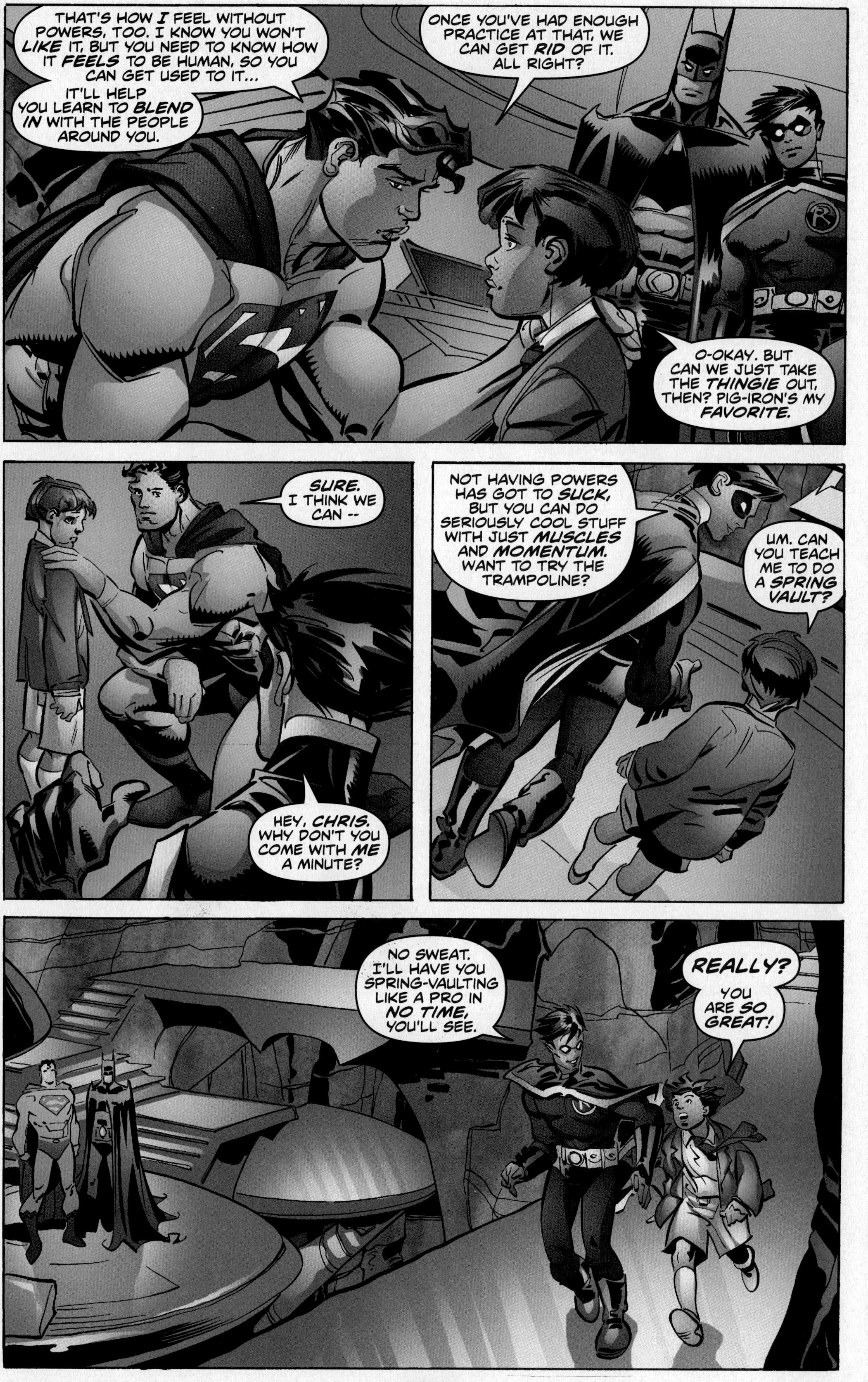
THAT'S HOW I FEEL WITHOUT POWERS, TOO. I KNOW YOU WON'T LIKE IT, BUT YOU NEED TO KNOW HOW IT FEELS TO BE HUMAN, SO YOU CAN GET USED TO IT...
IT'LL HELP YOU LEARN TO BLEND IN WITH THE PEOPLE AROUND YOU.
ONCE YOU'VE HAD ENOUGH PRACTICE AT THAT, WE CAN GET RID OF IT. ALL RIGHT?
O-OKAY. BUT CAN WE JUST TAKE THE THINGIE OUT, THEN? PIG-IRON'S MY FAVORITE.
SURE. I THINK WE CAN --
HEY, CHRIS. WHY DON'T YOU COME WITH ME A MINUTE?
NOT HAVING POWERS HAS GOT TO SUCK, BUT YOU CAN DO SERIOUSLY COOL STUFF WITH JUST MUSCLES AND MOMENTUM. WANT TO TRY THE TRAMPOLINE?
UM. CAN YOU TEACH ME TO DO A SPRING VAULT?
NO SWEAT. I'LL HAVE YOU SPRING-VAULTING LIKE A PRO IN NO TIME, YOU'LL SEE.
REALLY?
YOU ARE SO GREAT!

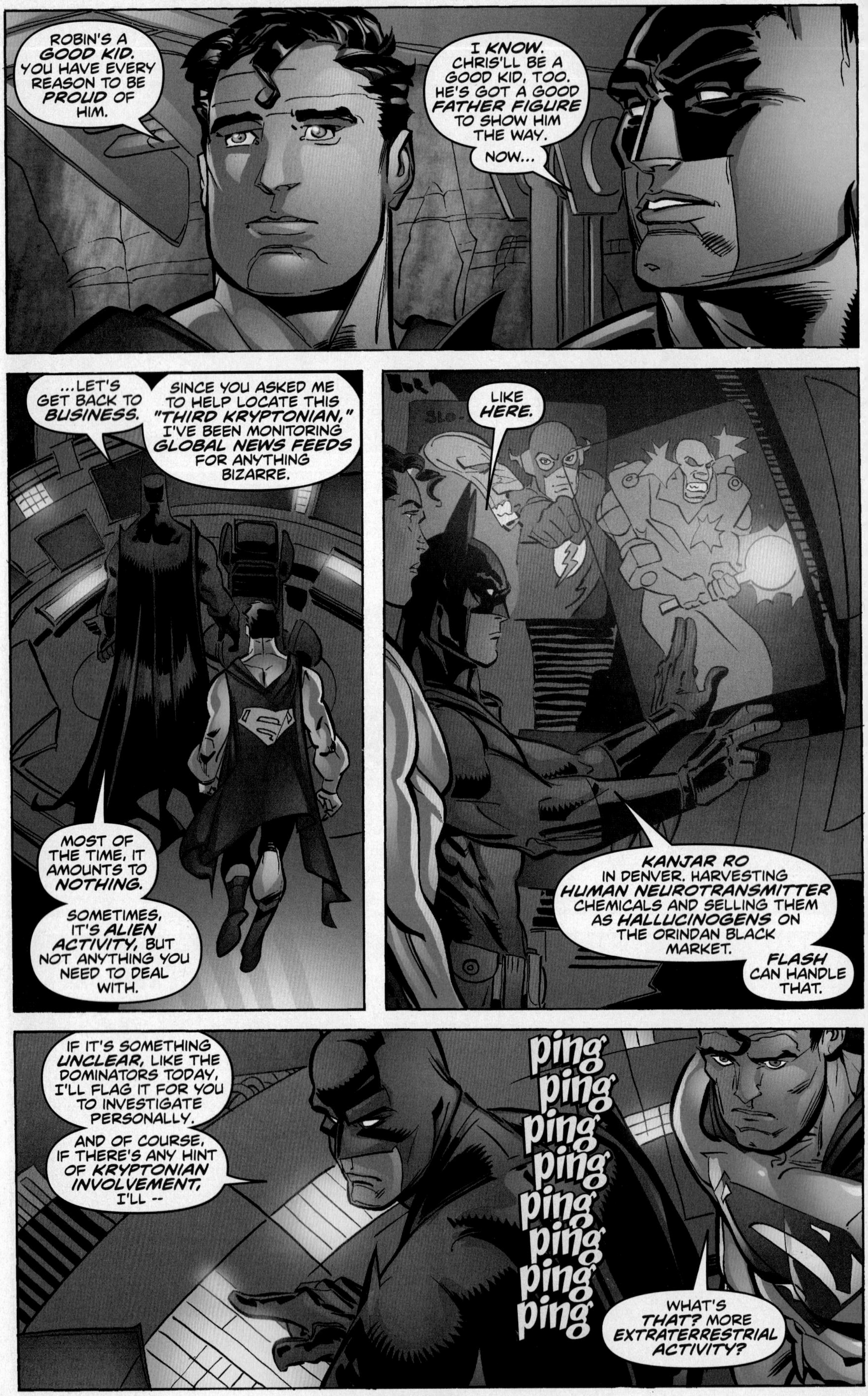
ROBIN'S A GOOD KID. YOU HAVE EVERY REASON TO BE PROUD OF HIM.
I KNOW. CHRIS'LL BE A GOOD KID, TOO. HE'S GOT A GOOD FATHER FIGURE TO SHOW HIM THE WAY.
NOW...
...LET'S GET BACK TO BUSINESS.
SINCE YOU ASKED ME TO HELP LOCATE THIS "THIRD KRYPTONIAN," I'VE BEEN MONITORING GLOBAL NEWS FEEDS FOR ANYTHING BIZARRE.
MOST OF THE TIME, IT AMOUNTS TO NOTHING.
SOMETIMES, IT'S ALIEN ACTIVITY, BUT NOT ANYTHING YOU NEED TO DEAL WITH.
LIKE HERE.
KANJAR RO IN DENVER. HARVESTING HUMAN NEUROTRANSMITTER CHEMICALS AND SELLING THEM AS HALLUCINOGENS ON THE ORINDAN BLACK MARKET.
FLASH CAN HANDLE THAT.
IF IT'S SOMETHING UNCLEAR, LIKE THE DOMINATORS TODAY, I'LL FLAG IT FOR YOU TO INVESTIGATE PERSONALLY.
AND OF COURSE, IF THERE'S ANY HINT OF KRYPTONIAN INVOLVEMENT, I'LL --
ping ping ping ping ping ping ping ping
WHAT'S THAT? MORE EXTRATERRESTRIAL ACTIVITY?

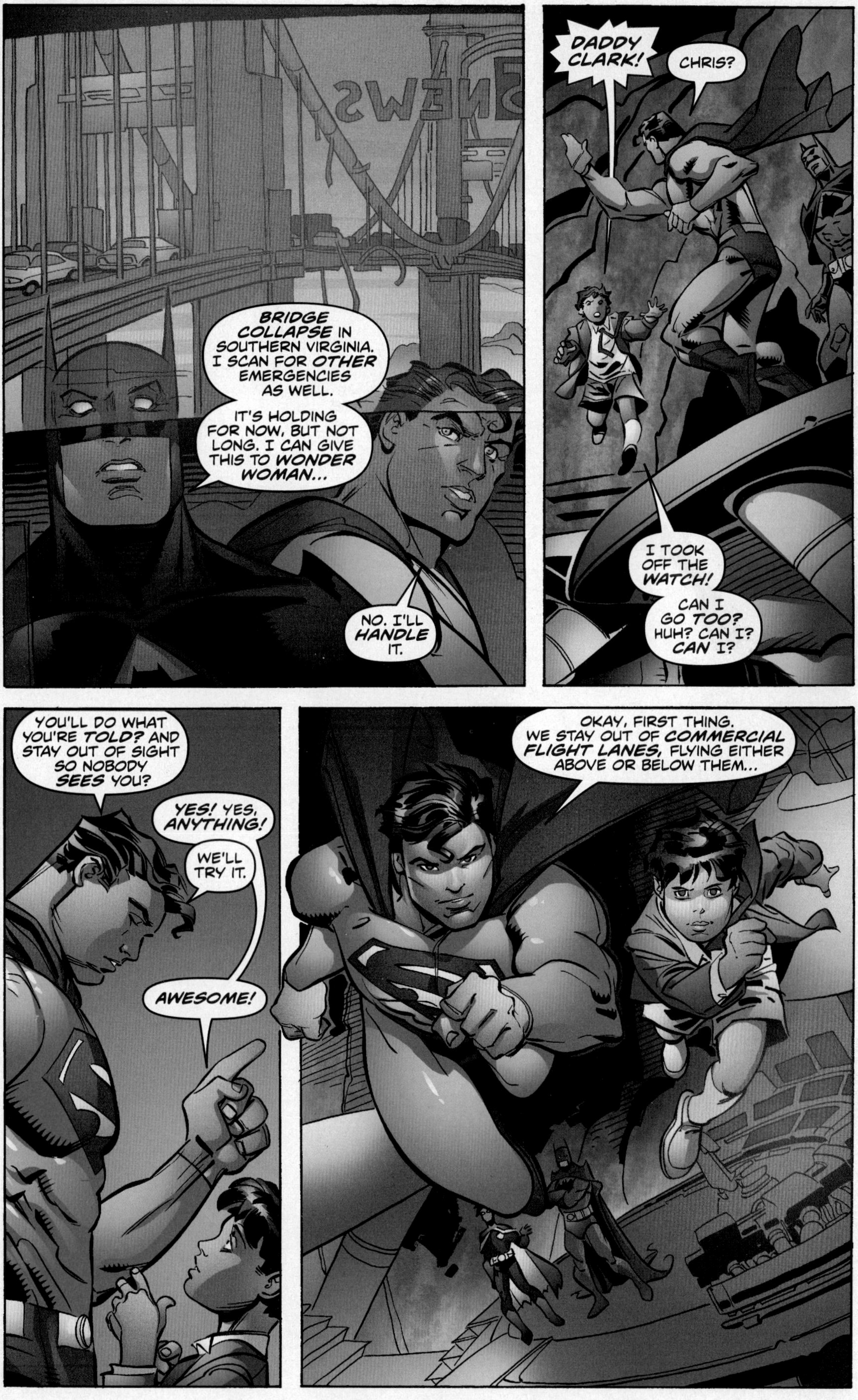
BRIDGE COLLAPSE IN SOUTHERN VIRGINIA. I SCAN FOR OTHER EMERGENCIES AS WELL.
IT'S HOLDING FOR NOW, BUT NOT LONG. I CAN GIVE THIS TO WONDER WOMAN...
NO. I'LL HANDLE IT.
DADDY CLARK!
CHRIS?
I TOOK OFF THE WATCH!
CAN I GO TOO? HUH? CAN I? CAN I?
YOU'LL DO WHAT YOU'RE TOLD? AND STAY OUT OF SIGHT SO NOBODY SEES YOU?
YES! YES, ANYTHING!
WE'LL TRY IT.
AWESOME!
OKAY, FIRST THING. WE STAY OUT OF COMMERCIAL FLIGHT LANES, FLYING EITHER ABOVE OR BELOW THEM...

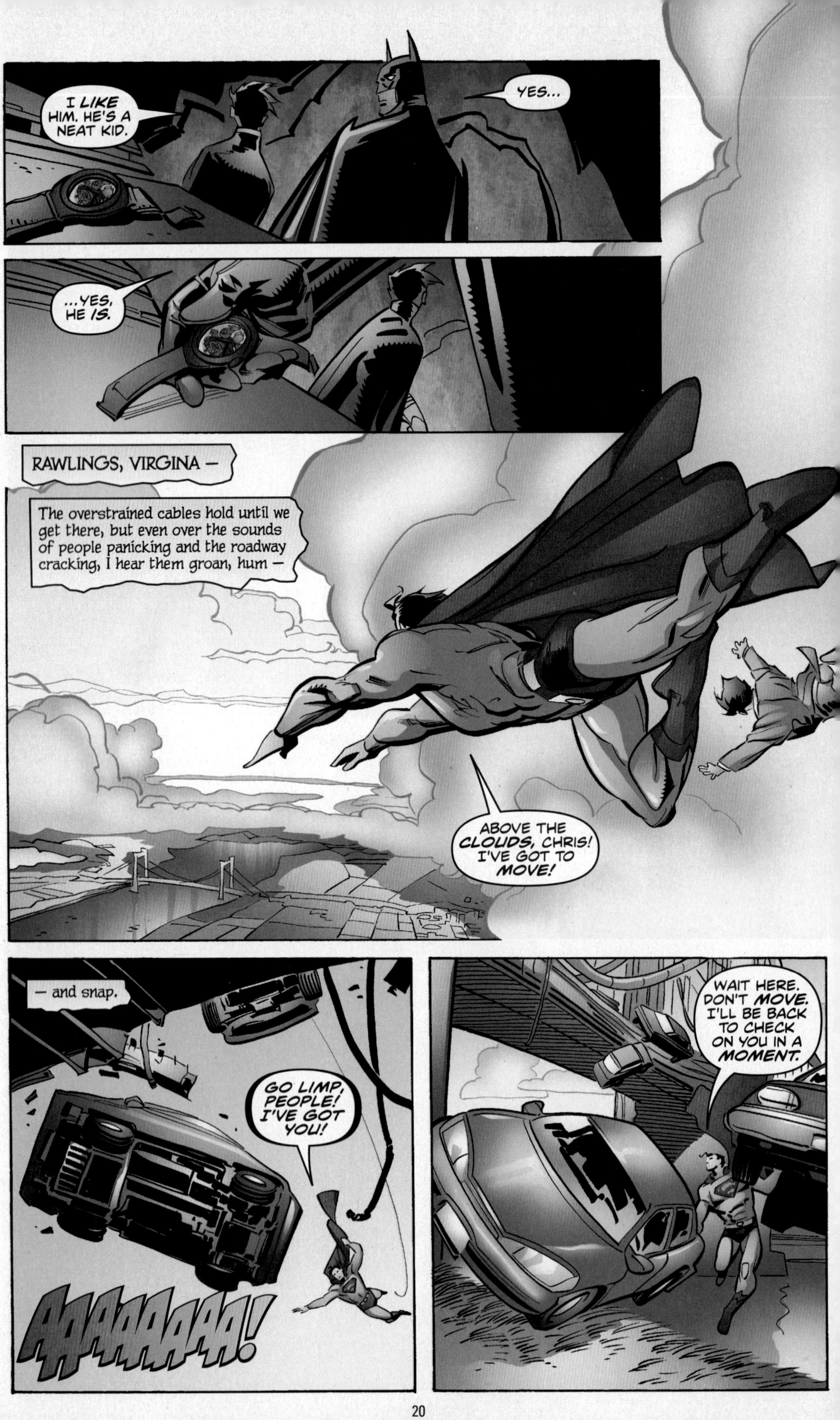
I LIKE HIM. HE'S A NEAT KID.
YES...
...YES, HE IS.
RAWLINGS, VIRGINA —
The overstrained cables hold until we get there, but even over the sounds of people panicking and the roadway cracking, I hear them groan, hum —
ABOVE THE CLOUDS, CHRIS! I'VE GOT TO MOVE!
— and snap.
GO LIMP, PEOPLE! I'VE GOT YOU!
AAAAAAAA!
WAIT HERE. DON'T MOVE. I'LL BE BACK TO CHECK ON YOU IN A MOMENT.

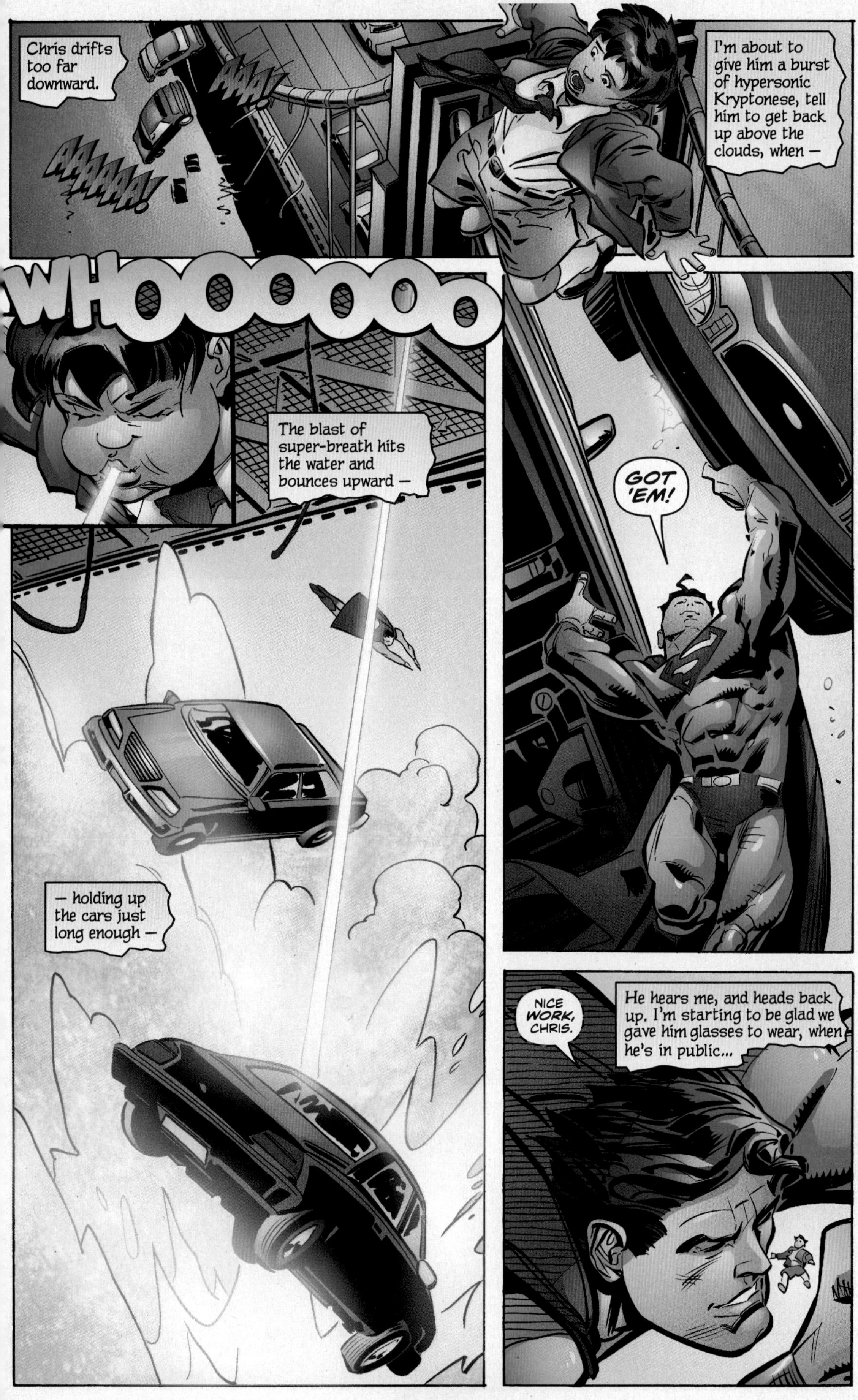

Chris drifts too far downward.
AAA!
AAAAAA!
I'm about to give him a burst of hypersonic Kryptonese, tell him to get back up above the clouds, when —
WHOOOOOO
The blast of super-breath hits the water and bounces upward —
GOT 'EM!
— holding up the cars just long enough —
NICE WORK, CHRIS.
He hears me, and heads back up. I'm starting to be glad we gave him glasses to wear, when he's in public...

A BOY.

THE INDIGENOUS MEDIA ACCOUNTS DO NOT CARRY *WORD* OF HIM.

NO. IT IS AN UNEXPECTED *TREASURE TROVE.* THE BOY, THE MAN, A GIRL, A *YOUNG WOMAN...*

WHY DO WE NOT *STRIKE,* COMMANDER? YOU CAME TO EARTH TO --

I CAME TO EARTH AFTER *SUPERMAN,* TALAM-SA.

WE PAID THE AUCTIONEER A *FORTUNE* FOR THE LOCATION OF THIS BACKWATER PLANET, AFTER HIS BROADCASTS REVEALED A *KRYPTONIAN* HERE.

BUT HE DID NOT SAY THERE WERE *MORE.*

A MAN, A BOY, A YOUNG WOMAN, A GIRL. AND AT LEAST *ONE OTHER,* WHOM THE MAN SEEKS *NOW.*

ONCE WE HAVE FOUND THEM *ALL,* WE STRIKE -- *CLEANSING* THIS PLANET OF *ALL LIFE,* IF NEED BE.

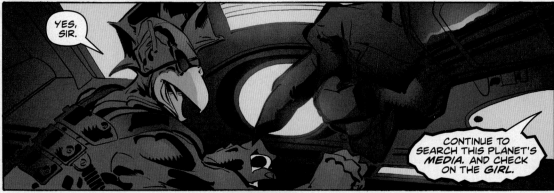

YES, SIR.

CONTINUE TO SEARCH THIS PLANET'S *MEDIA.* AND CHECK ON THE *GIRL.*

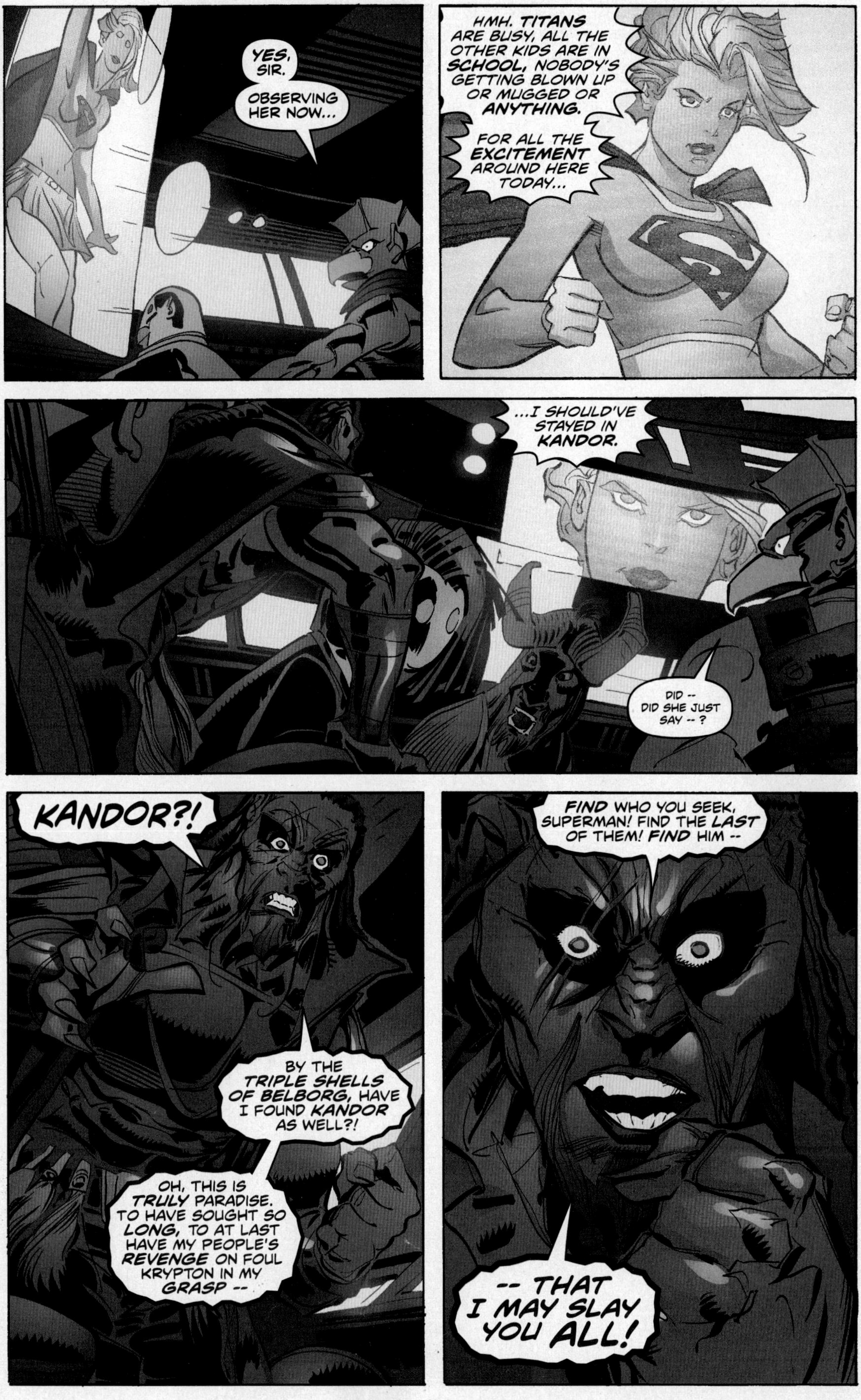
YES, SIR.
OBSERVING HER NOW...
HMH. TITANS ARE BUSY, ALL THE OTHER KIDS ARE IN SCHOOL, NOBODY'S GETTING BLOWN UP OR MUGGED OR ANYTHING.
FOR ALL THE EXCITEMENT AROUND HERE TODAY...
...I SHOULD'VE STAYED IN KANDOR.
DID -- DID SHE JUST SAY -- ?
KANDOR?!
BY THE TRIPLE SHELLS OF BELBORG, HAVE I FOUND KANDOR AS WELL?!
OH, THIS IS TRULY PARADISE. TO HAVE SOUGHT SO LONG, TO AT LAST HAVE MY PEOPLE'S REVENGE ON FOUL KRYPTON IN MY GRASP --
FIND WHO YOU SEEK, SUPERMAN! FIND THE LAST OF THEM! FIND HIM --
-- THAT I MAY SLAY YOU ALL!

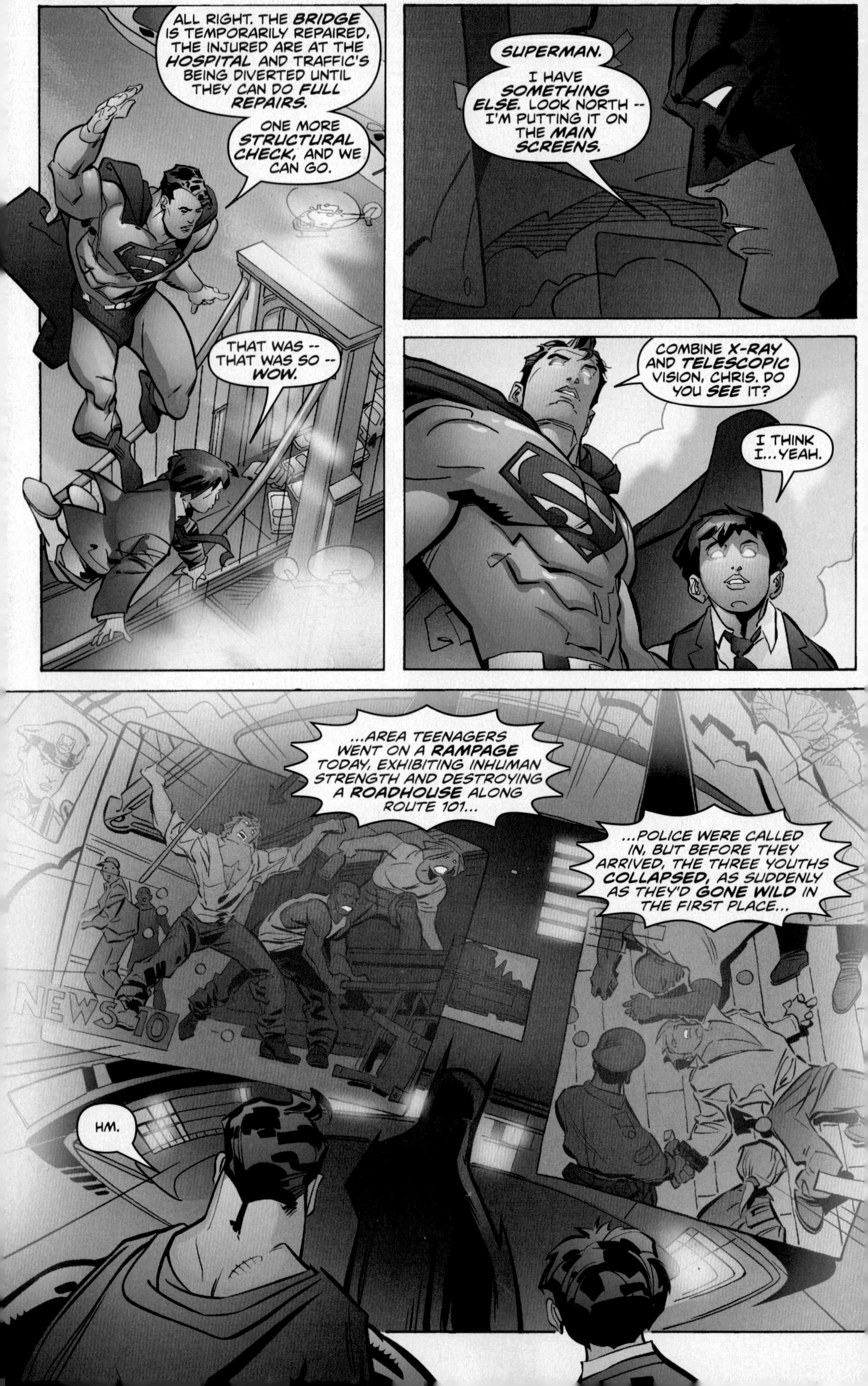
ALL RIGHT. THE BRIDGE IS TEMPORARILY REPAIRED, THE INJURED ARE AT THE HOSPITAL AND TRAFFIC'S BEING DIVERTED UNTIL THEY CAN DO FULL REPAIRS.
ONE MORE STRUCTURAL CHECK, AND WE CAN GO.
THAT WAS -- THAT WAS SO -- WOW.
SUPERMAN.
I HAVE SOMETHING ELSE. LOOK NORTH -- I'M PUTTING IT ON THE MAIN SCREENS.
COMBINE X-RAY AND TELESCOPIC VISION, CHRIS. DO YOU SEE IT?
I THINK I...YEAH.
...AREA TEENAGERS WENT ON A RAMPAGE TODAY, EXHIBITING INHUMAN STRENGTH AND DESTROYING A ROADHOUSE ALONG ROUTE 101...
...POLICE WERE CALLED IN, BUT BEFORE THEY ARRIVED, THE THREE YOUTHS COLLAPSED, AS SUDDENLY AS THEY'D GONE WILD IN THE FIRST PLACE...
NEWS 10
HM.

MEDICAL PERSONNEL ARE AT A LOSS TO EXPLAIN THE *WILD AGGRESSION,* OR THE *PRETERNATURAL ABILITIES...*

THIS HAPPENED *LAST NIGHT.*

THE PERPS WERE HIGH ON SOMETHING THEY *SMOKED.* I SECURED A COPY OF THE *TOXICOLOGY REPORT,* AND FOUND *THESE* MOLECULAR COMPOUNDS.

I SEE THEM. WHAT'S THE *SIGNIFICANCE?*

THEY'RE NOTHING *TERRESTRIAL.* BUT LOOK AT THE BLUE PARTS OF YOUR UNIFORM. LOOK AT THE MAKEUP OF THE *DYE.*

HUH?

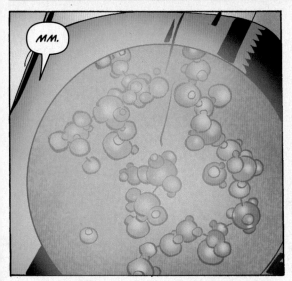

MM.

YOU REALLY *HAVE* BEEN STUDYING ME, HAVEN'T YOU?

I SEE THE *SIMILARITY.*

SO WHATEVER THESE KIDS GOT AHOLD OF, IT'S *KRYPTONIAN?*

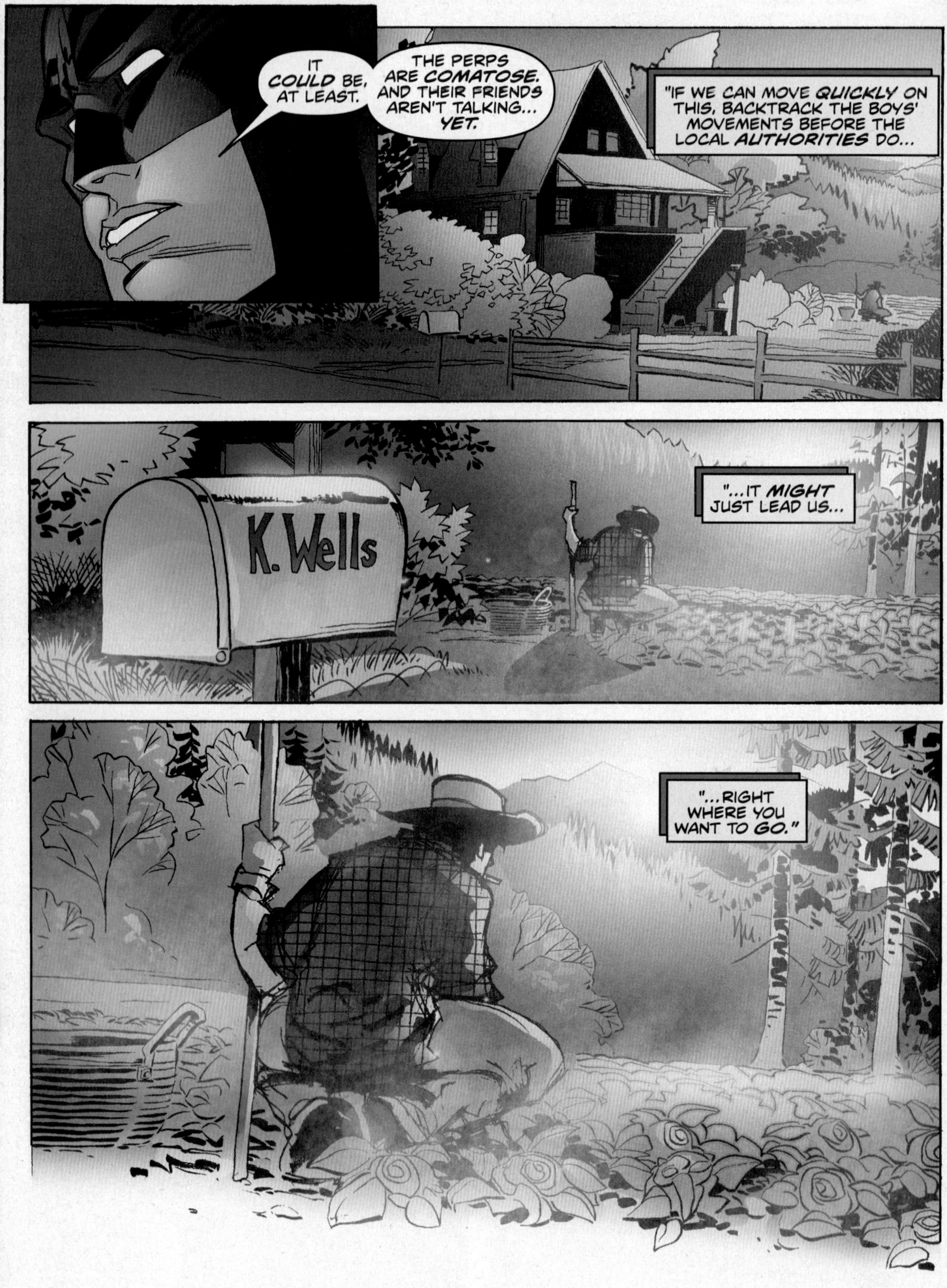
IT COULD BE, AT LEAST.
THE PERPS ARE COMATOSE. AND THEIR FRIENDS AREN'T TALKING... YET.
"IF WE CAN MOVE QUICKLY ON THIS, BACKTRACK THE BOYS' MOVEMENTS BEFORE THE LOCAL AUTHORITIES DO...
K. Wells
"...IT MIGHT JUST LEAD US...
"...RIGHT WHERE YOU WANT TO GO."

Cover art by Jesus Merino. Cover color by Alex Sinclair.

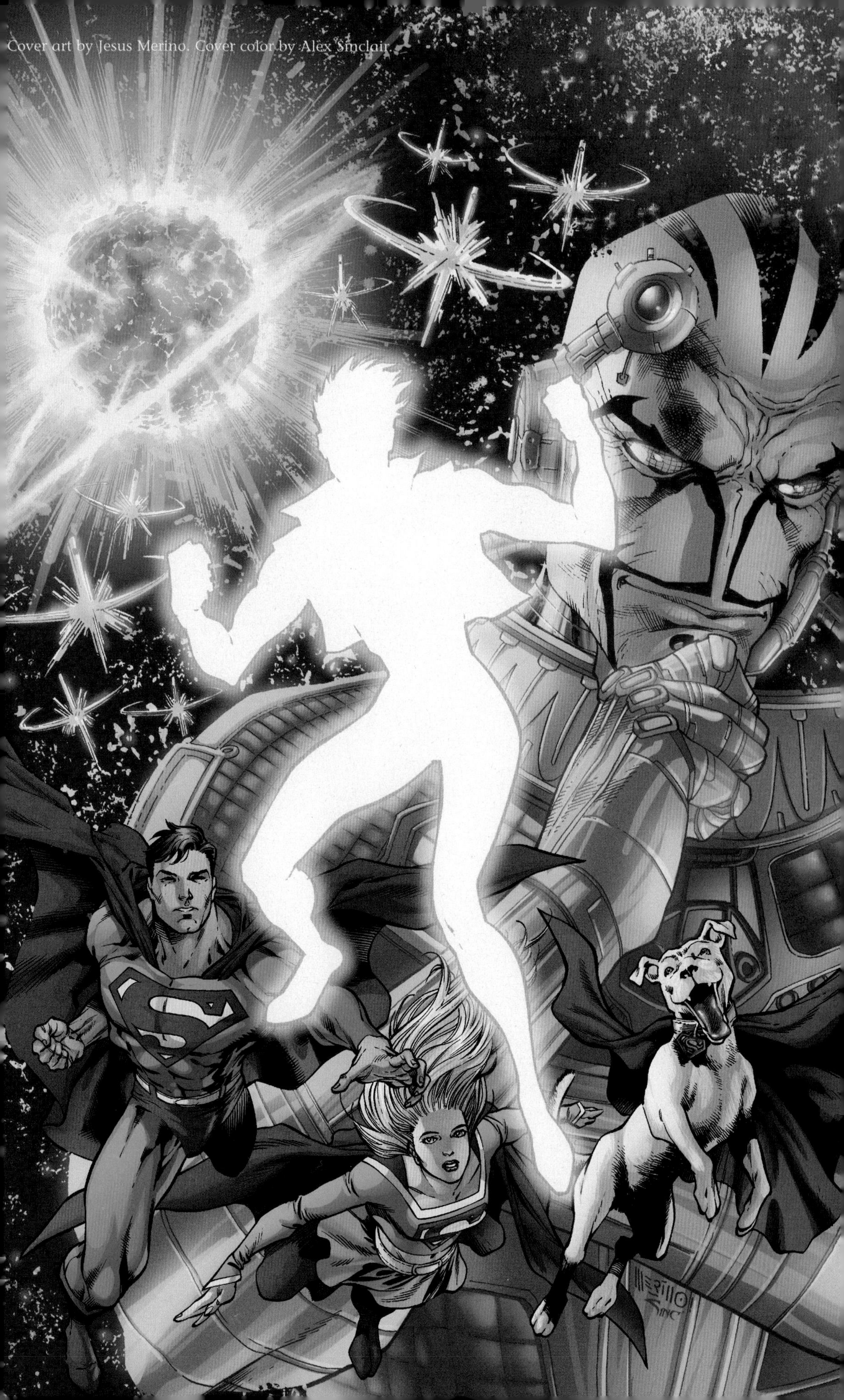

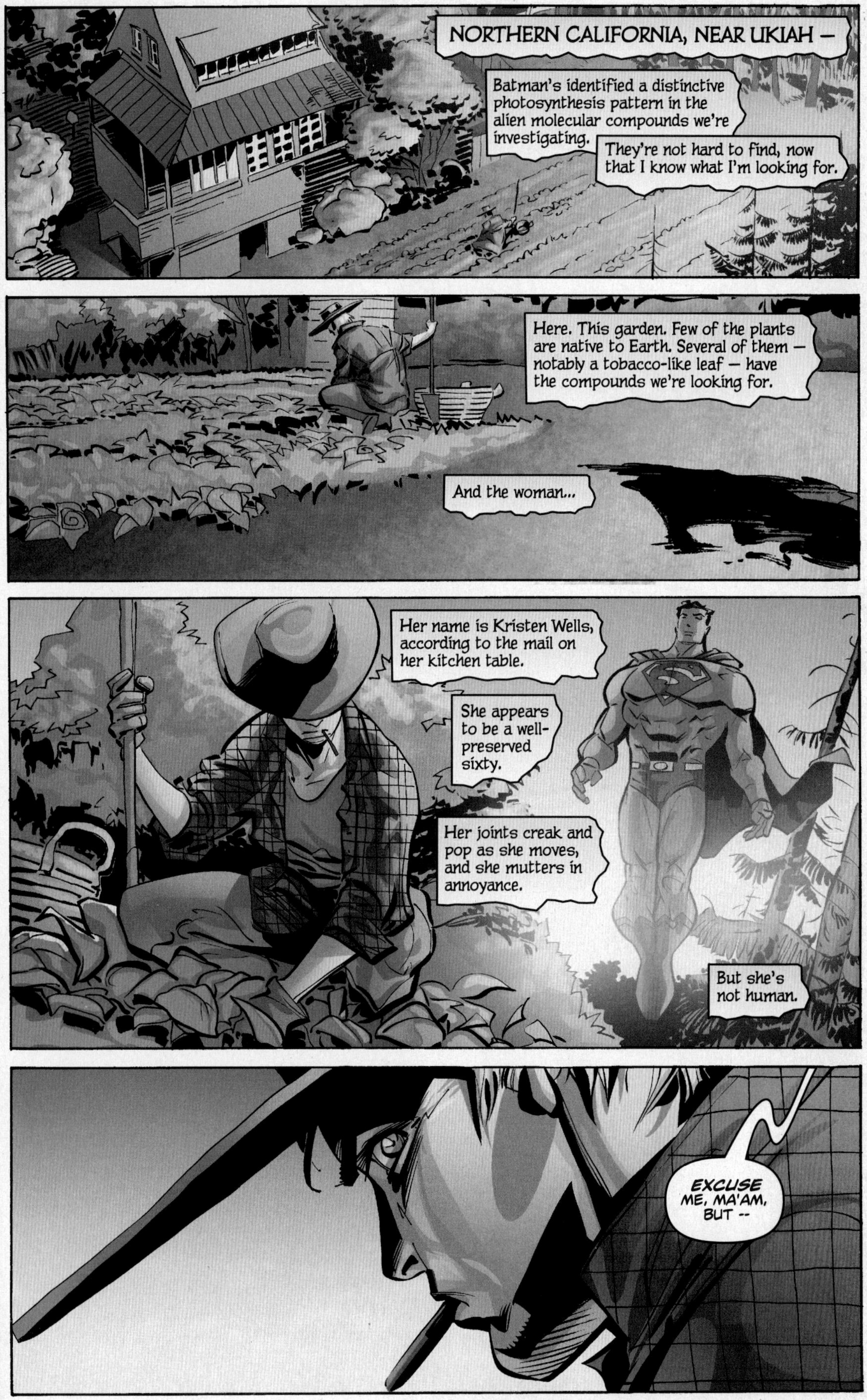
NORTHERN CALIFORNIA, NEAR UKIAH —
Batman's identified a distinctive photosynthesis pattern in the alien molecular compounds we're investigating.
They're not hard to find, now that I know what I'm looking for.
Here. This garden. Few of the plants are native to Earth. Several of them — notably a tobacco-like leaf — have the compounds we're looking for.
And the woman...
Her name is Kristen Wells, according to the mail on her kitchen table.
She appears to be a well-preserved sixty.
Her joints creak and pop as she moves, and she mutters in annoyance.
But she's not human.
EXCUSE ME, MA'AM, BUT --

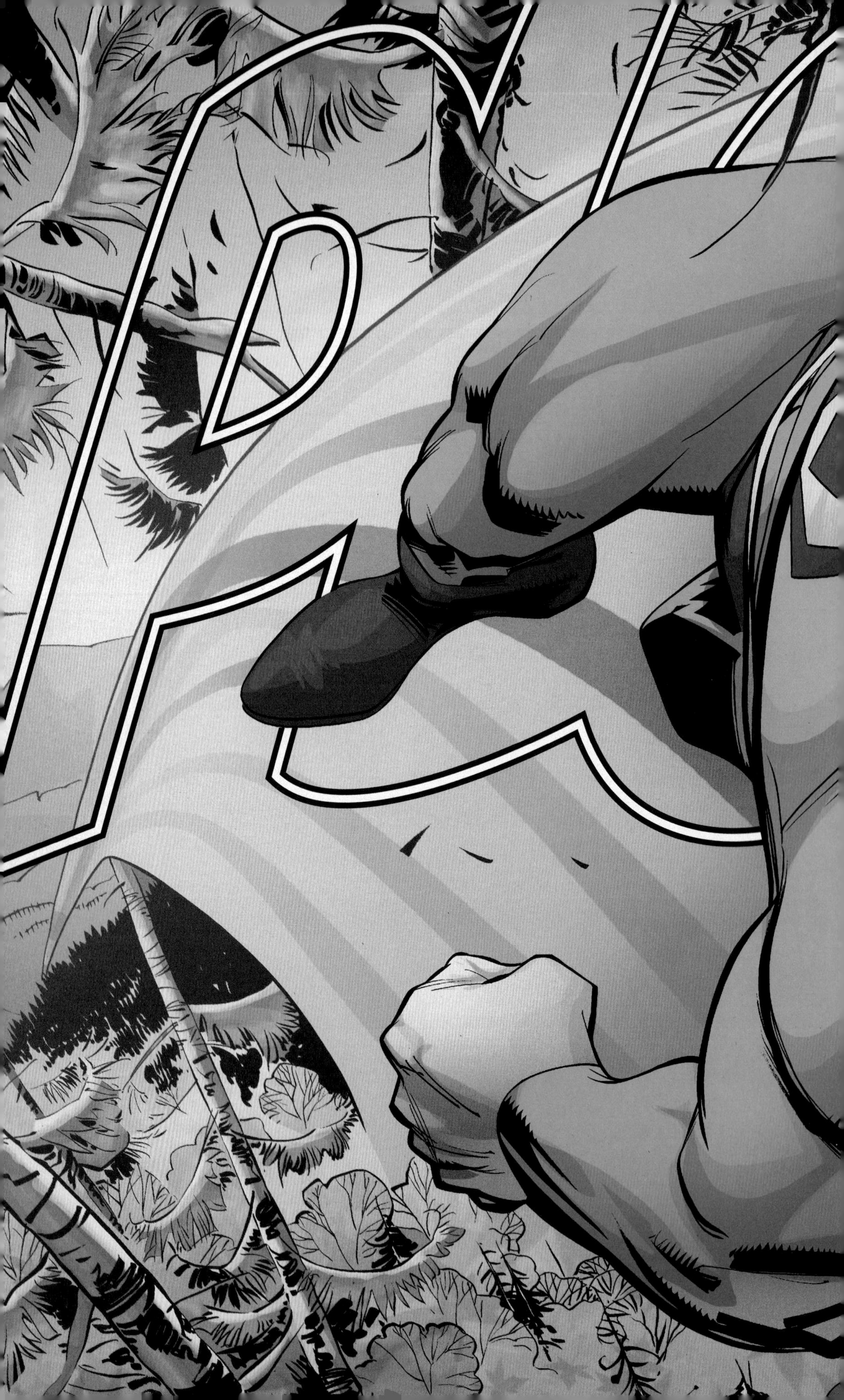

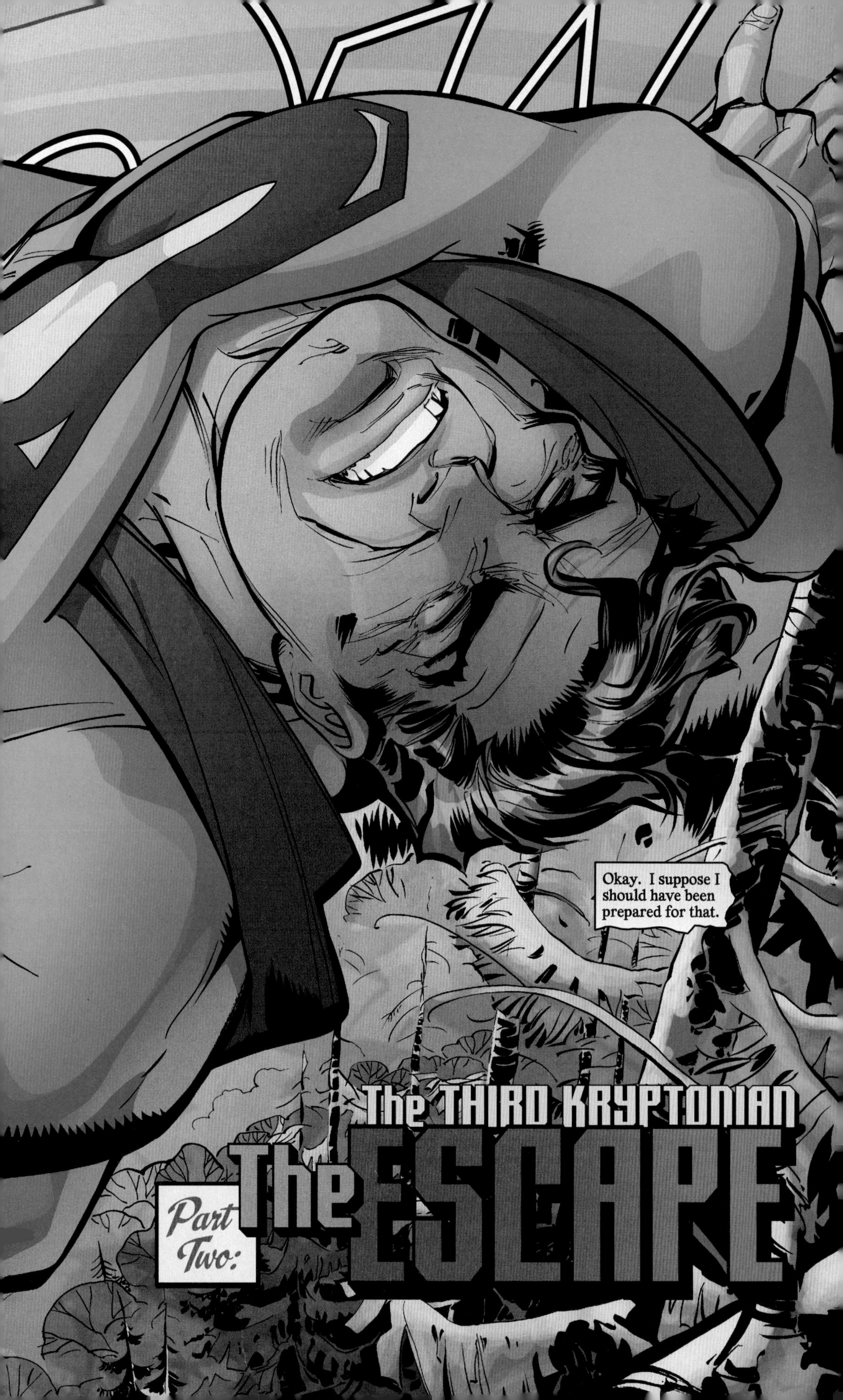

Okay. I suppose I should have been prepared for that.
The THIRD KRYPTONIAN
Part Two: The ESCAPE

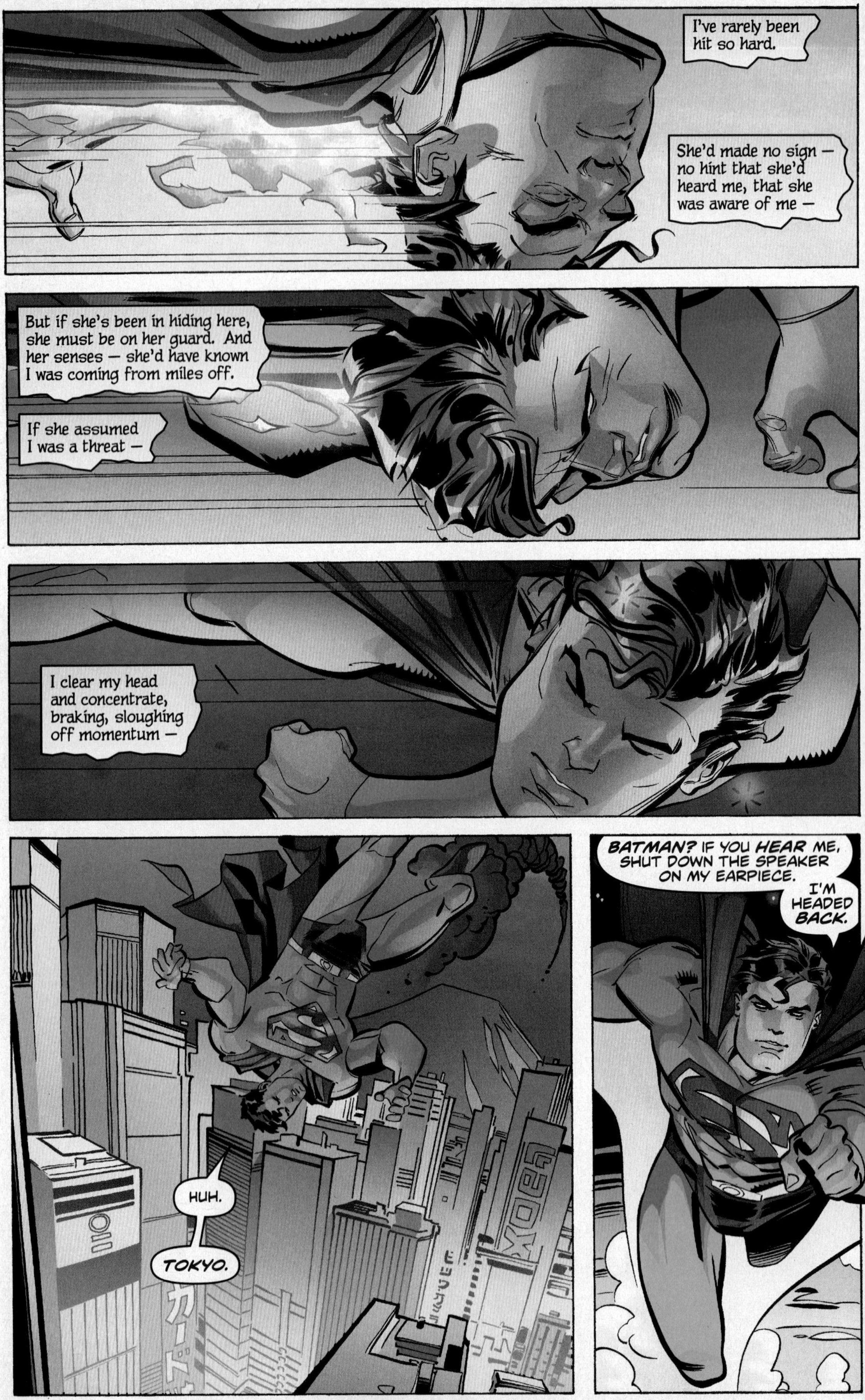
I've rarely been hit so hard.
She'd made no sign — no hint that she'd heard me, that she was aware of me —
But if she's been in hiding here, she must be on her guard. And her senses — she'd have known I was coming from miles off.
If she assumed I was a threat —
I clear my head and concentrate, braking, sloughing off momentum —
HUH.
TOKYO.
BATMAN? IF YOU HEAR ME, SHUT DOWN THE SPEAKER ON MY EARPIECE.
I'M HEADED BACK.

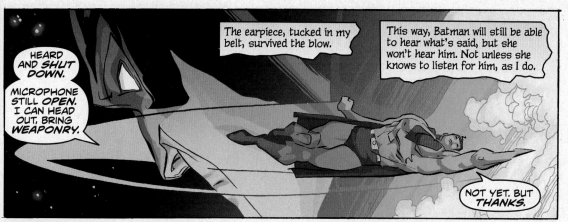

The earpiece, tucked in my belt, survived the blow.

This way, Batman will still be able to hear what's said, but she won't hear him. Not unless she knows to listen for him, as I do.

HEARD AND **SHUT DOWN.**

MICROPHONE STILL **OPEN.** I CAN HEAD OUT, BRING WEAPONRY.

NOT YET. BUT **THANKS.**

STOP *RIGHT THERE,* SUPERMAN. THIS BLASTER'S *DESIGNED* FOR USE ON OUR KIND -- AND I WON'T HESITATE TO USE IT!

I scan it. It is.

I'M NOT HERE TO FIGHT, MS. WELLS. JUST TO *TALK.*

IF YOU KNOW MY NAME, YOU KNOW *THAT,* TOO. I'M NO THREAT TO YOU.

K-KLK

THINK SO, HM?

WHAT THE HELL. WHAT MORE DO I HAVE TO *LOSE?* C'MON IN.

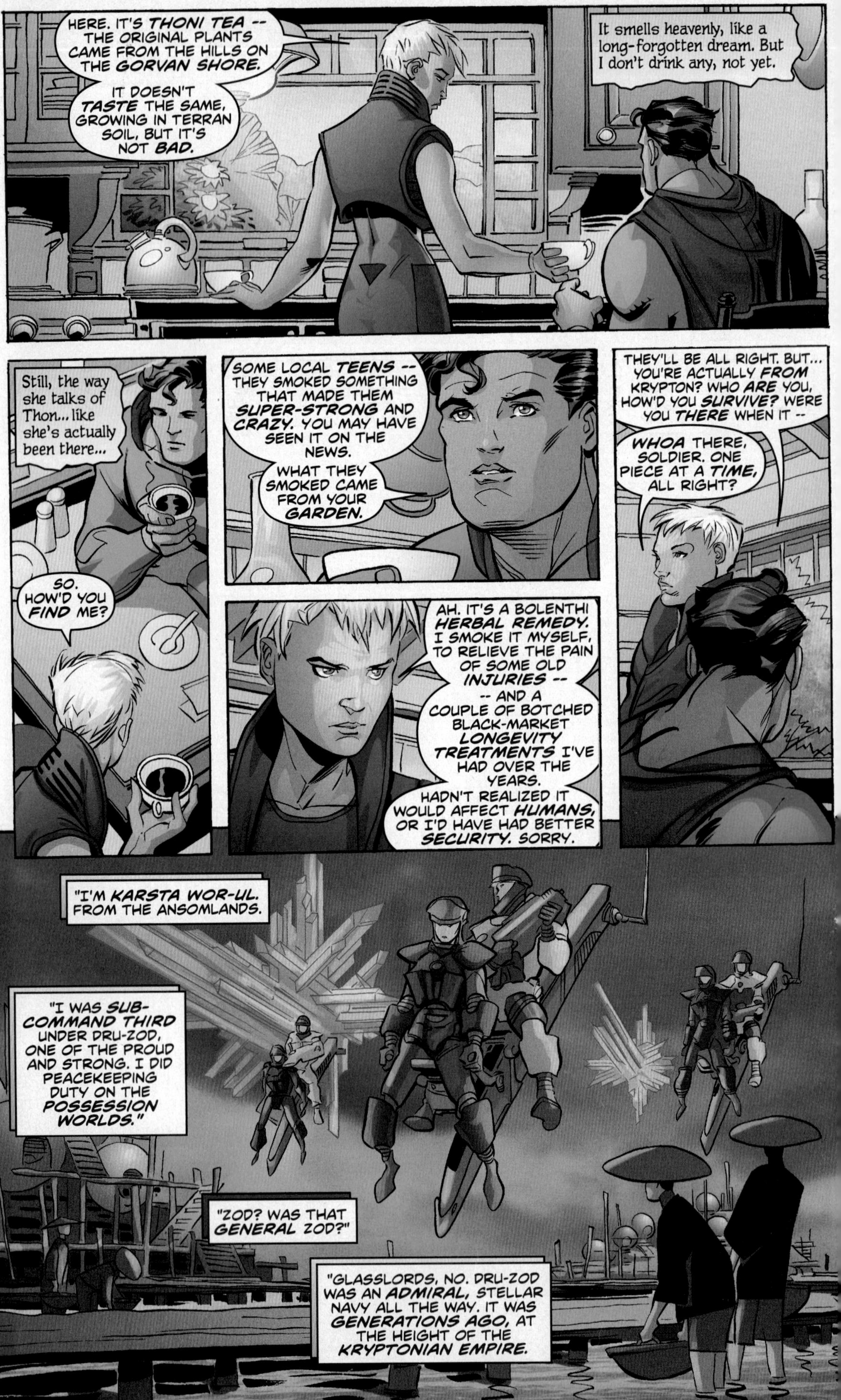
HERE. IT'S THONI TEA -- THE ORIGINAL PLANTS CAME FROM THE HILLS ON THE GORVAN SHORE.
IT DOESN'T TASTE THE SAME, GROWING IN TERRAN SOIL, BUT IT'S NOT BAD.
It smells heavenly, like a long-forgotten dream. But I don't drink any, not yet.
Still, the way she talks of Thon... like she's actually been there...
SO. HOW'D YOU FIND ME?
SOME LOCAL TEENS -- THEY SMOKED SOMETHING THAT MADE THEM SUPER-STRONG AND CRAZY. YOU MAY HAVE SEEN IT ON THE NEWS.
WHAT THEY SMOKED CAME FROM YOUR GARDEN.
AH. IT'S A BOLENTHI HERBAL REMEDY. I SMOKE IT MYSELF, TO RELIEVE THE PAIN OF SOME OLD INJURIES --
-- AND A COUPLE OF BOTCHED BLACK-MARKET LONGEVITY TREATMENTS I'VE HAD OVER THE YEARS.
HADN'T REALIZED IT WOULD AFFECT HUMANS, OR I'D HAVE HAD BETTER SECURITY. SORRY.
THEY'LL BE ALL RIGHT. BUT... YOU'RE ACTUALLY FROM KRYPTON? WHO ARE YOU, HOW'D YOU SURVIVE? WERE YOU THERE WHEN IT --
WHOA THERE, SOLDIER. ONE PIECE AT A TIME, ALL RIGHT?
"I'M KARSTA WOR-UL. FROM THE ANSOMLANDS.
"I WAS SUB-COMMAND THIRD UNDER DRU-ZOD, ONE OF THE PROUD AND STRONG. I DID PEACEKEEPING DUTY ON THE POSSESSION WORLDS."
"ZOD? WAS THAT GENERAL ZOD?"
"GLASSLORDS, NO. DRU-ZOD WAS AN ADMIRAL, STELLAR NAVY ALL THE WAY. IT WAS GENERATIONS AGO, AT THE HEIGHT OF THE KRYPTONIAN EMPIRE.

"OR BETTER I SHOULD SAY -- AT THE *END* OF THE EMPIRE..."

RECALLED TO *KRYPTON?* WHAT, *ALL* OF US? BUT *WHY?*

ELECTIONS. OLD HAR-ZOD THOUGHT HE HAD A *LOCK* ON HIS POSITION. HE THOUGHT *WRONG.*

MILITARY COUNCIL'S *OUT.* BAV SOR-EL'S *SCIENCE COUNCIL* IS IN.

NAVY'S *SHUTTING DOWN.*

BUT -- BUT --

"IT WAS *TRUE.*"

"THEY'D DECIDED, BACK HOME, THAT THE EMPIRE WAS IMMORAL. *TYRANNICAL.* THAT THE POWER WE HAD UNDER OTHER SUNS WAS *CORRUPTING.*"

"WE WERE ORDERED BACK TO LUNAR POSITION AROUND *WEGTHOR,* SO THE FLEET COULD BE *DECOMMISSIONED* AND *DISMANTLED.*"

E-SQUAD FOUR TO DESTROYER *FIREFALL.* WE REQUIRE ENTRY.

"BUT A *BUNCH* OF US, FROM ALL OVER THE FLEET, DIDN'T *WANT* TO BE GROUNDBOUND AND *POWERLESS.*"

"SO AS THE *ERADICATOR SQUAD* CAME IN PORTSIDE..."

GO! GO! WHILE THEIR SENSORS ARE BLOCKED BY *FIREFALL'S* MASS!

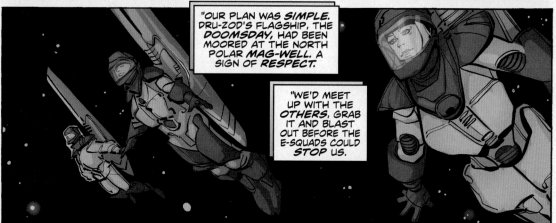

"OUR PLAN WAS *SIMPLE.* DRU-ZOD'S FLAGSHIP, THE *DOOMSDAY,* HAD BEEN MOORED AT THE NORTH POLAR *MAG-WELL.* A SIGN OF *RESPECT.*"

"WE'D MEET UP WITH THE *OTHERS,* GRAB IT AND BLAST OUT BEFORE THE E-SQUADS COULD *STOP* US."

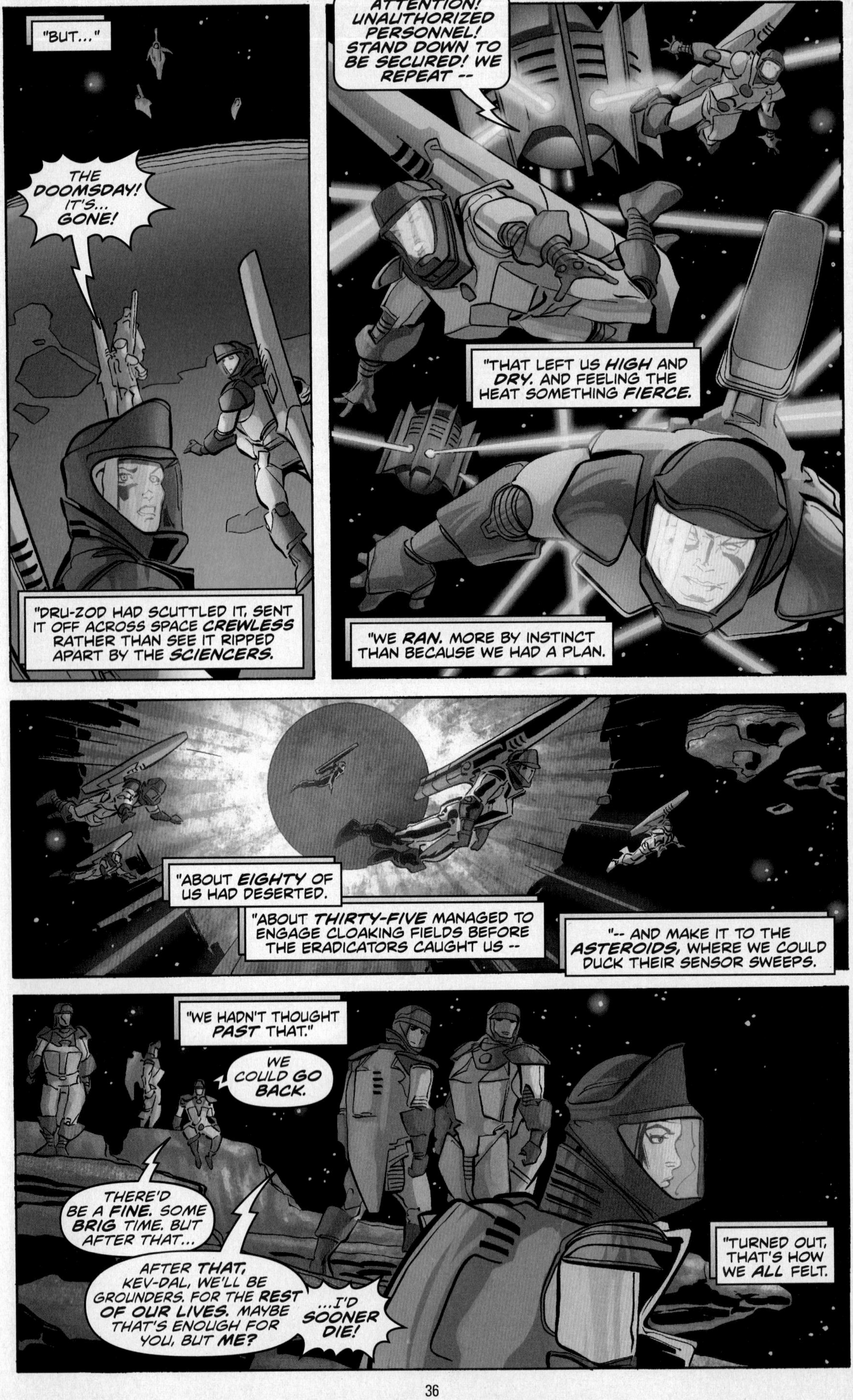
"BUT..."
THE DOOMSDAY! IT'S... GONE!
"DRU-ZOD HAD SCUTTLED IT, SENT IT OFF ACROSS SPACE CREWLESS RATHER THAN SEE IT RIPPED APART BY THE SCIENCERS.
ATTENTION! UNAUTHORIZED PERSONNEL! STAND DOWN TO BE SECURED! WE REPEAT --
"THAT LEFT US HIGH AND DRY. AND FEELING THE HEAT SOMETHING FIERCE.
"WE RAN. MORE BY INSTINCT THAN BECAUSE WE HAD A PLAN.
"ABOUT EIGHTY OF US HAD DESERTED.
"ABOUT THIRTY-FIVE MANAGED TO ENGAGE CLOAKING FIELDS BEFORE THE ERADICATORS CAUGHT US --
"-- AND MAKE IT TO THE ASTEROIDS, WHERE WE COULD DUCK THEIR SENSOR SWEEPS.
"WE HADN'T THOUGHT PAST THAT."
WE COULD GO BACK.
THERE'D BE A FINE. SOME BRIG TIME. BUT AFTER THAT...
AFTER THAT, KEV-DAL, WE'LL BE GROUNDERS. FOR THE REST OF OUR LIVES. MAYBE THAT'S ENOUGH FOR YOU, BUT ME?
...I'D SOONER DIE!
"TURNED OUT, THAT'S HOW WE ALL FELT.

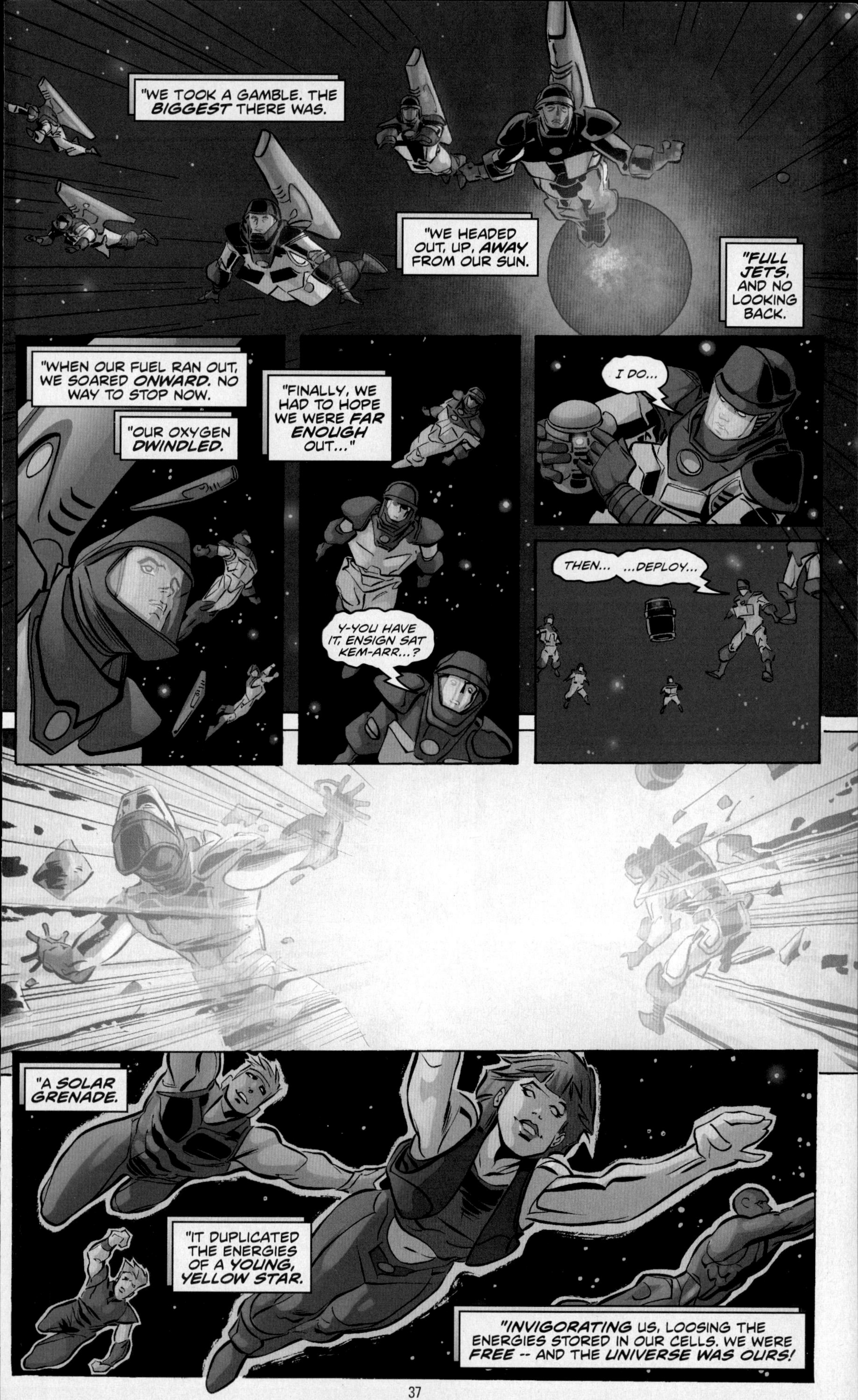
"WE TOOK A GAMBLE. THE *BIGGEST* THERE WAS.
"WE HEADED OUT, UP, *AWAY* FROM OUR SUN.
"*FULL JETS*, AND NO LOOKING BACK.
"WHEN OUR FUEL RAN OUT, WE SOARED *ONWARD*. NO WAY TO STOP NOW.
"OUR OXYGEN *DWINDLED*.
"FINALLY, WE HAD TO HOPE WE WERE *FAR ENOUGH* OUT..."
Y-YOU HAVE IT, ENSIGN SAT KEM-ARR...?
I DO...
THEN... ...DEPLOY...
"A *SOLAR GRENADE*.
"IT DUPLICATED THE ENERGIES OF A *YOUNG, YELLOW STAR*.
"*INVIGORATING* US, LOOSING THE ENERGIES STORED IN OUR CELLS. WE WERE *FREE* -- AND THE *UNIVERSE WAS OURS!*

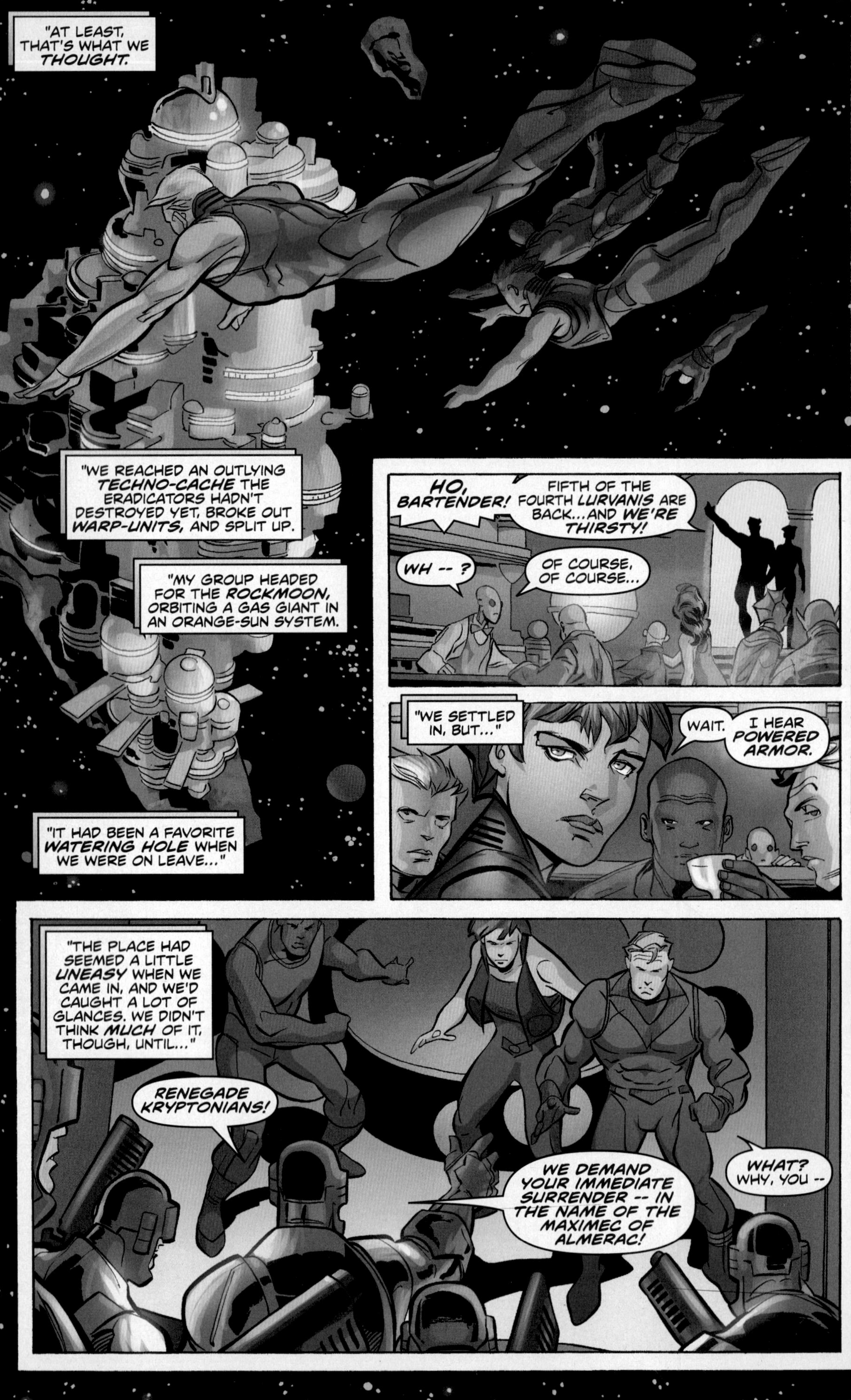
"AT LEAST, THAT'S WHAT WE THOUGHT.
"WE REACHED AN OUTLYING TECHNO-CACHE THE ERADICATORS HADN'T DESTROYED YET, BROKE OUT WARP-UNITS, AND SPLIT UP.
"MY GROUP HEADED FOR THE ROCKMOON, ORBITING A GAS GIANT IN AN ORANGE-SUN SYSTEM.
"IT HAD BEEN A FAVORITE WATERING HOLE WHEN WE WERE ON LEAVE..."
HO, BARTENDER!
FIFTH OF THE FOURTH LURVANIS ARE BACK...AND WE'RE THIRSTY!
WH -- ?
OF COURSE, OF COURSE...
"WE SETTLED IN, BUT..."
WAIT.
I HEAR POWERED ARMOR.
"THE PLACE HAD SEEMED A LITTLE UNEASY WHEN WE CAME IN, AND WE'D CAUGHT A LOT OF GLANCES. WE DIDN'T THINK MUCH OF IT, THOUGH, UNTIL..."
RENEGADE KRYPTONIANS!
WE DEMAND YOUR IMMEDIATE SURRENDER -- IN THE NAME OF THE MAXIMEC OF ALMERAC!
WHAT? WHY, YOU --

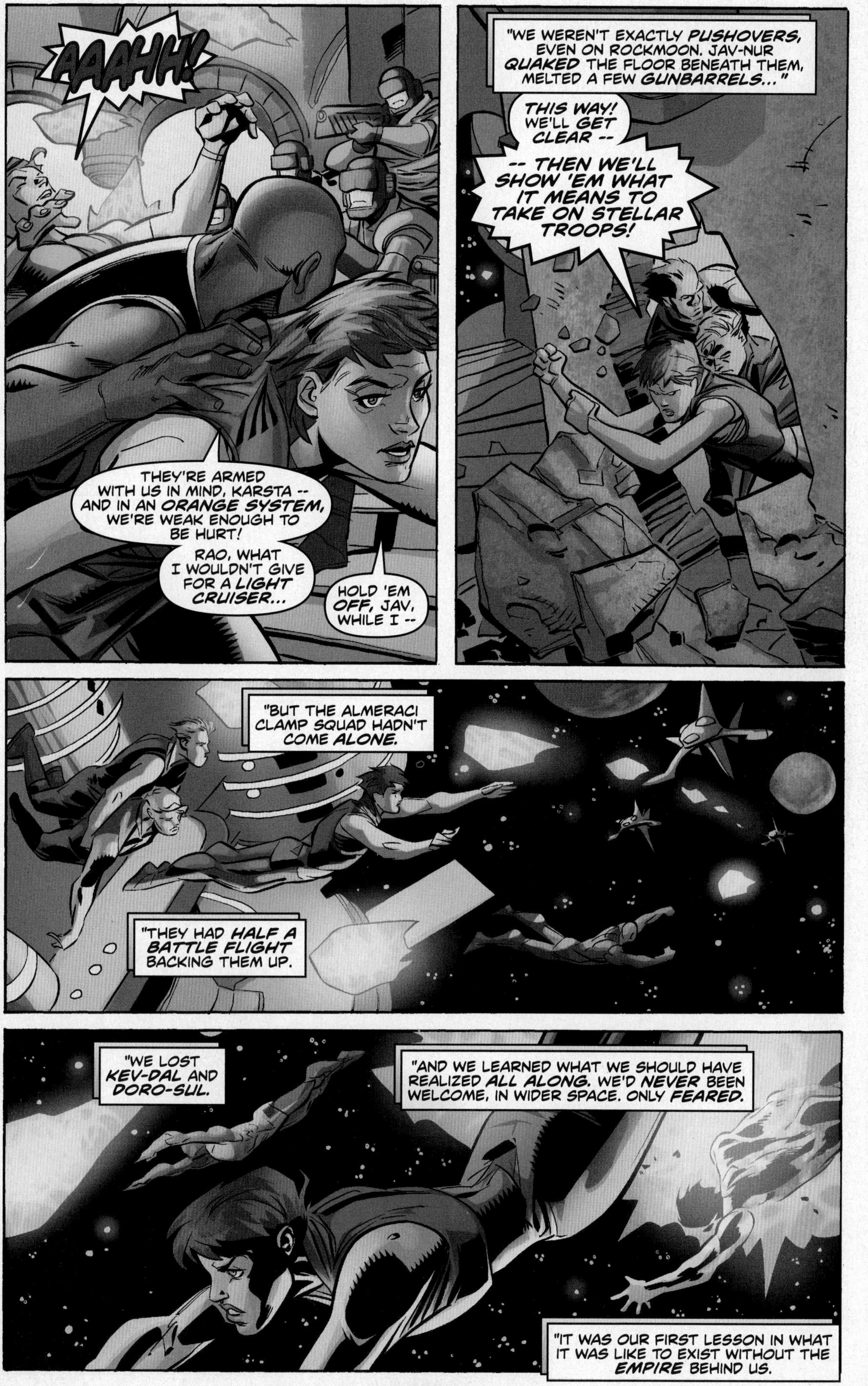
AAAHH!
THEY'RE ARMED WITH US IN MIND, KARSTA -- AND IN AN ORANGE SYSTEM, WE'RE WEAK ENOUGH TO BE HURT!
RAO, WHAT I WOULDN'T GIVE FOR A LIGHT CRUISER...
HOLD 'EM OFF, JAV, WHILE I --
"WE WEREN'T EXACTLY PUSHOVERS, EVEN ON ROCKMOON. JAV-NUR QUAKED THE FLOOR BENEATH THEM, MELTED A FEW GUNBARRELS..."
THIS WAY! WE'LL GET CLEAR --
-- THEN WE'LL SHOW 'EM WHAT IT MEANS TO TAKE ON STELLAR TROOPS!
"BUT THE ALMERACI CLAMP SQUAD HADN'T COME ALONE.
"THEY HAD HALF A BATTLE FLIGHT BACKING THEM UP.
"WE LOST KEV-DAL AND DORO-SUL.
"AND WE LEARNED WHAT WE SHOULD HAVE REALIZED ALL ALONG. WE'D NEVER BEEN WELCOME, IN WIDER SPACE. ONLY FEARED.
"IT WAS OUR FIRST LESSON IN WHAT IT WAS LIKE TO EXIST WITHOUT THE EMPIRE BEHIND US.

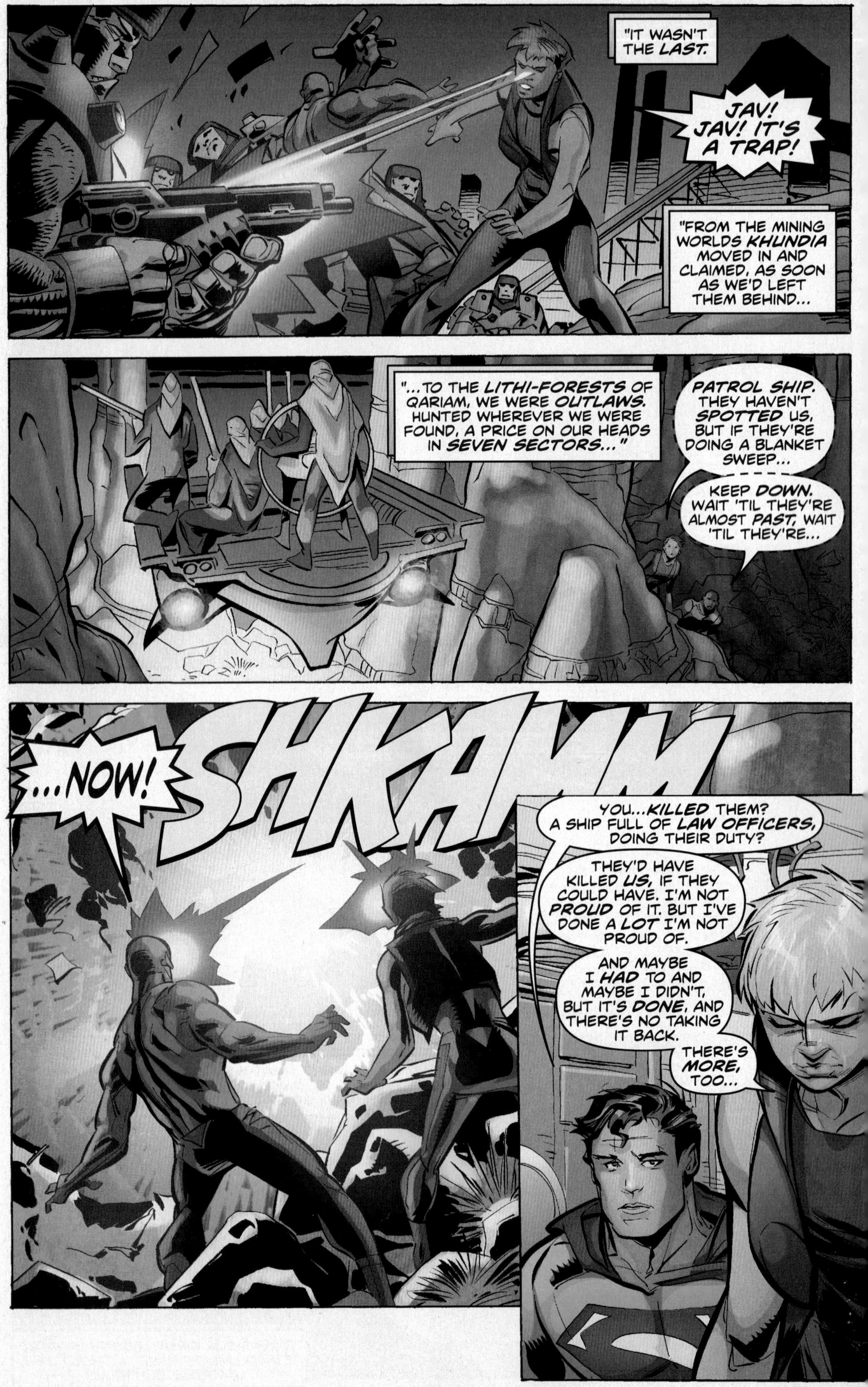
"IT WASN'T THE LAST.
JAV! JAV! IT'S A TRAP!
"FROM THE MINING WORLDS KHUNDIA MOVED IN AND CLAIMED, AS SOON AS WE'D LEFT THEM BEHIND...
"...TO THE LITHI-FORESTS OF QARIAM, WE WERE OUTLAWS. HUNTED WHEREVER WE WERE FOUND, A PRICE ON OUR HEADS IN SEVEN SECTORS..."
PATROL SHIP. THEY HAVEN'T SPOTTED US, BUT IF THEY'RE DOING A BLANKET SWEEP...
KEEP DOWN. WAIT 'TIL THEY'RE ALMOST PAST, WAIT 'TIL THEY'RE...
...NOW!
SHKAMM
YOU...KILLED THEM? A SHIP FULL OF LAW OFFICERS, DOING THEIR DUTY?
THEY'D HAVE KILLED US, IF THEY COULD HAVE. I'M NOT PROUD OF IT. BUT I'VE DONE A LOT I'M NOT PROUD OF.
AND MAYBE I HAD TO AND MAYBE I DIDN'T, BUT IT'S DONE, AND THERE'S NO TAKING IT BACK.
THERE'S MORE, TOO...

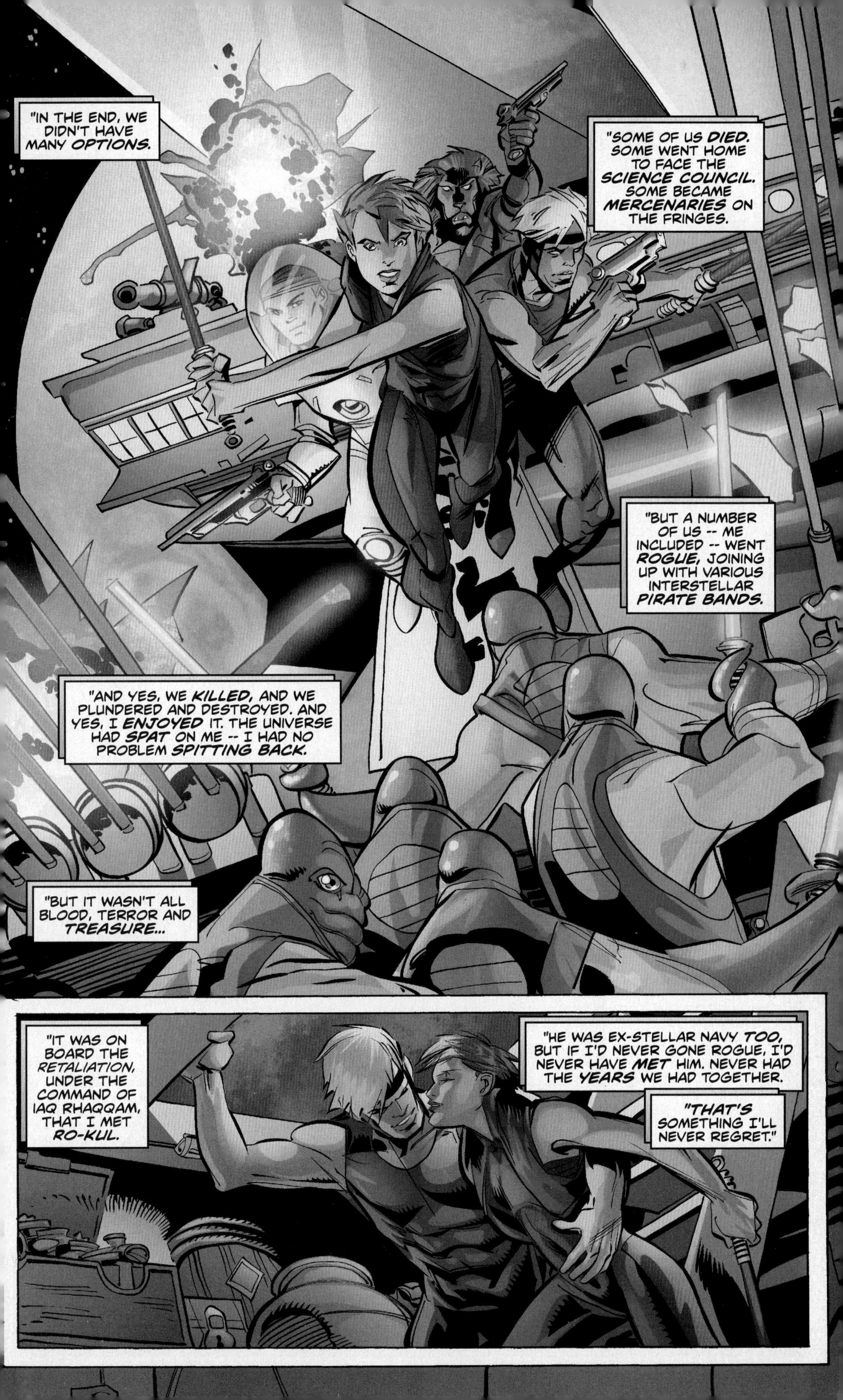
"IN THE END, WE DIDN'T HAVE MANY *OPTIONS*.
"SOME OF US *DIED*. SOME WENT HOME TO FACE THE *SCIENCE COUNCIL*. SOME BECAME *MERCENARIES* ON THE FRINGES.
"BUT A NUMBER OF US -- ME INCLUDED -- WENT *ROGUE*, JOINING UP WITH VARIOUS INTERSTELLAR *PIRATE BANDS*.
"AND YES, WE *KILLED*, AND WE PLUNDERED AND DESTROYED. AND YES, I *ENJOYED* IT. THE UNIVERSE HAD *SPAT* ON ME -- I HAD NO PROBLEM *SPITTING BACK*.
"BUT IT WASN'T ALL BLOOD, TERROR AND *TREASURE*...
"IT WAS ON BOARD THE *RETALIATION*, UNDER THE COMMAND OF IAQ RHAQQAM, THAT I MET *RO-KUL*.
"HE WAS EX-STELLAR NAVY *TOO*, BUT IF I'D NEVER GONE ROGUE, I'D NEVER HAVE *MET* HIM. NEVER HAD THE *YEARS* WE HAD TOGETHER.
"THAT'S SOMETHING I'LL NEVER REGRET."

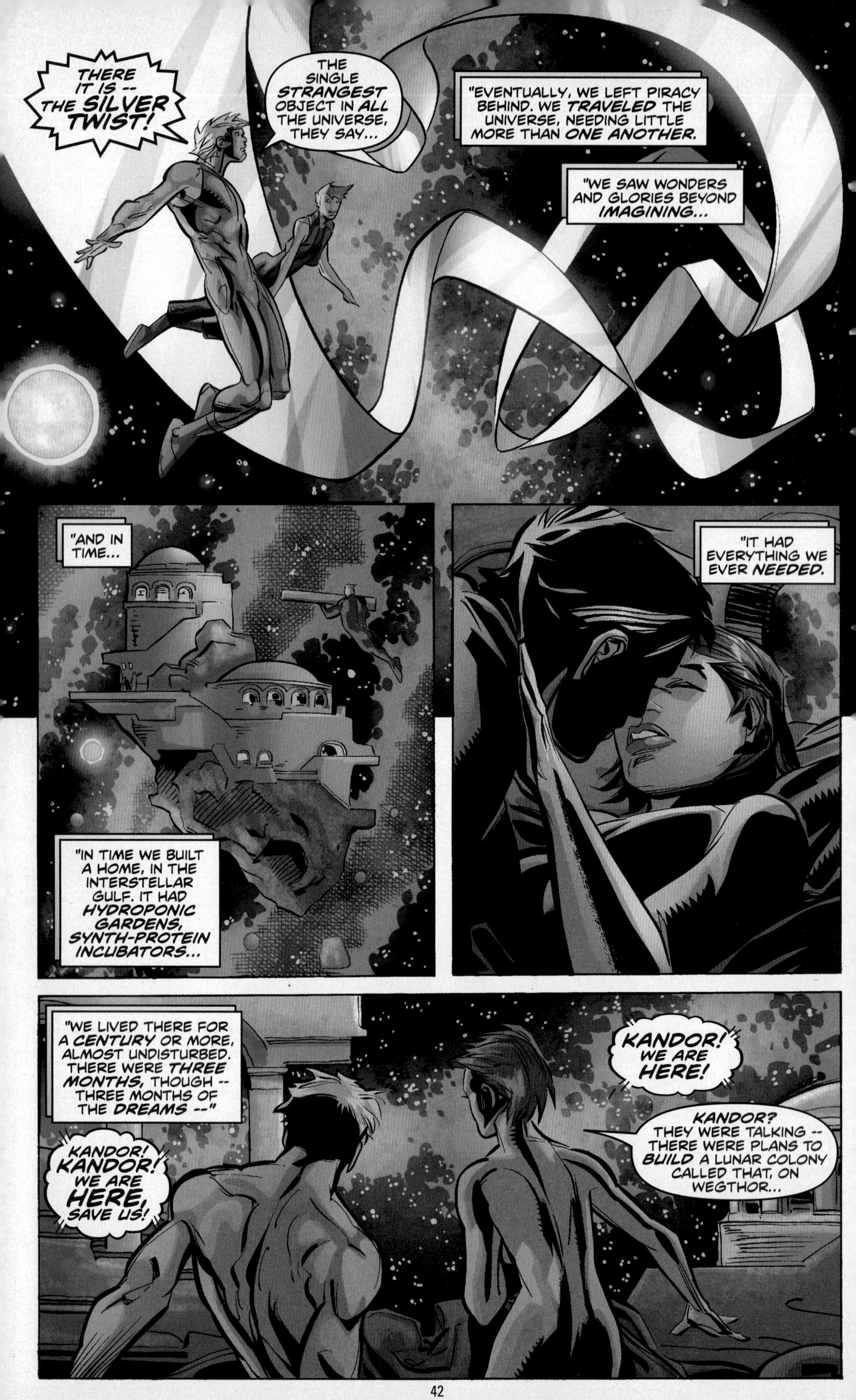
THERE IT IS -- THE SILVER TWIST!
THE SINGLE STRANGEST OBJECT IN ALL THE UNIVERSE, THEY SAY...
"EVENTUALLY, WE LEFT PIRACY BEHIND. WE TRAVELED THE UNIVERSE, NEEDING LITTLE MORE THAN ONE ANOTHER.
"WE SAW WONDERS AND GLORIES BEYOND IMAGINING...
"AND IN TIME...
"IN TIME WE BUILT A HOME, IN THE INTERSTELLAR GULF. IT HAD HYDROPONIC GARDENS, SYNTH-PROTEIN INCUBATORS...
"IT HAD EVERYTHING WE EVER NEEDED.
"WE LIVED THERE FOR A CENTURY OR MORE, ALMOST UNDISTURBED. THERE WERE THREE MONTHS, THOUGH -- THREE MONTHS OF THE DREAMS --"
KANDOR! WE ARE HERE!
KANDOR! KANDOR! WE ARE HERE, SAVE US!
KANDOR? THEY WERE TALKING -- THERE WERE PLANS TO BUILD A LUNAR COLONY CALLED THAT, ON WEGTHOR...

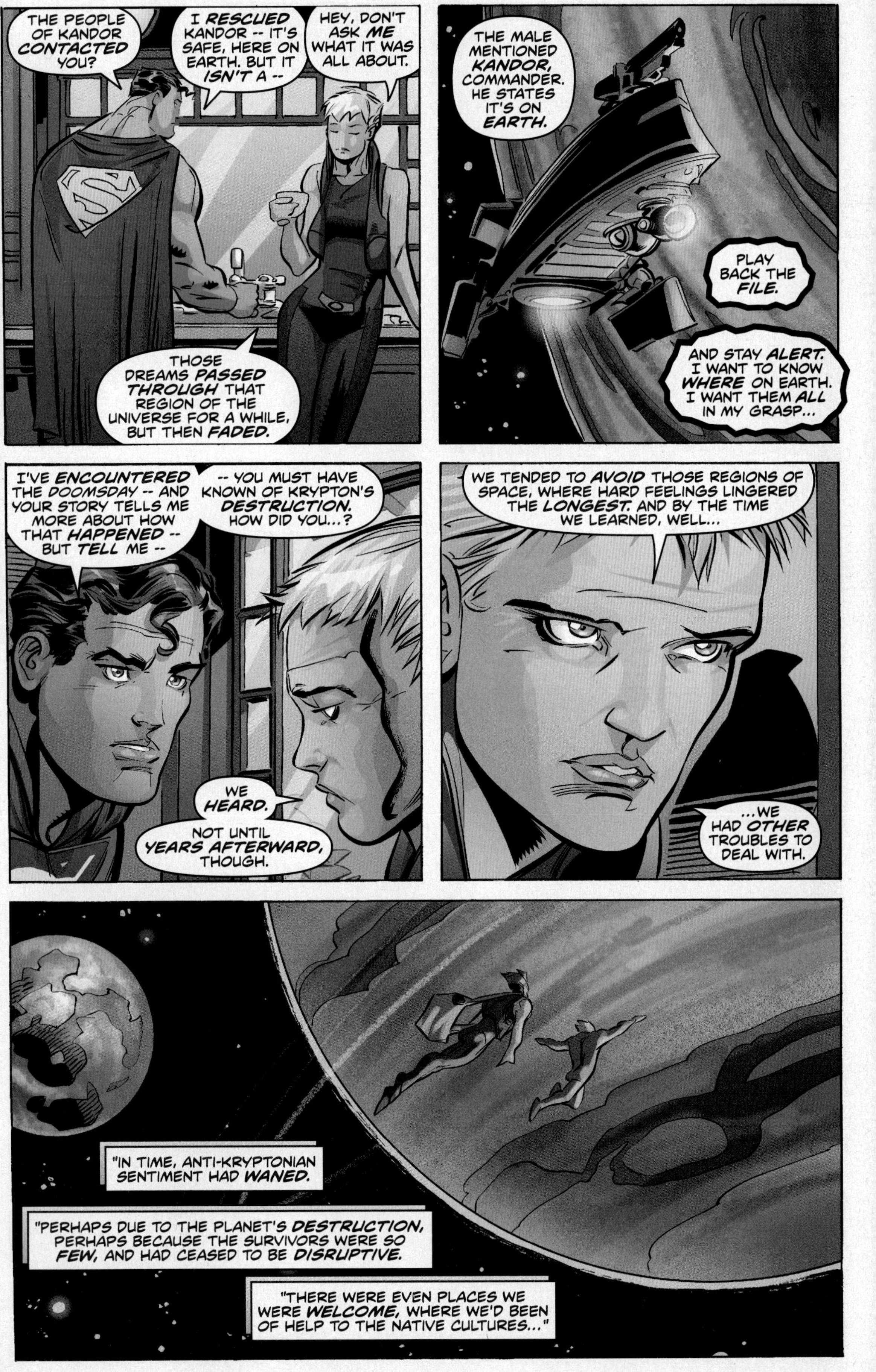
THE PEOPLE OF KANDOR CONTACTED YOU?
I RESCUED KANDOR -- IT'S SAFE, HERE ON EARTH. BUT IT ISN'T A --
HEY, DON'T ASK ME WHAT IT WAS ALL ABOUT.
THOSE DREAMS PASSED THROUGH THAT REGION OF THE UNIVERSE FOR A WHILE, BUT THEN FADED.
THE MALE MENTIONED KANDOR, COMMANDER. HE STATES IT'S ON EARTH.
PLAY BACK THE FILE.
AND STAY ALERT. I WANT TO KNOW WHERE ON EARTH. I WANT THEM ALL IN MY GRASP...
I'VE ENCOUNTERED THE DOOMSDAY -- AND YOUR STORY TELLS ME MORE ABOUT HOW THAT HAPPENED -- BUT TELL ME --
-- YOU MUST HAVE KNOWN OF KRYPTON'S DESTRUCTION. HOW DID YOU...?
WE HEARD.
NOT UNTIL YEARS AFTERWARD, THOUGH.
WE TENDED TO AVOID THOSE REGIONS OF SPACE, WHERE HARD FEELINGS LINGERED THE LONGEST. AND BY THE TIME WE LEARNED, WELL...
...WE HAD OTHER TROUBLES TO DEAL WITH.
"IN TIME, ANTI-KRYPTONIAN SENTIMENT HAD WANED.
"PERHAPS DUE TO THE PLANET'S DESTRUCTION, PERHAPS BECAUSE THE SURVIVORS WERE SO FEW, AND HAD CEASED TO BE DISRUPTIVE.
"THERE WERE EVEN PLACES WE WERE WELCOME, WHERE WE'D BEEN OF HELP TO THE NATIVE CULTURES..."

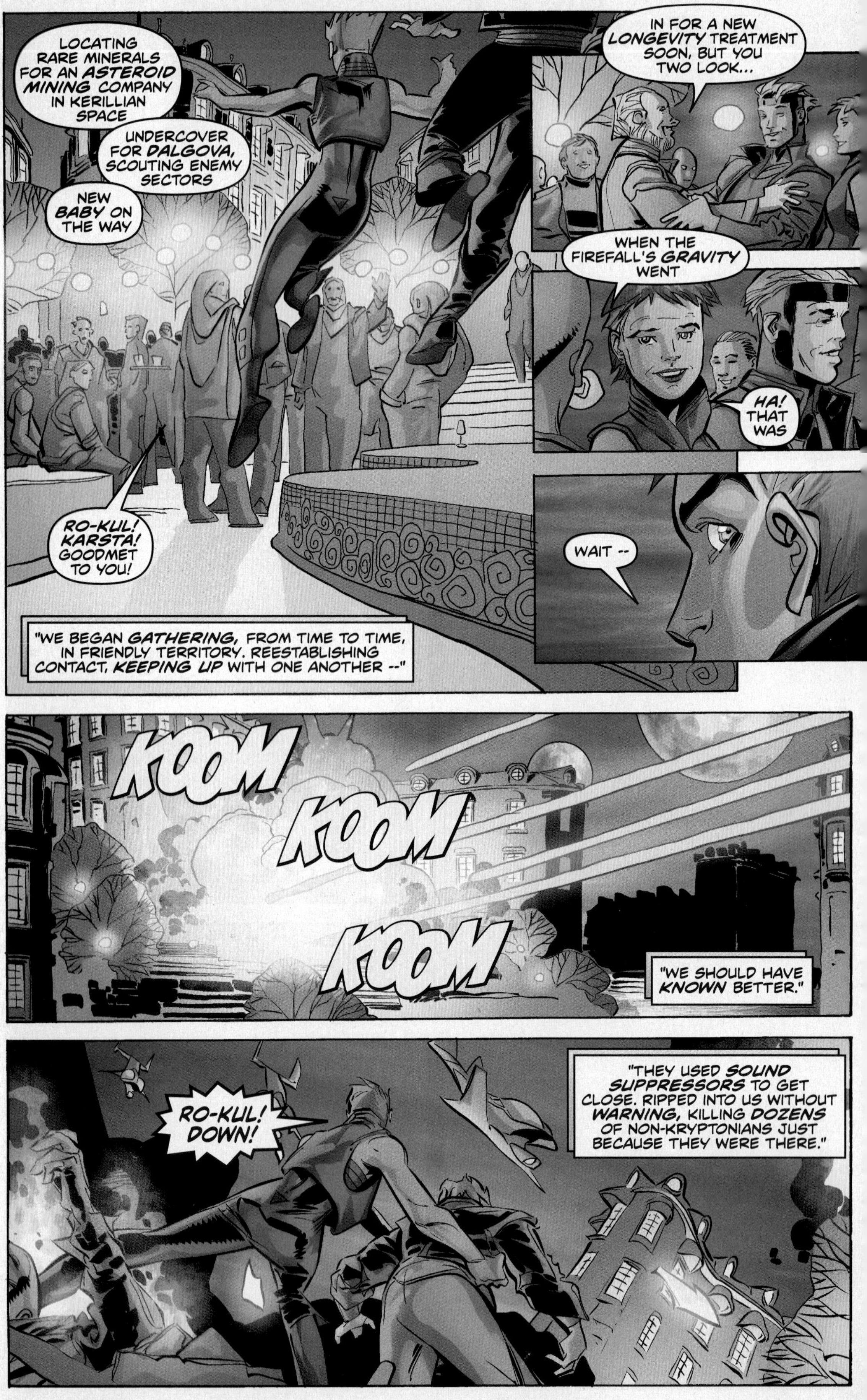

LOCATING RARE MINERALS FOR AN ASTEROID MINING COMPANY IN KERILLIAN SPACE
UNDERCOVER FOR DALGOVA, SCOUTING ENEMY SECTORS
NEW BABY ON THE WAY
RO-KUL! KARSTA! GOODMET TO YOU!
"WE BEGAN GATHERING, FROM TIME TO TIME, IN FRIENDLY TERRITORY. REESTABLISHING CONTACT, KEEPING UP WITH ONE ANOTHER --"
IN FOR A NEW LONGEVITY TREATMENT SOON, BUT YOU TWO LOOK...
WHEN THE FIREFALL'S GRAVITY WENT
HA! THAT WAS
WAIT --
KOOM
KOOM
KOOM
"WE SHOULD HAVE KNOWN BETTER."
RO-KUL! DOWN!
"THEY USED SOUND SUPPRESSORS TO GET CLOSE. RIPPED INTO US WITHOUT WARNING, KILLING DOZENS OF NON-KRYPTONIANS JUST BECAUSE THEY WERE THERE."

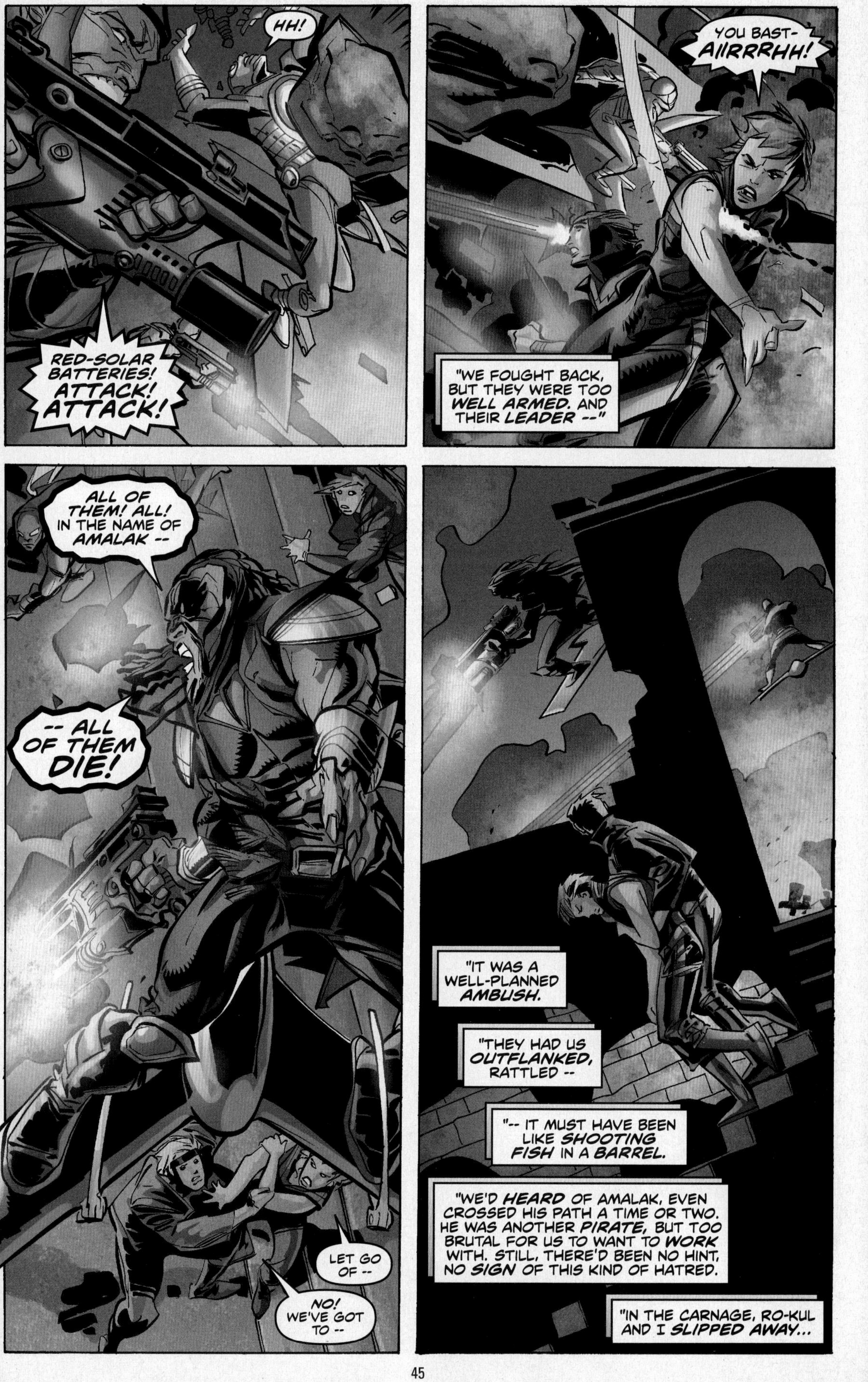
HH!
RED-SOLAR BATTERIES! ATTACK! ATTACK!
YOU BAST- AIIRRRHH!
"WE FOUGHT BACK, BUT THEY WERE TOO WELL ARMED. AND THEIR LEADER --"
ALL OF THEM! ALL! IN THE NAME OF AMALAK --
-- ALL OF THEM DIE!
LET GO OF --
NO! WE'VE GOT TO --
"IT WAS A WELL-PLANNED AMBUSH.
"THEY HAD US OUTFLANKED, RATTLED --
"-- IT MUST HAVE BEEN LIKE SHOOTING FISH IN A BARREL.
"WE'D HEARD OF AMALAK, EVEN CROSSED HIS PATH A TIME OR TWO. HE WAS ANOTHER PIRATE, BUT TOO BRUTAL FOR US TO WANT TO WORK WITH. STILL, THERE'D BEEN NO HINT, NO SIGN OF THIS KIND OF HATRED.
"IN THE CARNAGE, RO-KUL AND I SLIPPED AWAY...

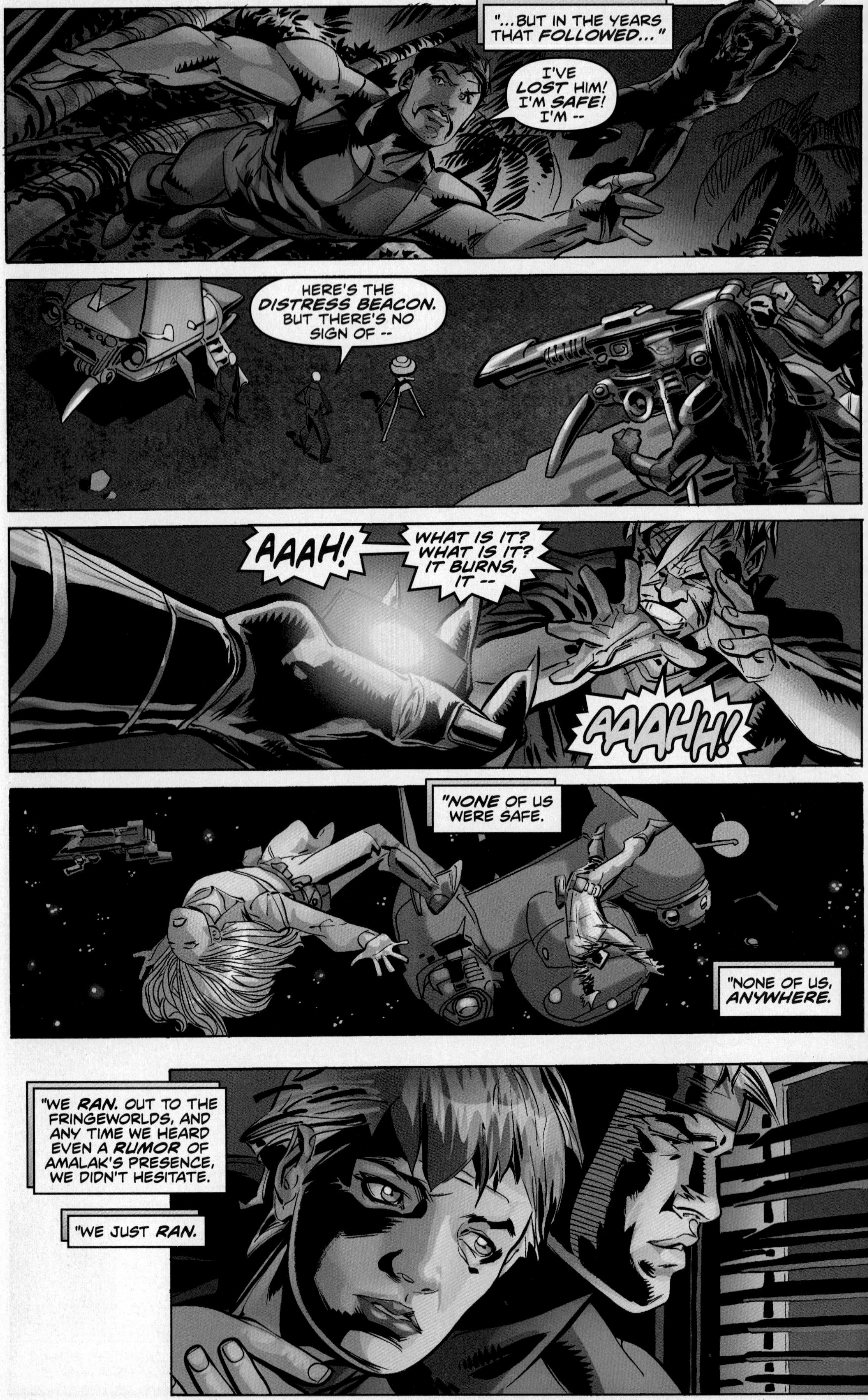
"...BUT IN THE YEARS THAT FOLLOWED..."
I'VE LOST HIM! I'M SAFE! I'M --
HERE'S THE DISTRESS BEACON. BUT THERE'S NO SIGN OF --
AAAH!
WHAT IS IT? WHAT IS IT? IT BURNS, IT --
AAAHH!
"NONE OF US WERE SAFE.
"NONE OF US, ANYWHERE.
"WE RAN. OUT TO THE FRINGEWORLDS, AND ANY TIME WE HEARD EVEN A RUMOR OF AMALAK'S PRESENCE, WE DIDN'T HESITATE.
"WE JUST RAN.

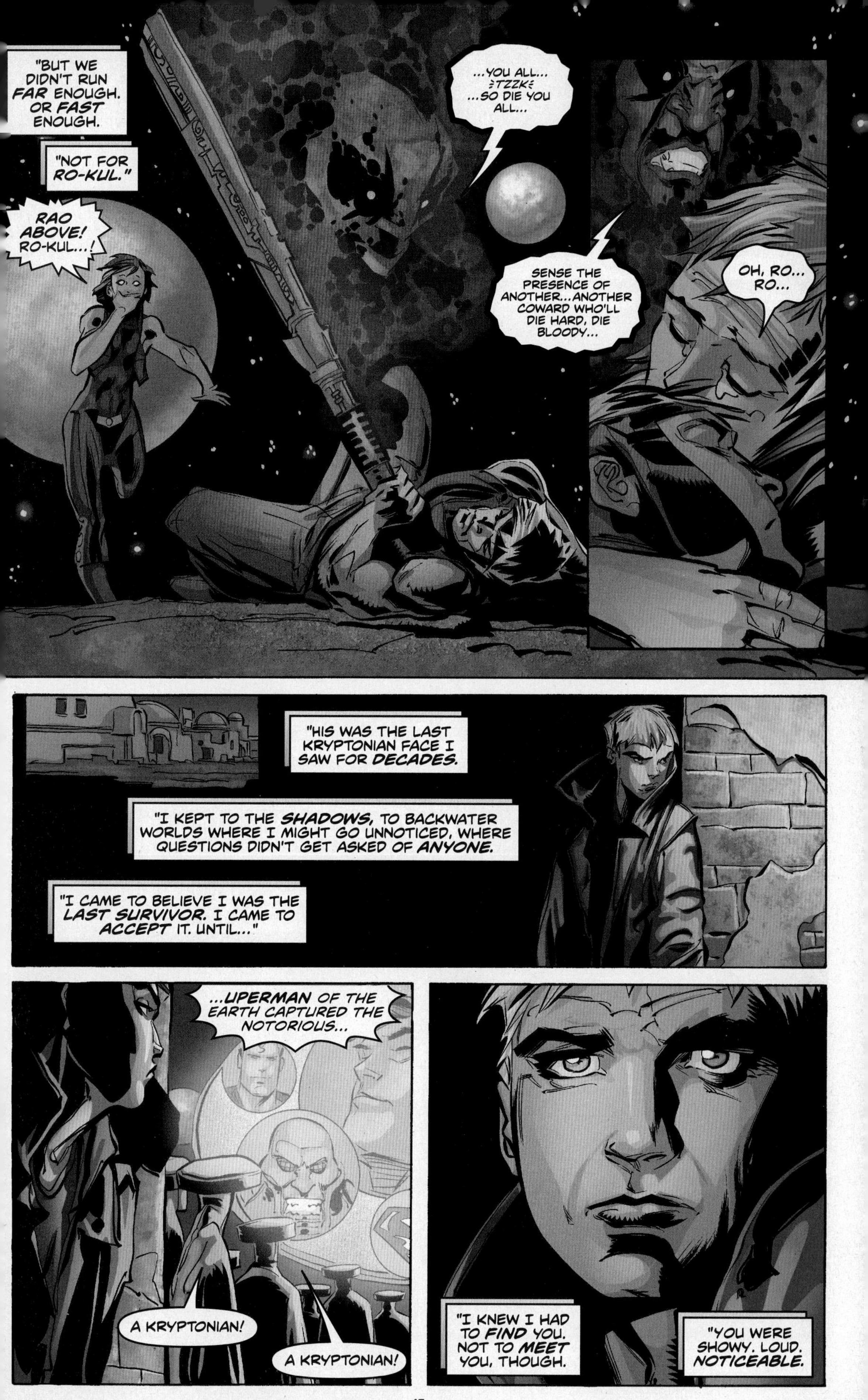
"BUT WE DIDN'T RUN FAR ENOUGH. OR FAST ENOUGH.
"NOT FOR RO-KUL."
RAO ABOVE! RO-KUL...!
...YOU ALL... ƷTZZKƸ ...SO DIE YOU ALL...
SENSE THE PRESENCE OF ANOTHER...ANOTHER COWARD WHO'LL DIE HARD, DIE BLOODY...
OH, RO... RO...
"HIS WAS THE LAST KRYPTONIAN FACE I SAW FOR DECADES.
"I KEPT TO THE SHADOWS, TO BACKWATER WORLDS WHERE I MIGHT GO UNNOTICED, WHERE QUESTIONS DIDN'T GET ASKED OF ANYONE.
"I CAME TO BELIEVE I WAS THE LAST SURVIVOR. I CAME TO ACCEPT IT. UNTIL..."
...UPERMAN OF THE EARTH CAPTURED THE NOTORIOUS...
A KRYPTONIAN!
A KRYPTONIAN!
"I KNEW I HAD TO FIND YOU. NOT TO MEET YOU, THOUGH.
"YOU WERE SHOWY. LOUD. NOTICEABLE.

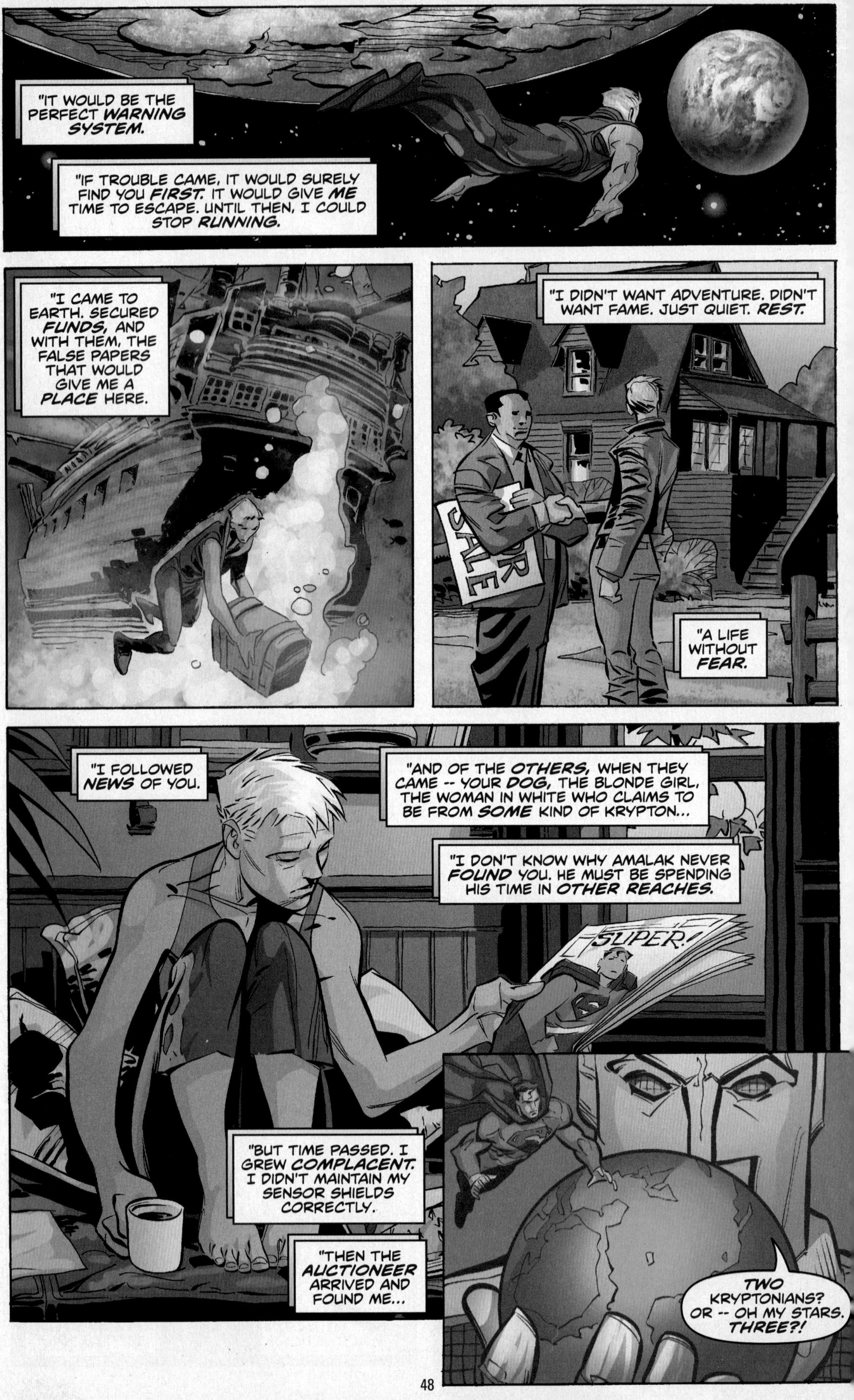

"IT WOULD BE THE PERFECT WARNING SYSTEM.
"IF TROUBLE CAME, IT WOULD SURELY FIND YOU FIRST. IT WOULD GIVE ME TIME TO ESCAPE. UNTIL THEN, I COULD STOP RUNNING.
"I CAME TO EARTH. SECURED FUNDS, AND WITH THEM, THE FALSE PAPERS THAT WOULD GIVE ME A PLACE HERE.
"I DIDN'T WANT ADVENTURE. DIDN'T WANT FAME. JUST QUIET. REST.
"A LIFE WITHOUT FEAR.
"I FOLLOWED NEWS OF YOU.
"AND OF THE OTHERS, WHEN THEY CAME -- YOUR DOG, THE BLONDE GIRL, THE WOMAN IN WHITE WHO CLAIMS TO BE FROM SOME KIND OF KRYPTON...
"I DON'T KNOW WHY AMALAK NEVER FOUND YOU. HE MUST BE SPENDING HIS TIME IN OTHER REACHES.
SUPER
"BUT TIME PASSED. I GREW COMPLACENT. I DIDN'T MAINTAIN MY SENSOR SHIELDS CORRECTLY.
"THEN THE AUCTIONEER ARRIVED AND FOUND ME...
TWO KRYPTONIANS? OR -- OH MY STARS. THREE?!

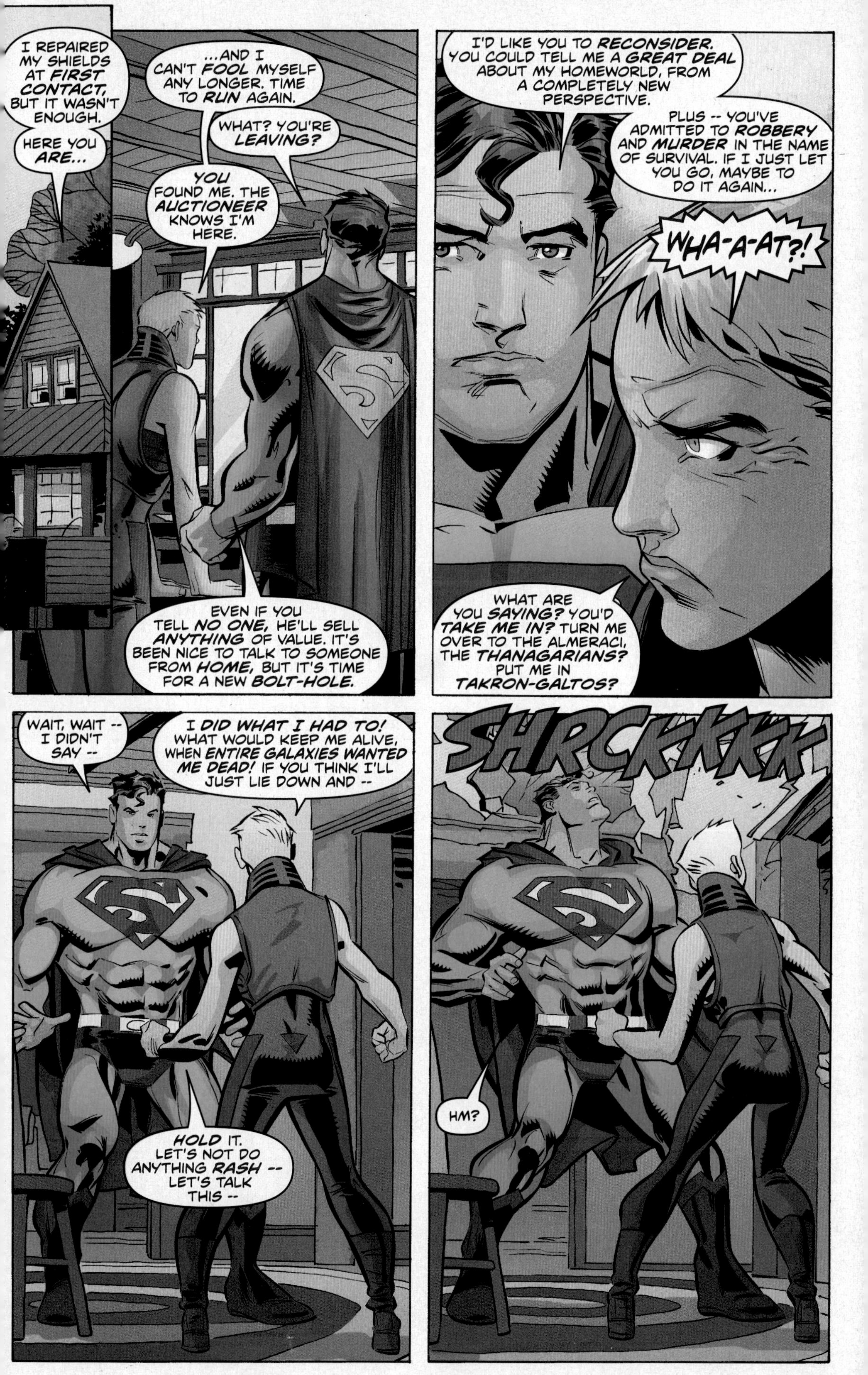

I REPAIRED MY SHIELDS AT FIRST CONTACT, BUT IT WASN'T ENOUGH.
HERE YOU ARE...
...AND I CAN'T FOOL MYSELF ANY LONGER. TIME TO RUN AGAIN.
WHAT? YOU'RE LEAVING?
YOU FOUND ME. THE AUCTIONEER KNOWS I'M HERE.
EVEN IF YOU TELL NO ONE, HE'LL SELL ANYTHING OF VALUE. IT'S BEEN NICE TO TALK TO SOMEONE FROM HOME, BUT IT'S TIME FOR A NEW BOLT-HOLE.
I'D LIKE YOU TO RECONSIDER. YOU COULD TELL ME A GREAT DEAL ABOUT MY HOMEWORLD, FROM A COMPLETELY NEW PERSPECTIVE.
PLUS -- YOU'VE ADMITTED TO ROBBERY AND MURDER IN THE NAME OF SURVIVAL. IF I JUST LET YOU GO, MAYBE TO DO IT AGAIN...
WHA-A-AT?!
WHAT ARE YOU SAYING? YOU'D TAKE ME IN? TURN ME OVER TO THE ALMERACI, THE THANAGARIANS? PUT ME IN TAKRON-GALTOS?
WAIT, WAIT -- I DIDN'T SAY --
I DID WHAT I HAD TO! WHAT WOULD KEEP ME ALIVE, WHEN ENTIRE GALAXIES WANTED ME DEAD! IF YOU THINK I'LL JUST LIE DOWN AND --
HOLD IT. LET'S NOT DO ANYTHING RASH -- LET'S TALK THIS --
SHRCKKKK
HM?

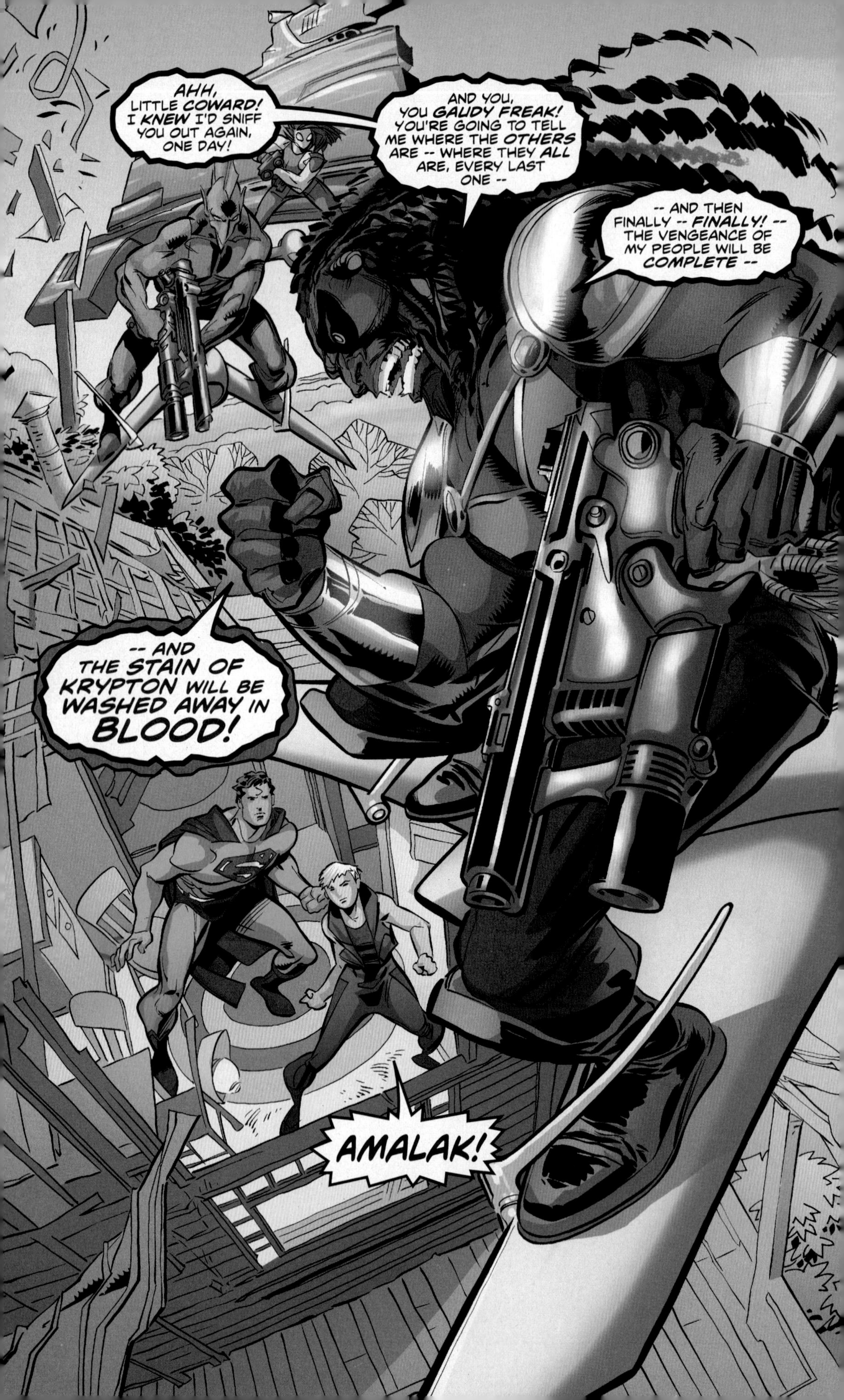
AHH, LITTLE COWARD! I KNEW I'D SNIFF YOU OUT AGAIN, ONE DAY!
AND YOU, YOU GAUDY FREAK! YOU'RE GOING TO TELL ME WHERE THE OTHERS ARE -- WHERE THEY ALL ARE, EVERY LAST ONE --
-- AND THEN FINALLY -- FINALLY! -- THE VENGEANCE OF MY PEOPLE WILL BE COMPLETE --
-- AND THE STAIN OF KRYPTON WILL BE WASHED AWAY IN BLOOD!
AMALAK!

Cover art by Jesus Merino. Cover color by Guy Major.

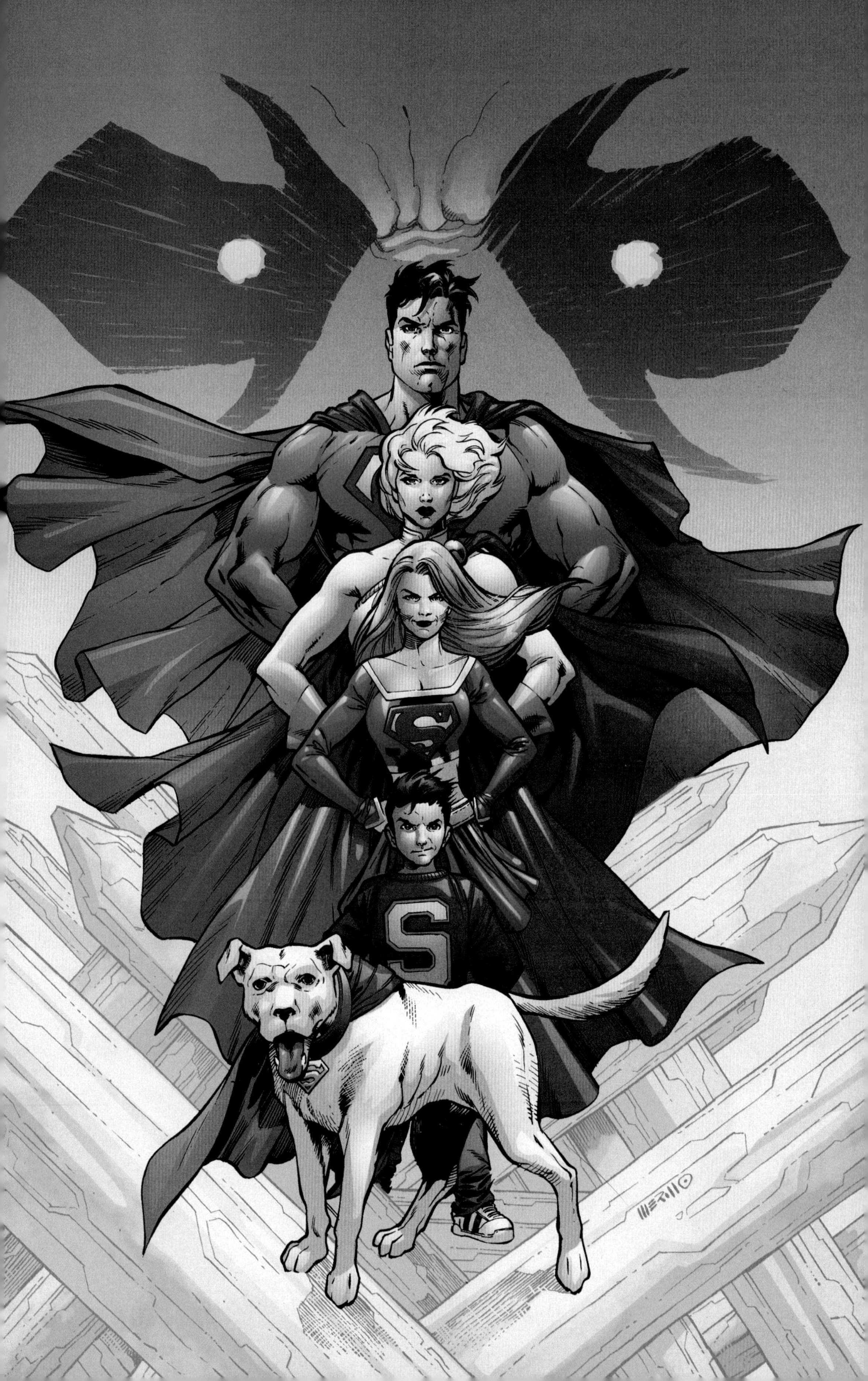

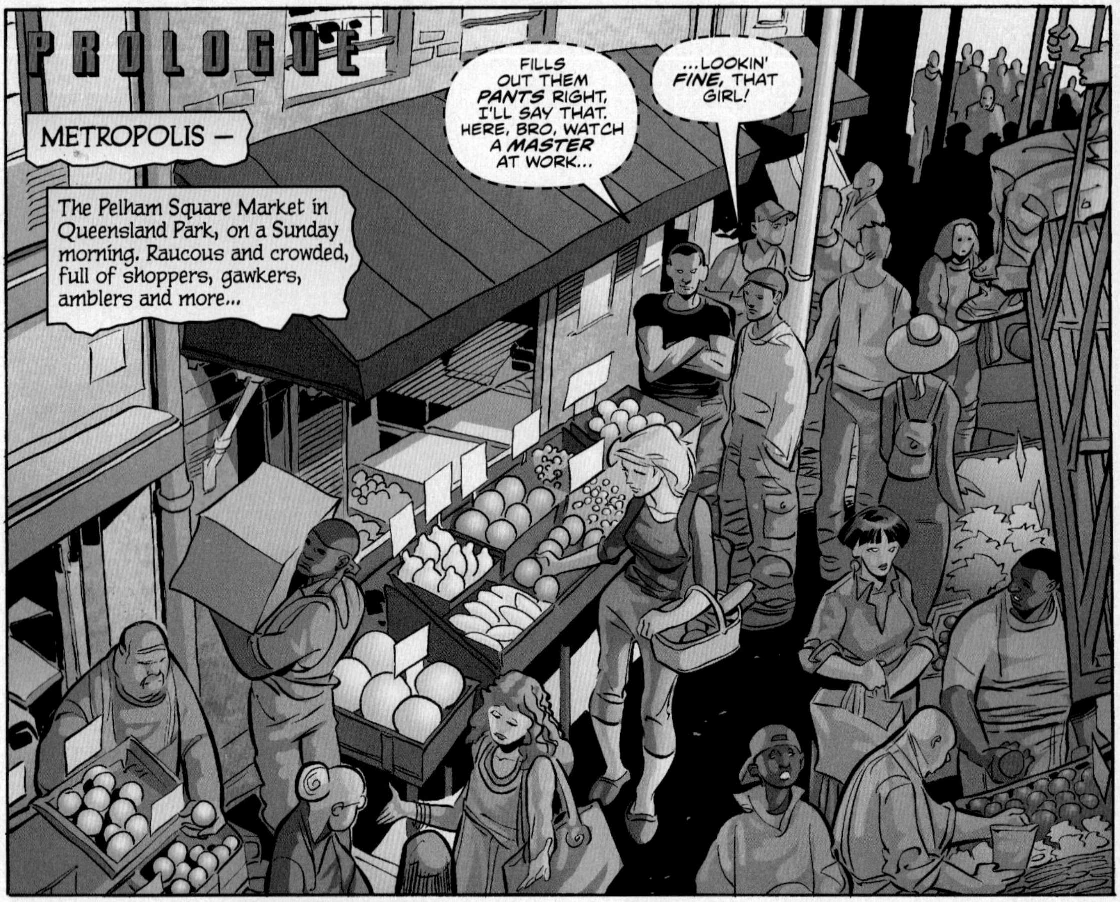
PROLOGUE
METROPOLIS —
The Pelham Square Market in Queensland Park, on a Sunday morning. Raucous and crowded, full of shoppers, gawkers, amblers and more...
FILLS OUT THEM PANTS RIGHT, I'LL SAY THAT. HERE, BRO, WATCH A MASTER AT WORK...
...LOOKIN' FINE, THAT GIRL!

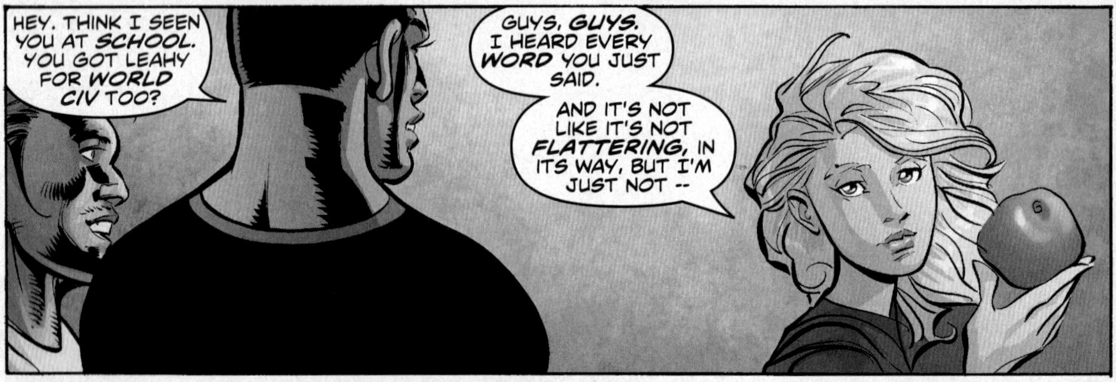
HEY. THINK I SEEN YOU AT SCHOOL. YOU GOT LEAHY FOR WORLD CIV TOO?
GUYS, GUYS. I HEARD EVERY WORD YOU JUST SAID.
AND IT'S NOT LIKE IT'S NOT FLATTERING, IN ITS WAY, BUT I'M JUST NOT --

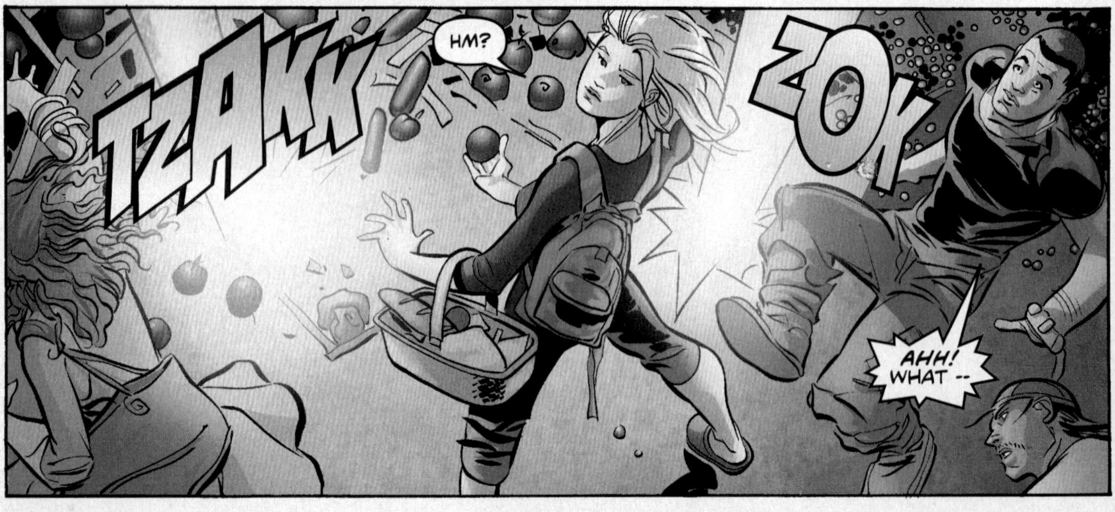
HM?
TZAKK
ZOK
AHH! WHAT --

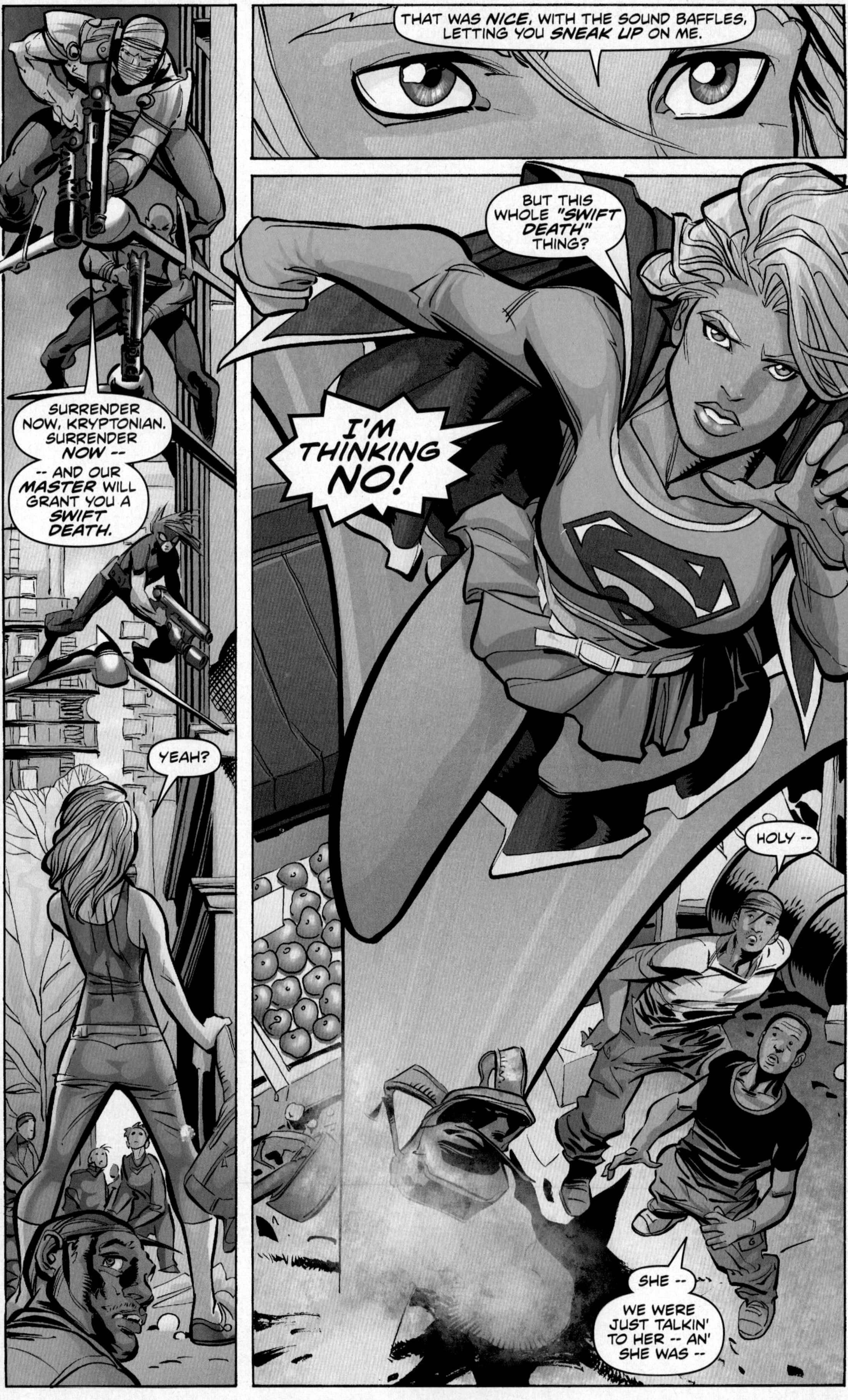
SURRENDER NOW, KRYPTONIAN. SURRENDER NOW --
-- AND OUR MASTER WILL GRANT YOU A SWIFT DEATH.
YEAH?
THAT WAS NICE, WITH THE SOUND BAFFLES, LETTING YOU SNEAK UP ON ME.
BUT THIS WHOLE "SWIFT DEATH" THING?
I'M THINKING NO!
HOLY --
SHE --
WE WERE JUST TALKIN' TO HER -- AN' SHE WAS --

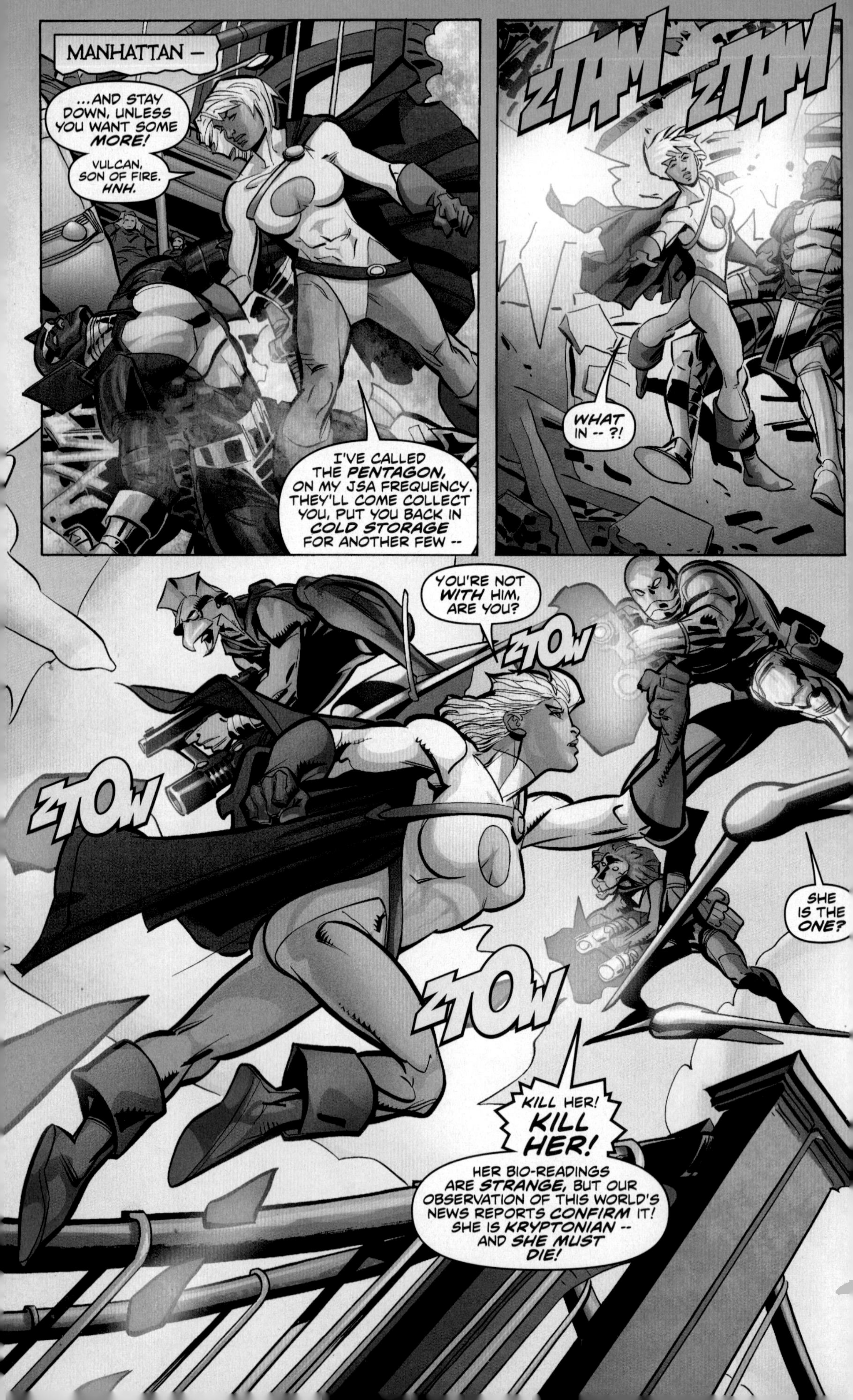
MANHATTAN —
...AND STAY DOWN, UNLESS YOU WANT SOME MORE!
VULCAN, SON OF FIRE. HNH.
I'VE CALLED THE PENTAGON, ON MY JSA FREQUENCY. THEY'LL COME COLLECT YOU, PUT YOU BACK IN COLD STORAGE FOR ANOTHER FEW --
ZTAM ZTAM
WHAT IN -- ?!
YOU'RE NOT WITH HIM, ARE YOU?
ZTOW
ZTOW
SHE IS THE ONE?
ZTOW
KILL HER! KILL HER!
HER BIO-READINGS ARE STRANGE, BUT OUR OBSERVATION OF THIS WORLD'S NEWS REPORTS CONFIRM IT! SHE IS KRYPTONIAN -- AND SHE MUST DIE!

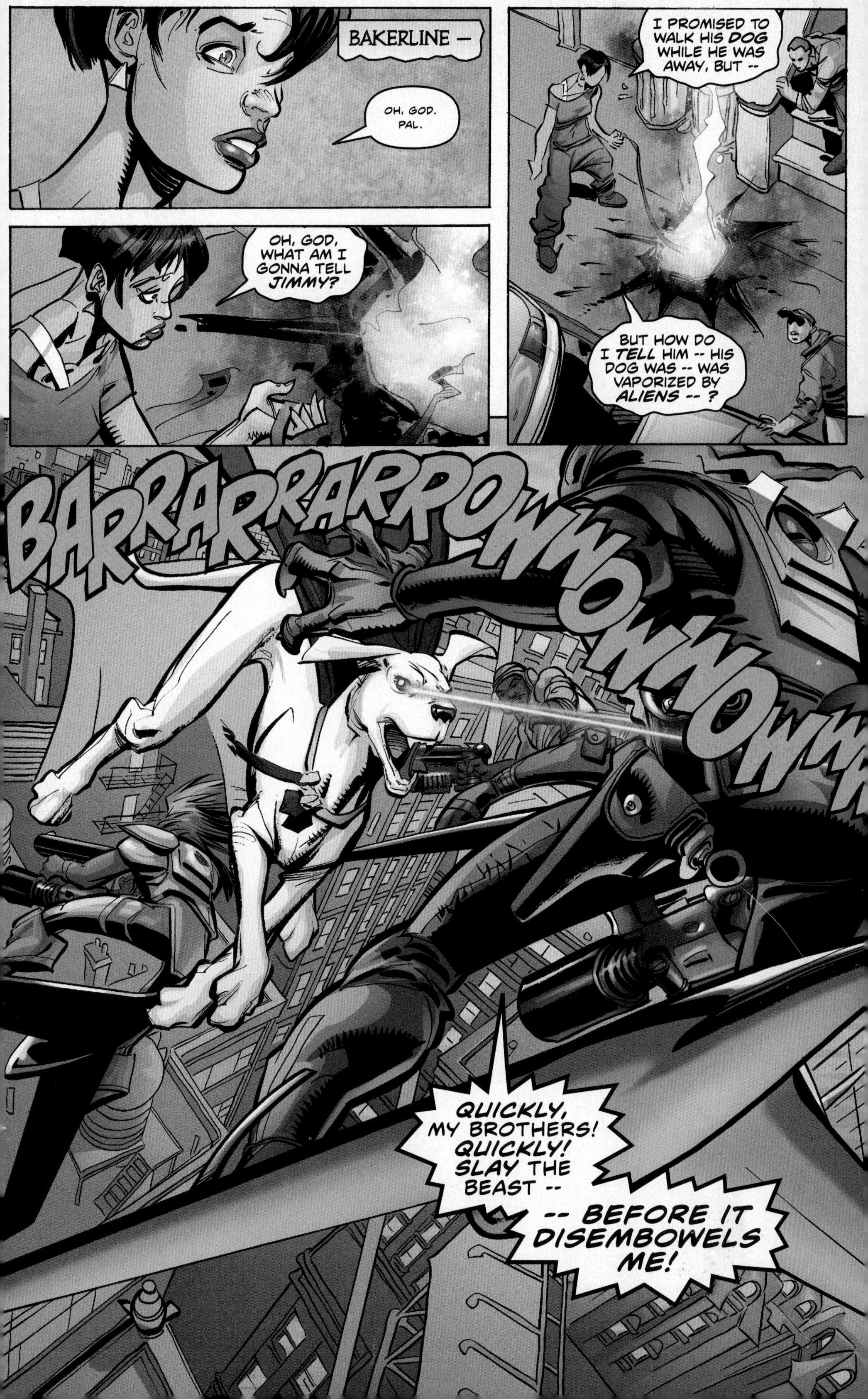
BAKERLINE —
OH, GOD. PAL.
I PROMISED TO WALK HIS DOG WHILE HE WAS AWAY, BUT --
OH, GOD, WHAT AM I GONNA TELL JIMMY?
BUT HOW DO I TELL HIM -- HIS DOG WAS -- WAS VAPORIZED BY ALIENS -- ?
BARRARRARROWWOWWOWW
QUICKLY, MY BROTHERS! QUICKLY! SLAY THE BEAST --
-- BEFORE IT DISEMBOWELS ME!

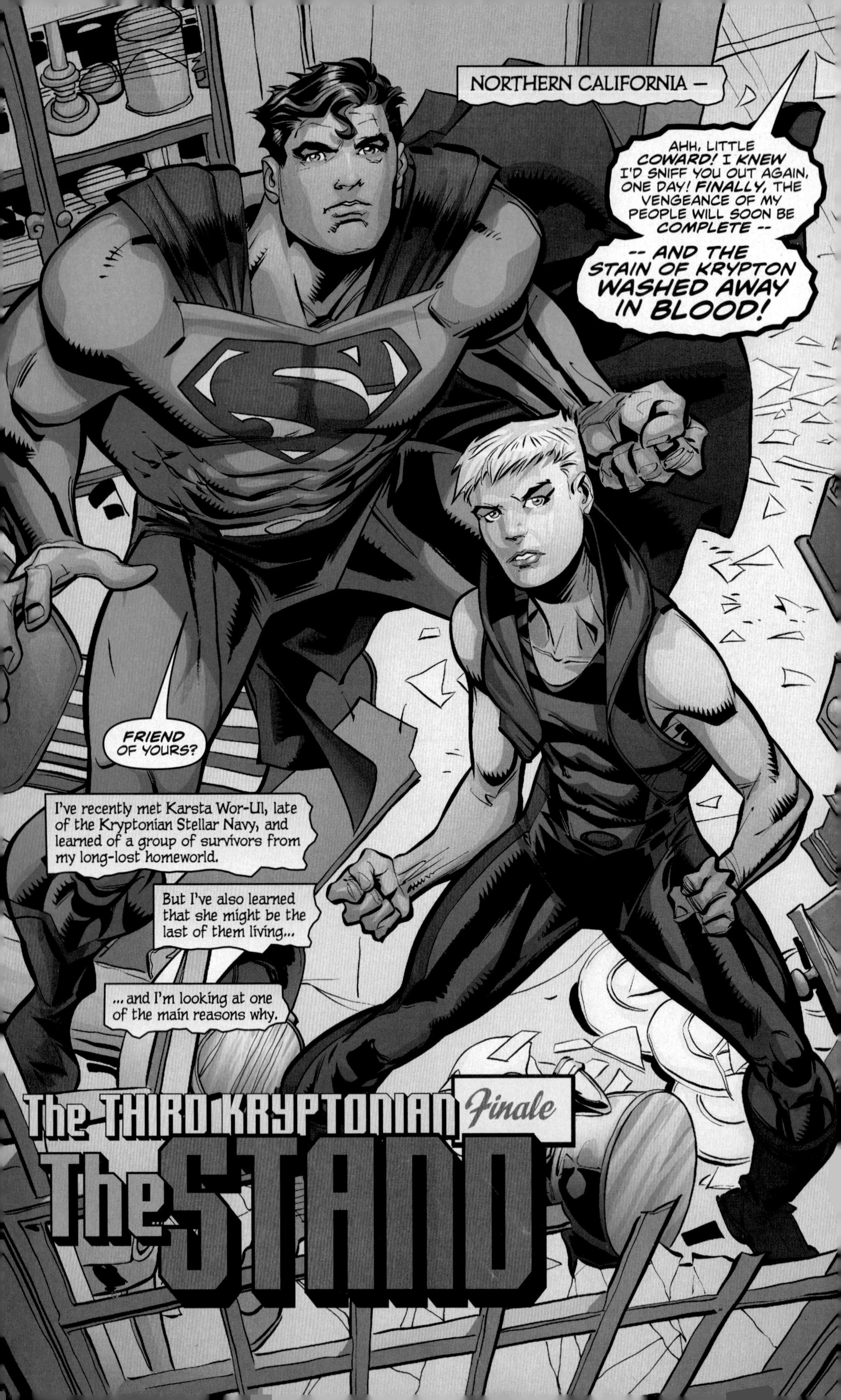
NORTHERN CALIFORNIA —
AHH, LITTLE COWARD! I KNEW I'D SNIFF YOU OUT AGAIN, ONE DAY! FINALLY, THE VENGEANCE OF MY PEOPLE WILL SOON BE COMPLETE --
-- AND THE STAIN OF KRYPTON WASHED AWAY IN BLOOD!
FRIEND OF YOURS?
I've recently met Karsta Wor-Ul, late of the Kryptonian Stellar Navy, and learned of a group of survivors from my long-lost homeworld.
But I've also learned that she might be the last of them living...
...and I'm looking at one of the main reasons why.
The THIRD KRYPTONIAN Finale
The STAND

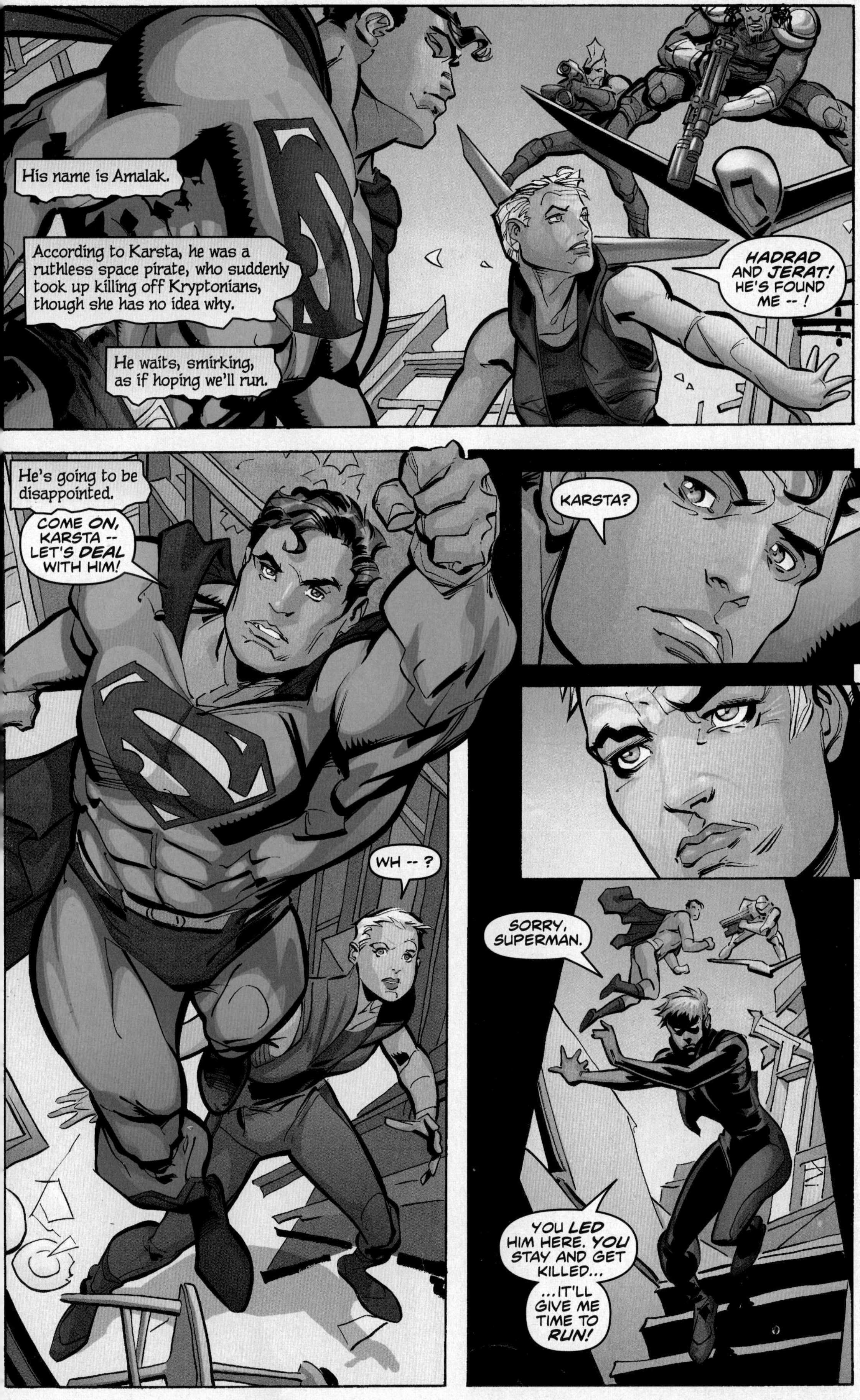
His name is Amalak.
According to Karsta, he was a ruthless space pirate, who suddenly took up killing off Kryptonians, though she has no idea why.
He waits, smirking, as if hoping we'll run.
HADRAD AND JERAT! HE'S FOUND ME -- !
He's going to be disappointed.
COME ON, KARSTA -- LET'S DEAL WITH HIM!
WH -- ?
KARSTA?
SORRY, SUPERMAN.
YOU LED HIM HERE. YOU STAY AND GET KILLED...
...IT'LL GIVE ME TIME TO RUN!

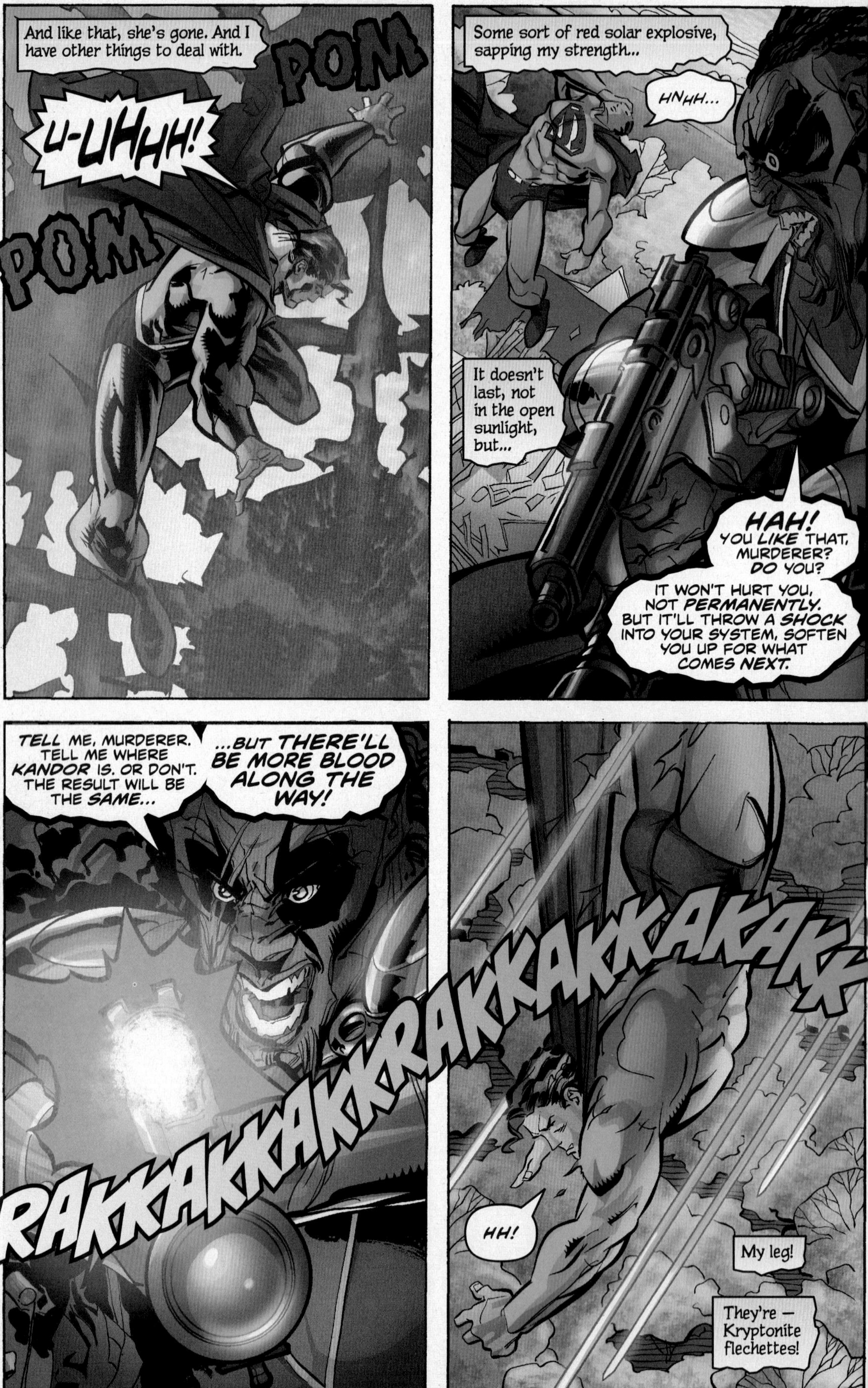

And like that, she's gone. And I have other things to deal with.
POM
U-UHHH!
POM
Some sort of red solar explosive, sapping my strength...
HNHH...
It doesn't last, not in the open sunlight, but...
HAH! YOU LIKE THAT, MURDERER? DO YOU?
IT WON'T HURT YOU, NOT PERMANENTLY. BUT IT'LL THROW A SHOCK INTO YOUR SYSTEM, SOFTEN YOU UP FOR WHAT COMES NEXT.
TELL ME, MURDERER. TELL ME WHERE KANDOR IS. OR DON'T. THE RESULT WILL BE THE SAME...
...BUT THERE'LL BE MORE BLOOD ALONG THE WAY!
RAKKAKKAKKRAKKAKKAKAKK
HH!
My leg!
They're — Kryptonite flechettes!

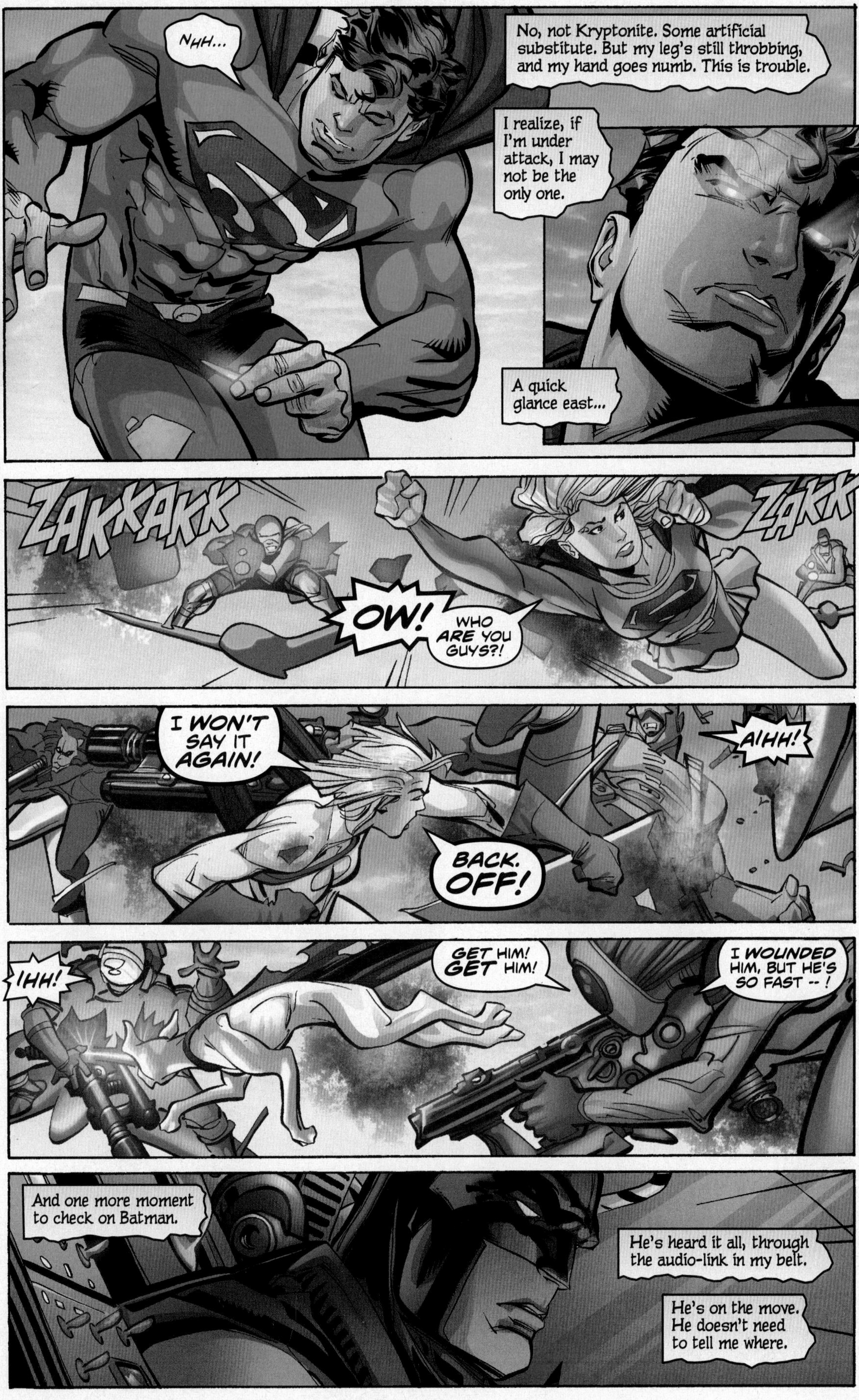
NHH...
No, not Kryptonite. Some artificial substitute. But my leg's still throbbing, and my hand goes numb. This is trouble.
I realize, if I'm under attack, I may not be the only one.
A quick glance east...
ZAKKAKK
ZAKK
OW!
WHO ARE YOU GUYS?!
I WON'T SAY IT AGAIN!
AIHH!
BACK. OFF!
IHH!
GET HIM! GET HIM!
I WOUNDED HIM, BUT HE'S SO FAST -- !
And one more moment to check on Batman.
He's heard it all, through the audio-link in my belt.
He's on the move. He doesn't need to tell me where.

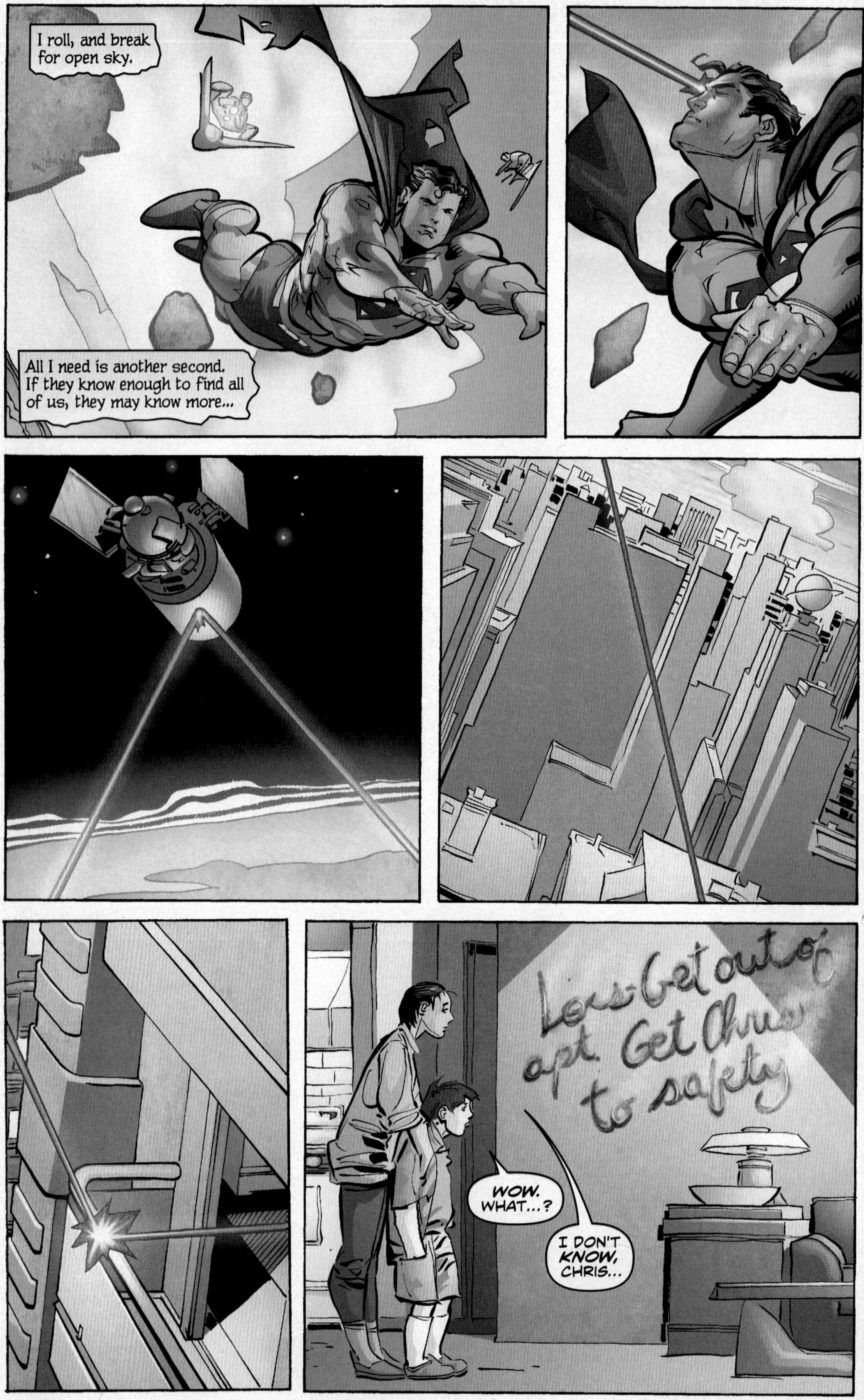
I roll, and break for open sky.
All I need is another second. If they know enough to find all of us, they may know more...
Lois-Get out of apt. Get Chris to safety
WOW. WHAT...?
I DON'T KNOW, CHRIS...

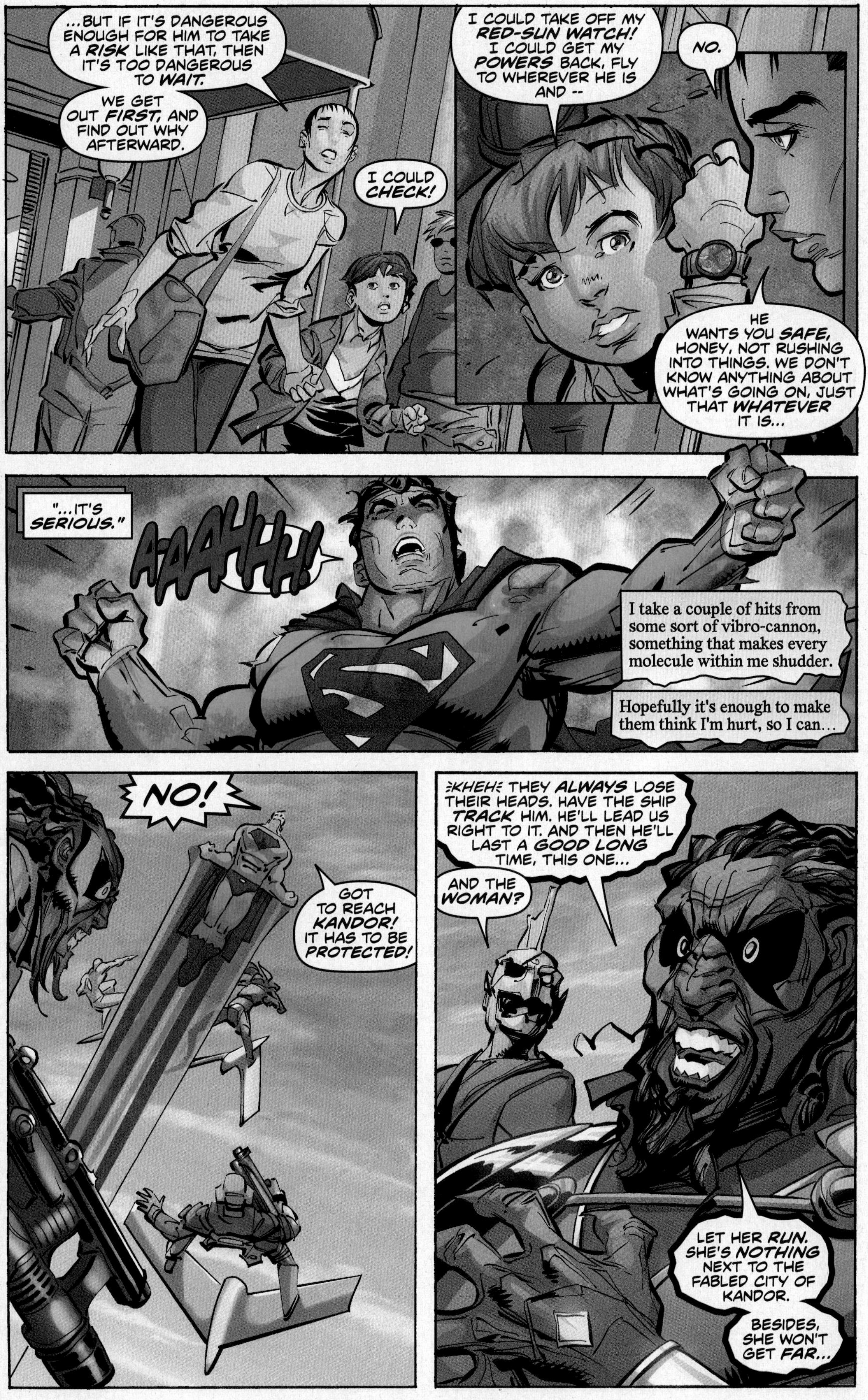

...BUT IF IT'S DANGEROUS ENOUGH FOR HIM TO TAKE A RISK LIKE THAT, THEN IT'S TOO DANGEROUS TO WAIT.
WE GET OUT FIRST, AND FIND OUT WHY AFTERWARD.
I COULD CHECK!
I COULD TAKE OFF MY RED-SUN WATCH! I COULD GET MY POWERS BACK, FLY TO WHEREVER HE IS AND --
NO.
HE WANTS YOU SAFE, HONEY, NOT RUSHING INTO THINGS. WE DON'T KNOW ANYTHING ABOUT WHAT'S GOING ON, JUST THAT WHATEVER IT IS...
"...IT'S SERIOUS."
AAAHHH!
I take a couple of hits from some sort of vibro-cannon, something that makes every molecule within me shudder.
Hopefully it's enough to make them think I'm hurt, so I can...
NO!
GOT TO REACH KANDOR! IT HAS TO BE PROTECTED!
KHEH! THEY ALWAYS LOSE THEIR HEADS. HAVE THE SHIP TRACK HIM. HE'LL LEAD US RIGHT TO IT. AND THEN HE'LL LAST A GOOD LONG TIME, THIS ONE...
AND THE WOMAN?
LET HER RUN. SHE'S NOTHING NEXT TO THE FABLED CITY OF KANDOR.
BESIDES, SHE WON'T GET FAR...

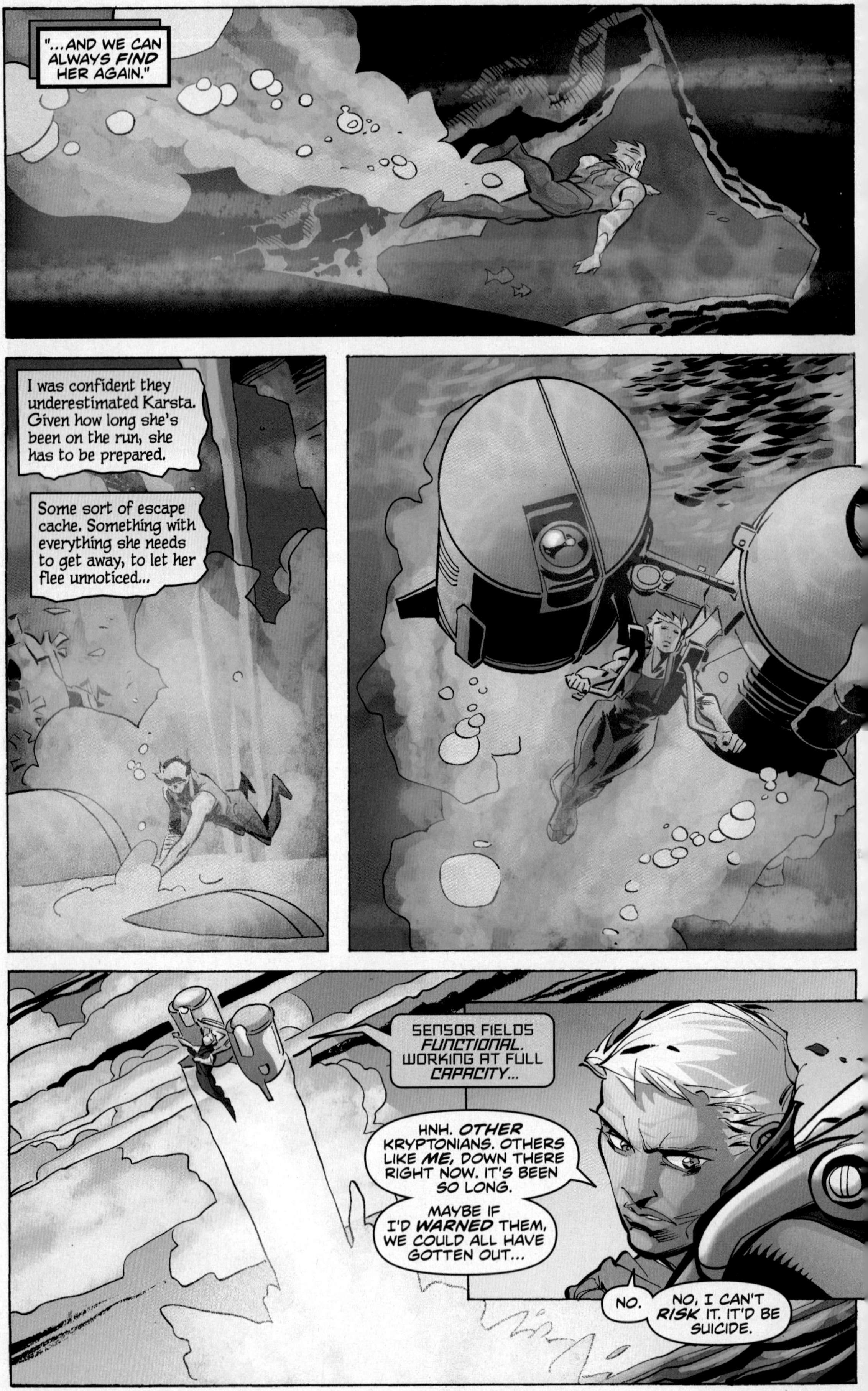
"...AND WE CAN ALWAYS FIND HER AGAIN."
I was confident they underestimated Karsta. Given how long she's been on the run, she has to be prepared.
Some sort of escape cache. Something with everything she needs to get away, to let her flee unnoticed...
SENSOR FIELDS FUNCTIONAL. WORKING AT FULL CAPACITY...
HNH. OTHER KRYPTONIANS. OTHERS LIKE ME, DOWN THERE RIGHT NOW. IT'S BEEN SO LONG.
MAYBE IF I'D WARNED THEM, WE COULD ALL HAVE GOTTEN OUT...
NO.
NO, I CAN'T RISK IT. IT'D BE SUICIDE.

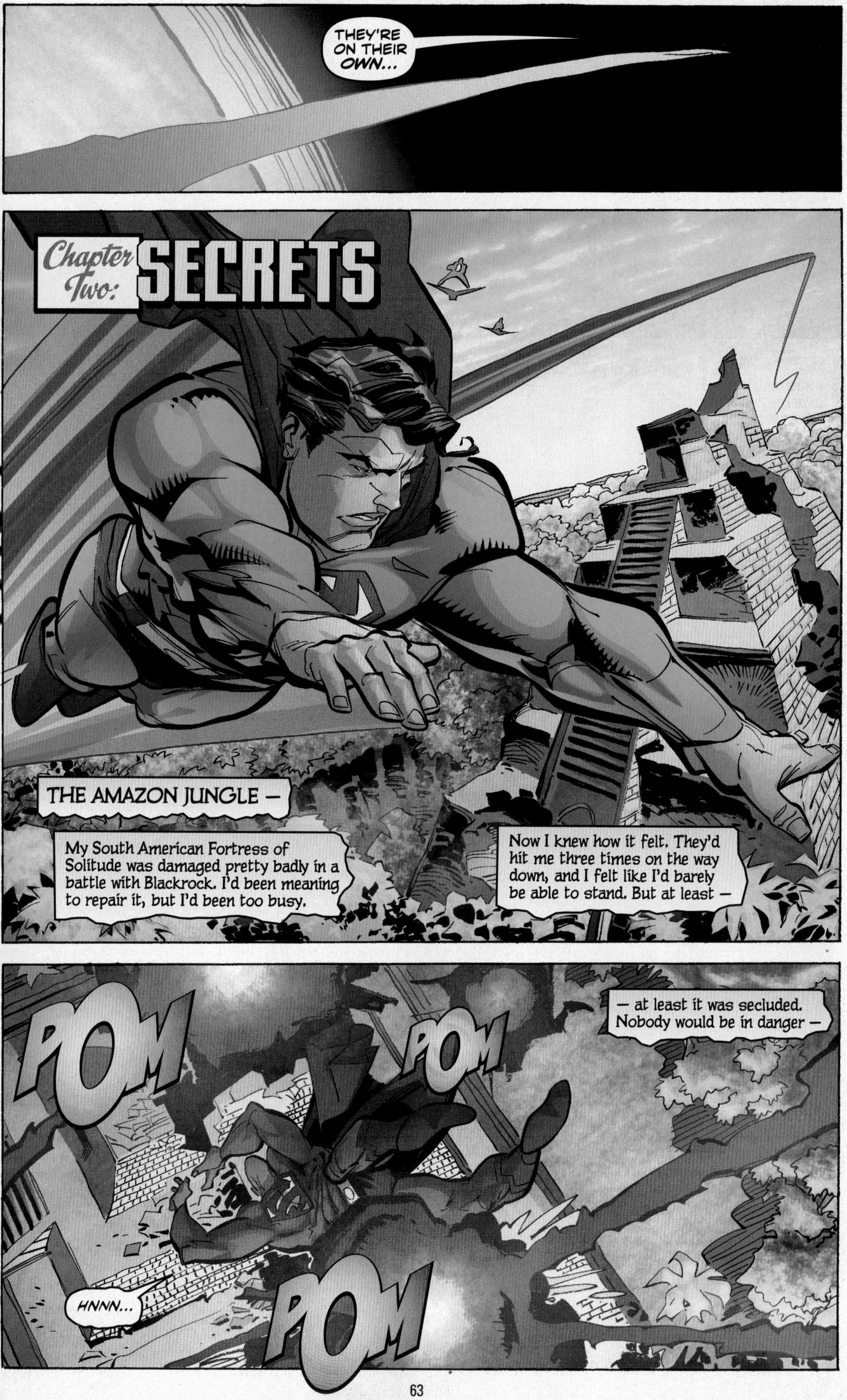
THEY'RE ON THEIR OWN...
Chapter Two: SECRETS
THE AMAZON JUNGLE —
My South American Fortress of Solitude was damaged pretty badly in a battle with Blackrock. I'd been meaning to repair it, but I'd been too busy.
Now I knew how it felt. They'd hit me three times on the way down, and I felt like I'd barely be able to stand. But at least —
POM
POM
— at least it was secluded. Nobody would be in danger —
HNNN...
POM

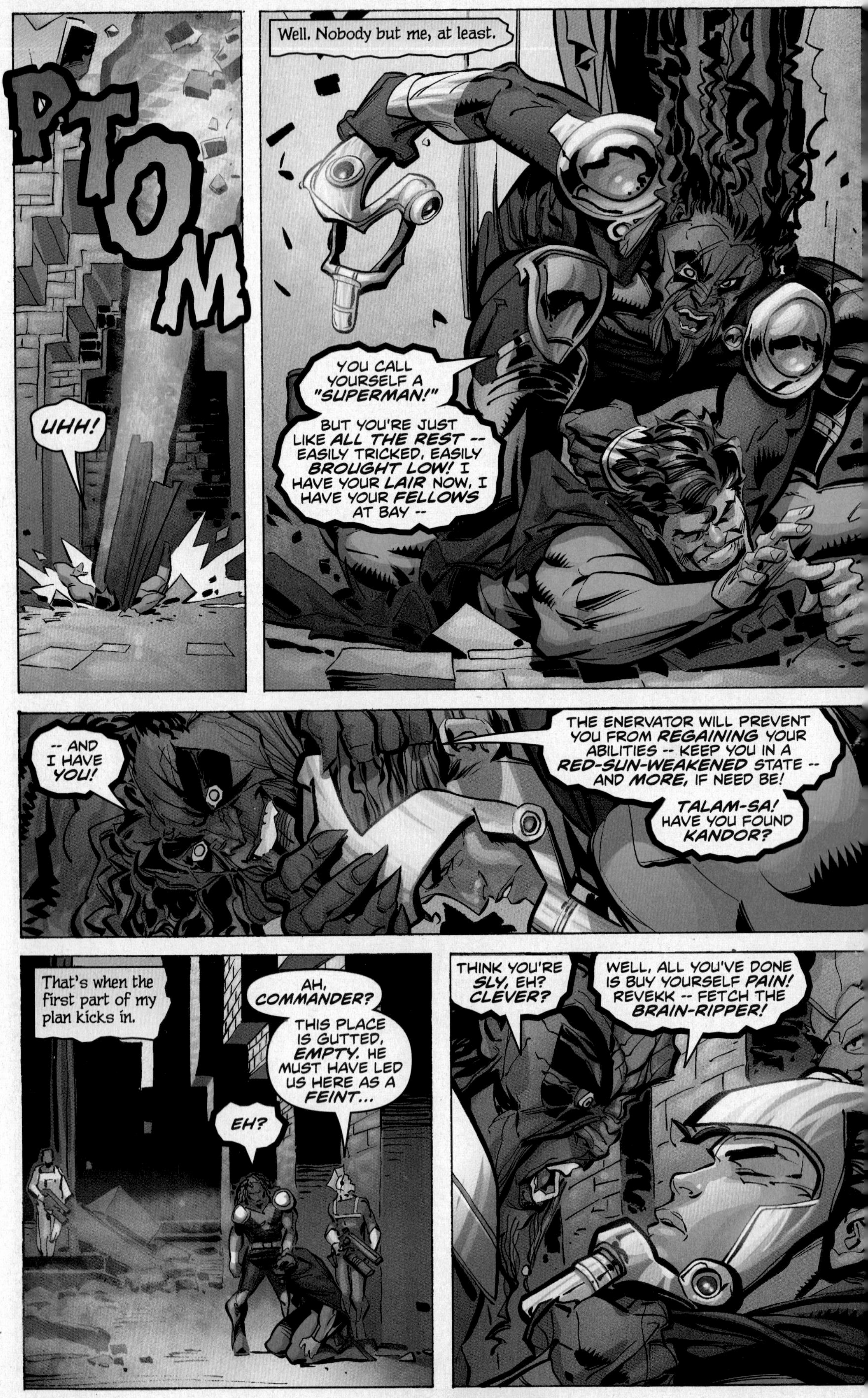
PTOM
UHH!
Well. Nobody but me, at least.
YOU CALL YOURSELF A "SUPERMAN!"
BUT YOU'RE JUST LIKE ALL THE REST -- EASILY TRICKED, EASILY BROUGHT LOW! I HAVE YOUR LAIR NOW, I HAVE YOUR FELLOWS AT BAY --
-- AND I HAVE YOU!
THE ENERVATOR WILL PREVENT YOU FROM REGAINING YOUR ABILITIES -- KEEP YOU IN A RED-SUN-WEAKENED STATE -- AND MORE, IF NEED BE!
TALAM-SA! HAVE YOU FOUND KANDOR?
That's when the first part of my plan kicks in.
AH, COMMANDER?
THIS PLACE IS GUTTED, EMPTY. HE MUST HAVE LED US HERE AS A FEINT...
EH?
THINK YOU'RE SLY, EH? CLEVER?
WELL, ALL YOU'VE DONE IS BUY YOURSELF PAIN! REVEKK -- FETCH THE BRAIN-RIPPER!

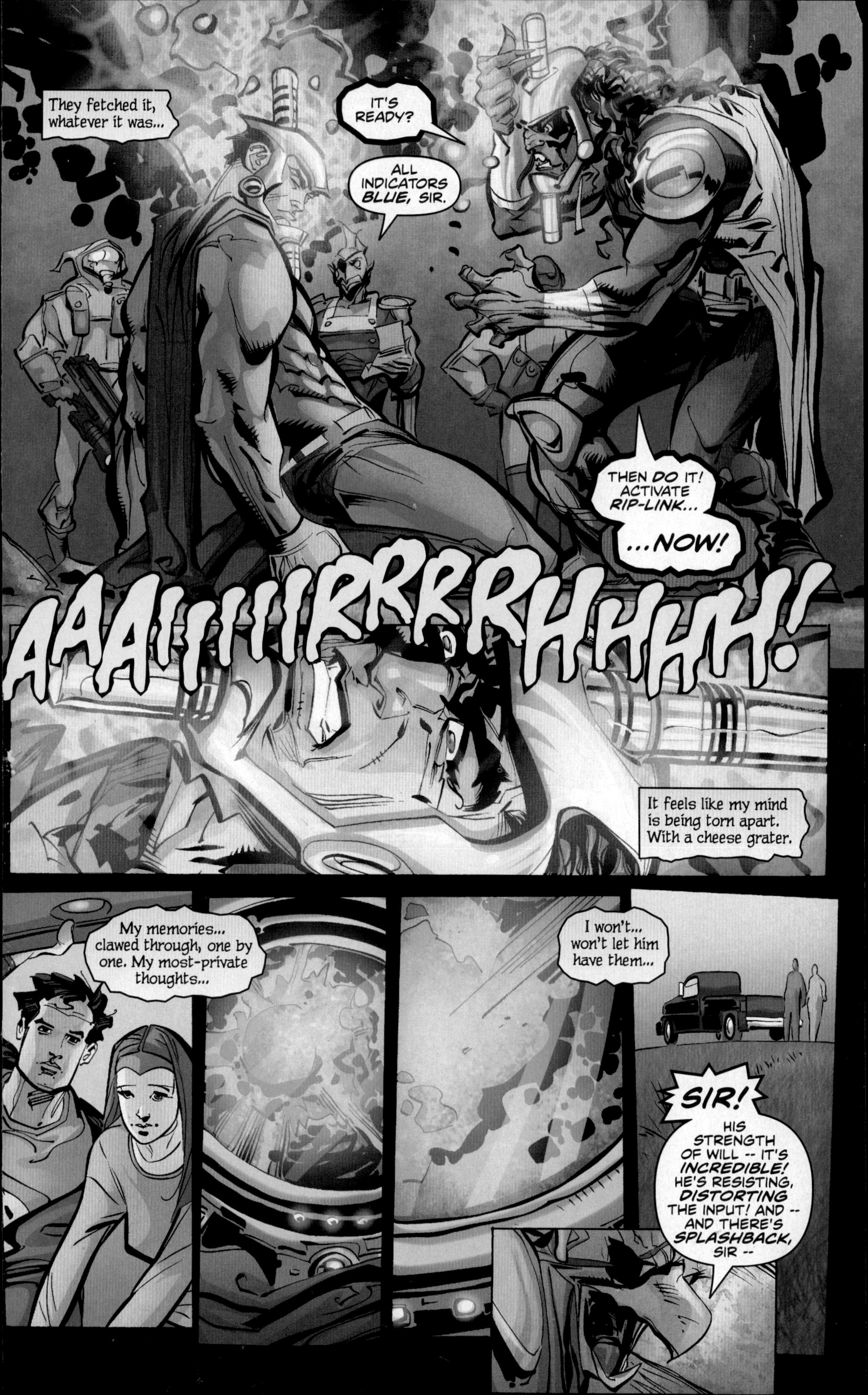
They fetched it, whatever it was...
IT'S READY?
ALL INDICATORS BLUE, SIR.
THEN DO IT! ACTIVATE RIP-LINK...
...NOW!
AAAIIIIIRRRRRHHHHH!
It feels like my mind is being torn apart. With a cheese grater.
My memories... clawed through, one by one. My most-private thoughts...
I won't... won't let him have them...
SIR!
HIS STRENGTH OF WILL -- IT'S INCREDIBLE! HE'S RESISTING, DISTORTING THE INPUT! AND -- AND THERE'S SPLASHBACK, SIR --

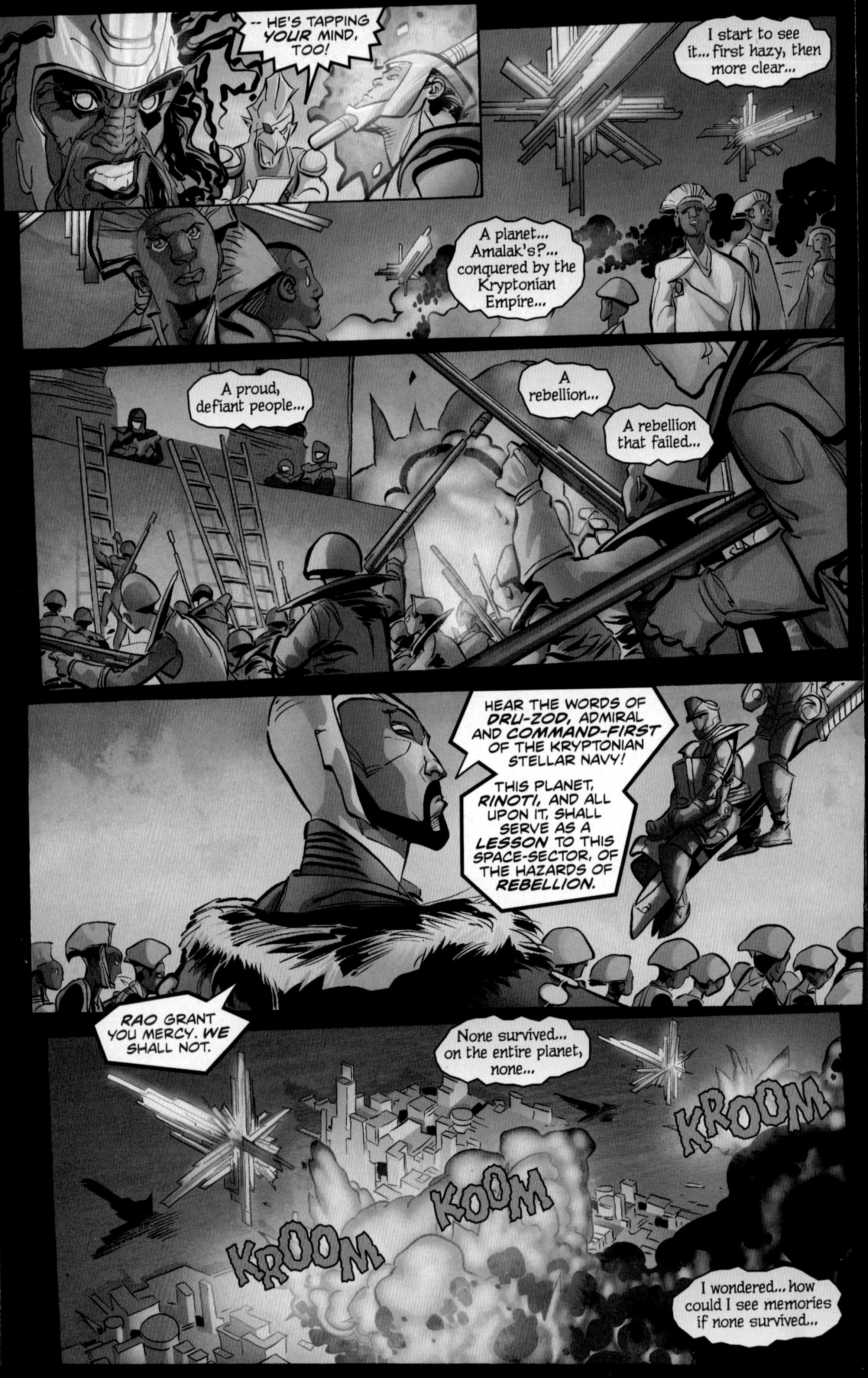
-- HE'S TAPPING YOUR MIND, TOO!
I start to see it... first hazy, then more clear...
A planet... Amalak's?... conquered by the Kryptonian Empire...
A proud, defiant people...
A rebellion...
A rebellion that failed...
HEAR THE WORDS OF DRU-ZOD, ADMIRAL AND COMMAND-FIRST OF THE KRYPTONIAN STELLAR NAVY!
THIS PLANET, RINOTI, AND ALL UPON IT, SHALL SERVE AS A LESSON TO THIS SPACE-SECTOR, OF THE HAZARDS OF REBELLION.
RAO GRANT YOU MERCY. WE SHALL NOT.
None survived... on the entire planet, none...
KROOM
KOOM
KROOM
I wondered... how could I see memories if none survived...

But then...a ship...

NO... NO...

MINE... NOT FOR YOU...

A ship, after so long... a homecomer?...

SHFF

IT -- IT CANNOT BE!

I WAS HERE -- ONLY *FIFTY ORBITS* BACK! THE PLANET -- IT WAS HEALTHY, *THRIVING!* THE PEOPLE, THE TRADESMEN -- WHAT *HAPPENED* HERE?

The dust... there was no wind, but it rises... cries...

SHFF

SHAA

SHAA SHAA

WHAT -- WHO --

KILLED US

OUR SOULS

OUR BLOOD

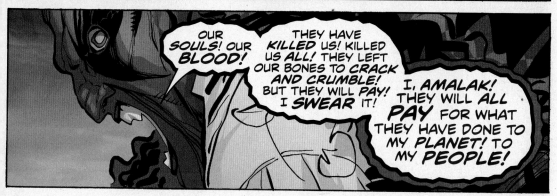

OUR SOULS! OUR BLOOD!

THEY HAVE *KILLED US!* KILLED US *ALL!* THEY LEFT OUR BONES TO *CRACK* AND CRUMBLE! BUT THEY WILL *PAY!* I *SWEAR* IT!

I, *AMALAK!* THEY WILL *ALL PAY* FOR WHAT THEY HAVE DONE TO MY *PLANET!* TO MY *PEOPLE!*

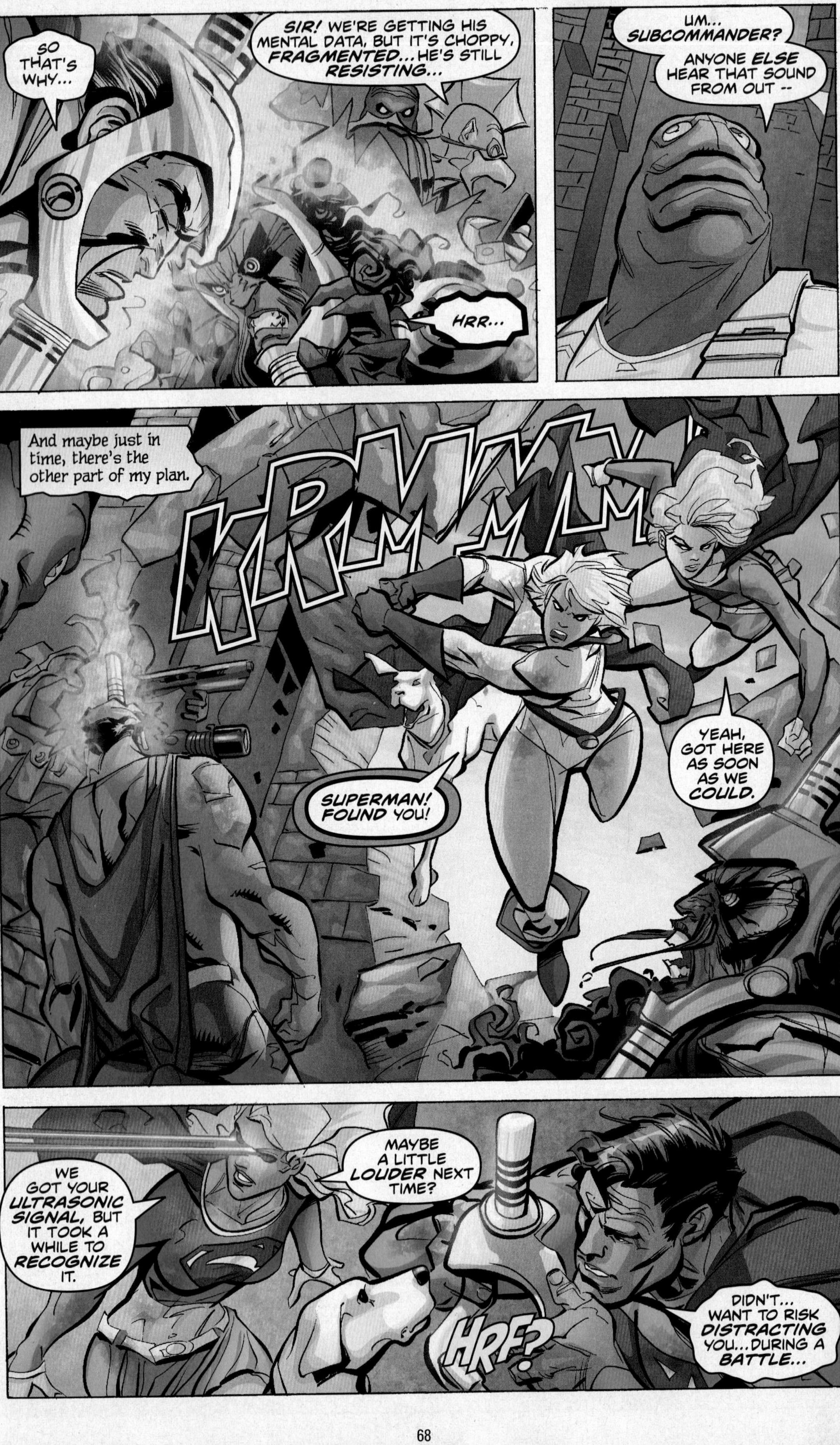
SO THAT'S WHY...
SIR! WE'RE GETTING HIS MENTAL DATA, BUT IT'S CHOPPY, FRAGMENTED... HE'S STILL RESISTING...
HRR...
UM... SUBCOMMANDER?
ANYONE ELSE HEAR THAT SOUND FROM OUT --
And maybe just in time, there's the other part of my plan.
KRMMM
SUPERMAN! FOUND YOU!
YEAH, GOT HERE AS SOON AS WE COULD.
WE GOT YOUR ULTRASONIC SIGNAL, BUT IT TOOK A WHILE TO RECOGNIZE IT.
MAYBE A LITTLE LOUDER NEXT TIME?
HRF?
DIDN'T... WANT TO RISK DISTRACTING YOU...DURING A BATTLE...

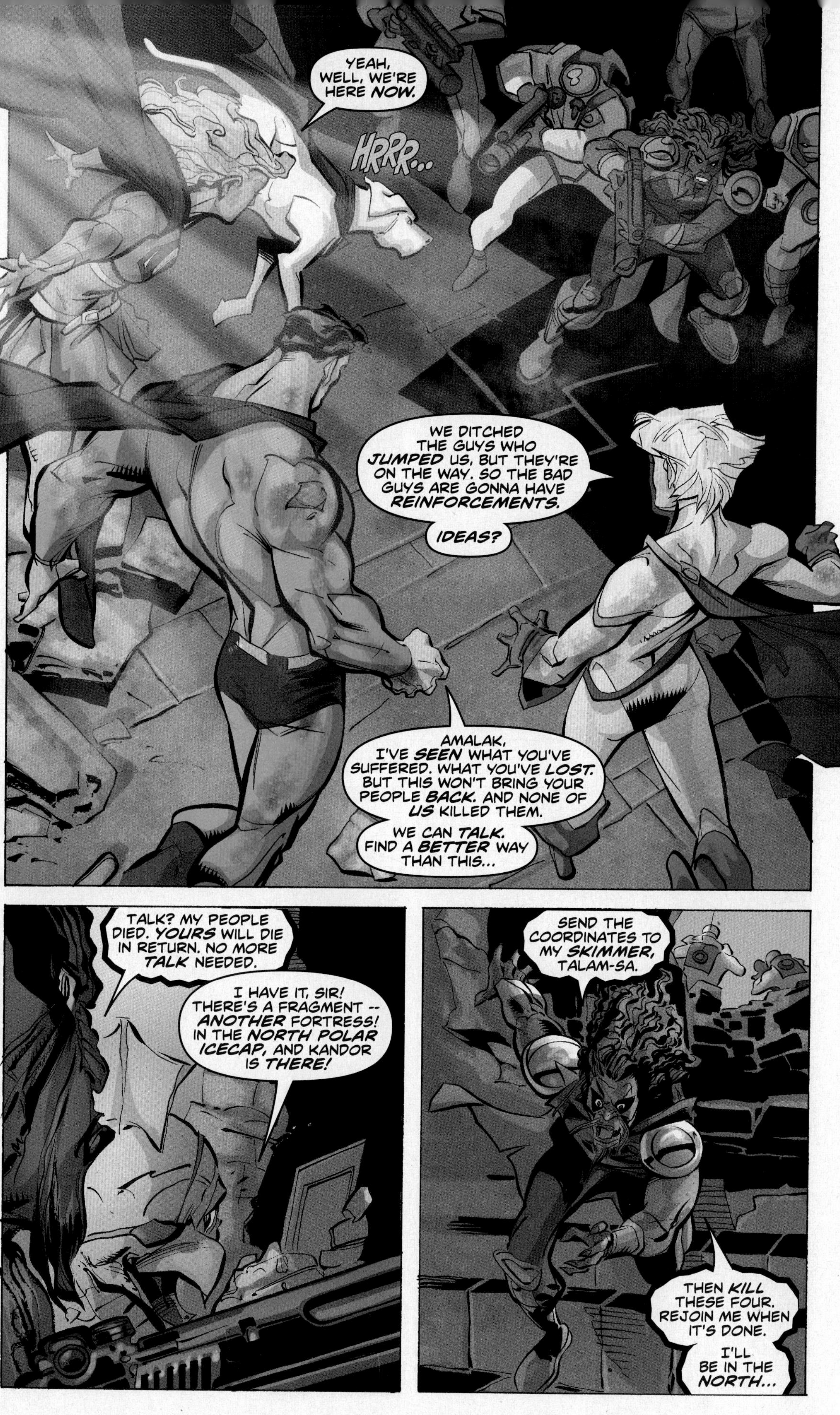

YEAH, WELL, WE'RE HERE NOW.
HRRR...
WE DITCHED THE GUYS WHO JUMPED US, BUT THEY'RE ON THE WAY. SO THE BAD GUYS ARE GONNA HAVE REINFORCEMENTS.
IDEAS?
AMALAK, I'VE SEEN WHAT YOU'VE SUFFERED. WHAT YOU'VE LOST. BUT THIS WON'T BRING YOUR PEOPLE BACK. AND NONE OF US KILLED THEM.
WE CAN TALK. FIND A BETTER WAY THAN THIS...
TALK? MY PEOPLE DIED. YOURS WILL DIE IN RETURN. NO MORE TALK NEEDED.
I HAVE IT, SIR! THERE'S A FRAGMENT -- ANOTHER FORTRESS! IN THE NORTH POLAR ICECAP, AND KANDOR IS THERE!
SEND THE COORDINATES TO MY SKIMMER, TALAM-SA.
THEN KILL THESE FOUR. REJOIN ME WHEN IT'S DONE.
I'LL BE IN THE NORTH...

And, above...

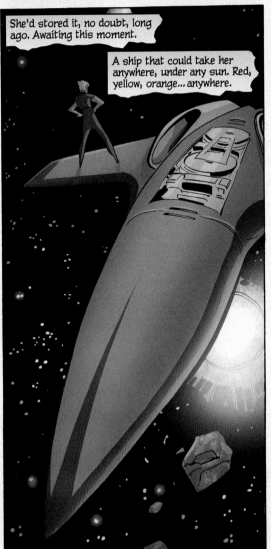

She'd stored it, no doubt, long ago. Awaiting this moment.

A ship that could take her anywhere, under any sun. Red, yellow, orange... anywhere.

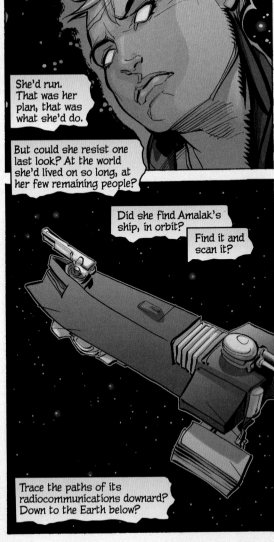

She'd run. That was her plan, that was what she'd do.

But could she resist one last look? At the world she'd lived on so long, at her few remaining people?

Did she find Amalak's ship, in orbit?

Find it and scan it?

Trace the paths of its radiocomunications downward? Down to the Earth below?

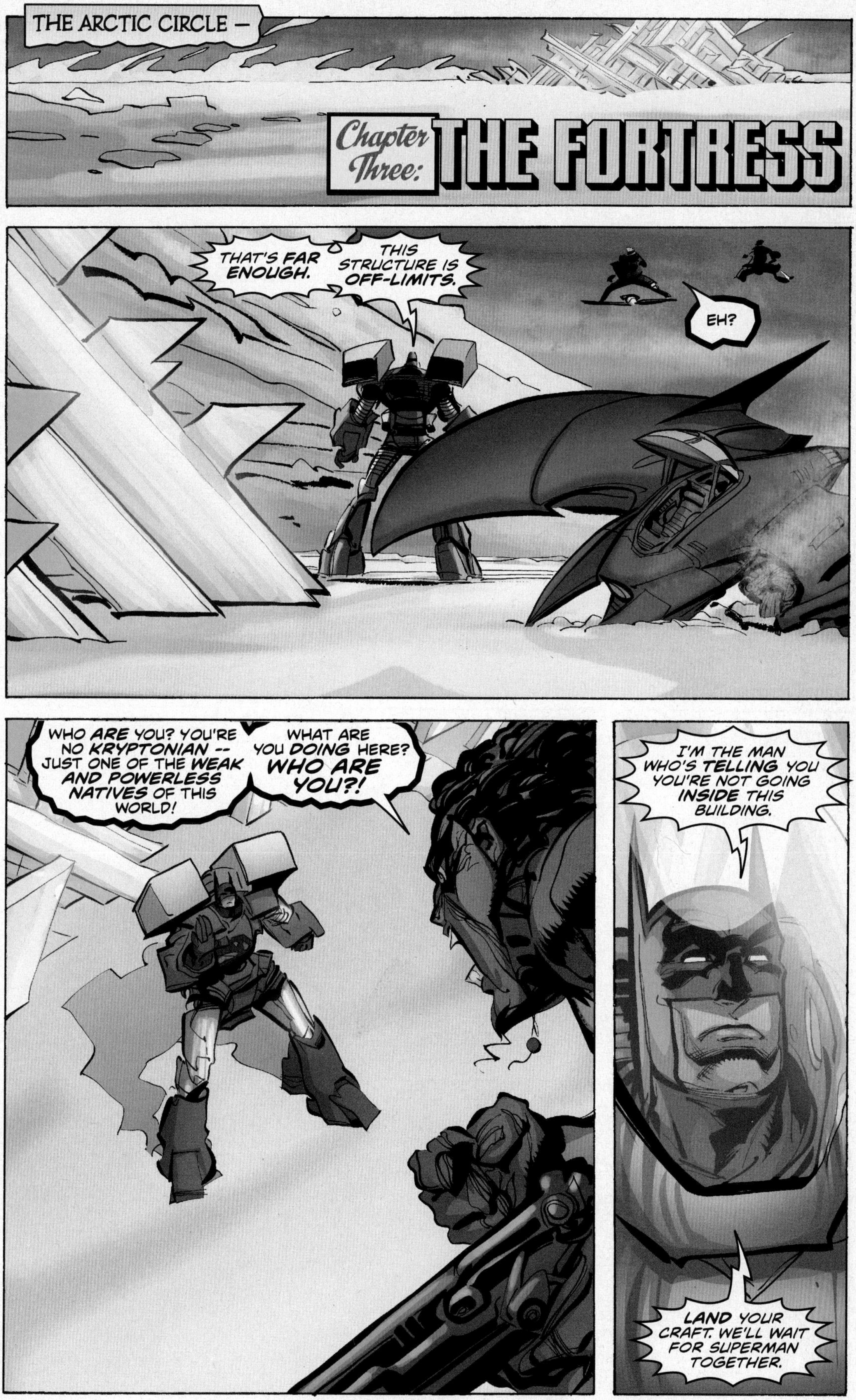

THE ARCTIC CIRCLE –
Chapter Three: THE FORTRESS
THAT'S FAR ENOUGH.
THIS STRUCTURE IS OFF-LIMITS.
EH?
WHO ARE YOU? YOU'RE NO KRYPTONIAN -- JUST ONE OF THE WEAK AND POWERLESS NATIVES OF THIS WORLD!
WHAT ARE YOU DOING HERE? WHO ARE YOU?!
I'M THE MAN WHO'S TELLING YOU YOU'RE NOT GOING INSIDE THIS BUILDING.
LAND YOUR CRAFT. WE'LL WAIT FOR SUPERMAN TOGETHER.

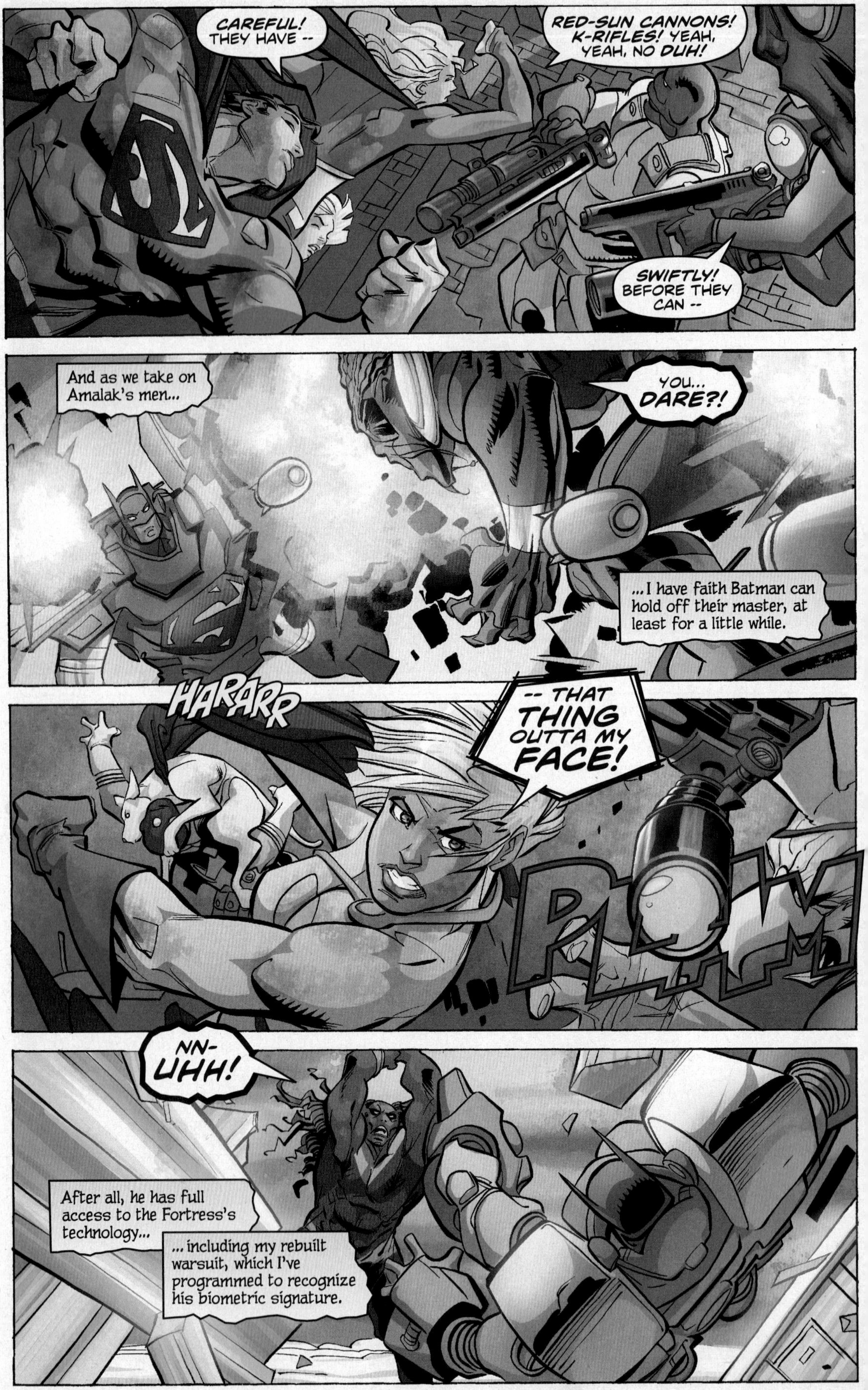
CAREFUL! THEY HAVE --
RED-SUN CANNONS! K-RIFLES! YEAH, YEAH, NO DUH!
SWIFTLY! BEFORE THEY CAN --
And as we take on Amalak's men...
YOU... DARE?!
...I have faith Batman can hold off their master, at least for a little while.
HARARR
-- THAT THING OUTTA MY FACE!
BLAM
NN-UHH!
After all, he has full access to the Fortress's technology...
...including my rebuilt warsuit, which I've programmed to recognize his biometric signature.

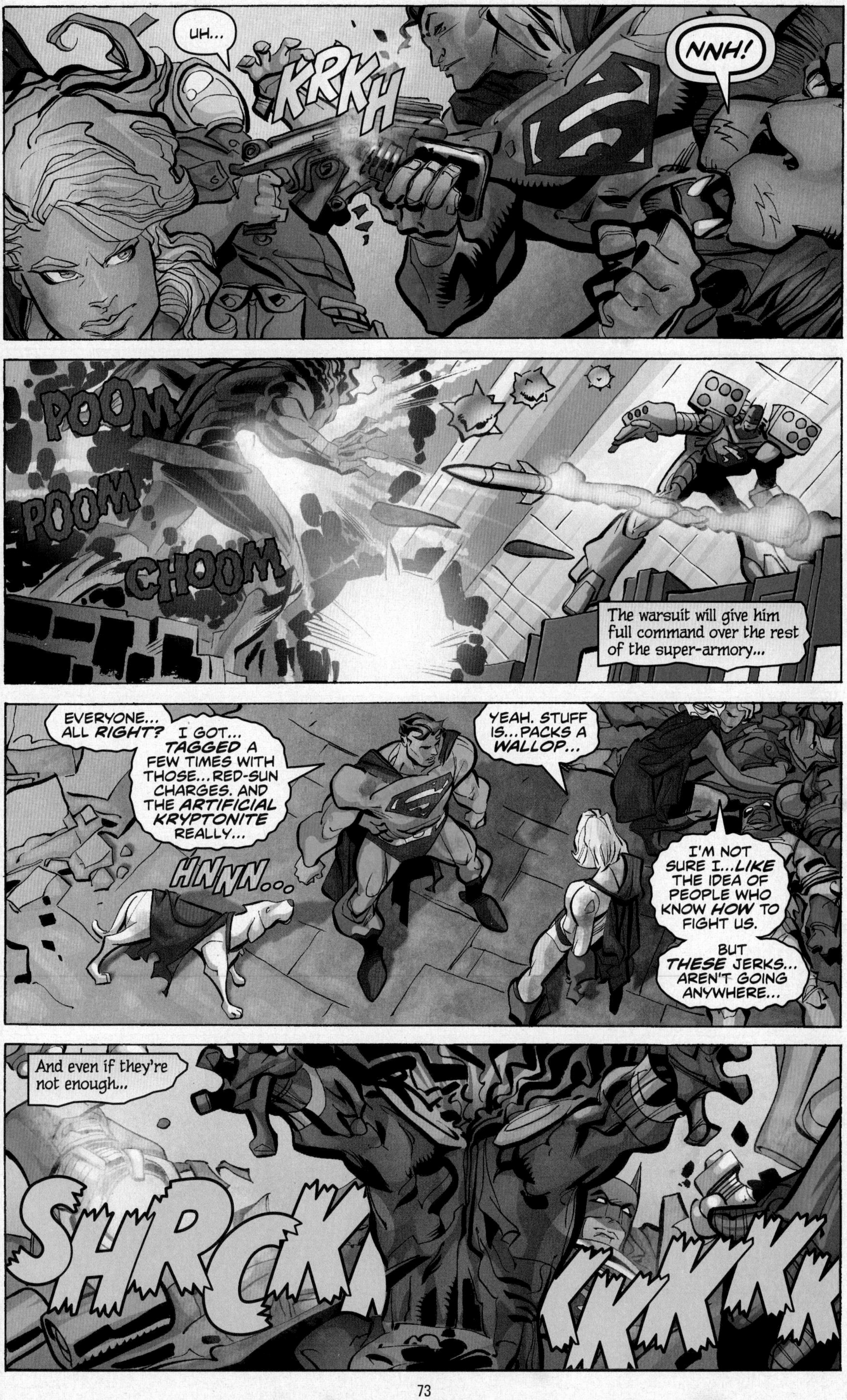
UH...
KRKH
NNH!
POOM
POOM
CHOOM
The warsuit will give him full command over the rest of the super-armory...
EVERYONE... ALL RIGHT? I GOT... TAGGED A FEW TIMES WITH THOSE...RED-SUN CHARGES. AND THE ARTIFICIAL KRYPTONITE REALLY...
YEAH. STUFF IS...PACKS A WALLOP...
HNNN...
I'M NOT SURE I...LIKE THE IDEA OF PEOPLE WHO KNOW HOW TO FIGHT US.
BUT THESE JERKS... AREN'T GOING ANYWHERE...
And even if they're not enough...
SHRCKKKK

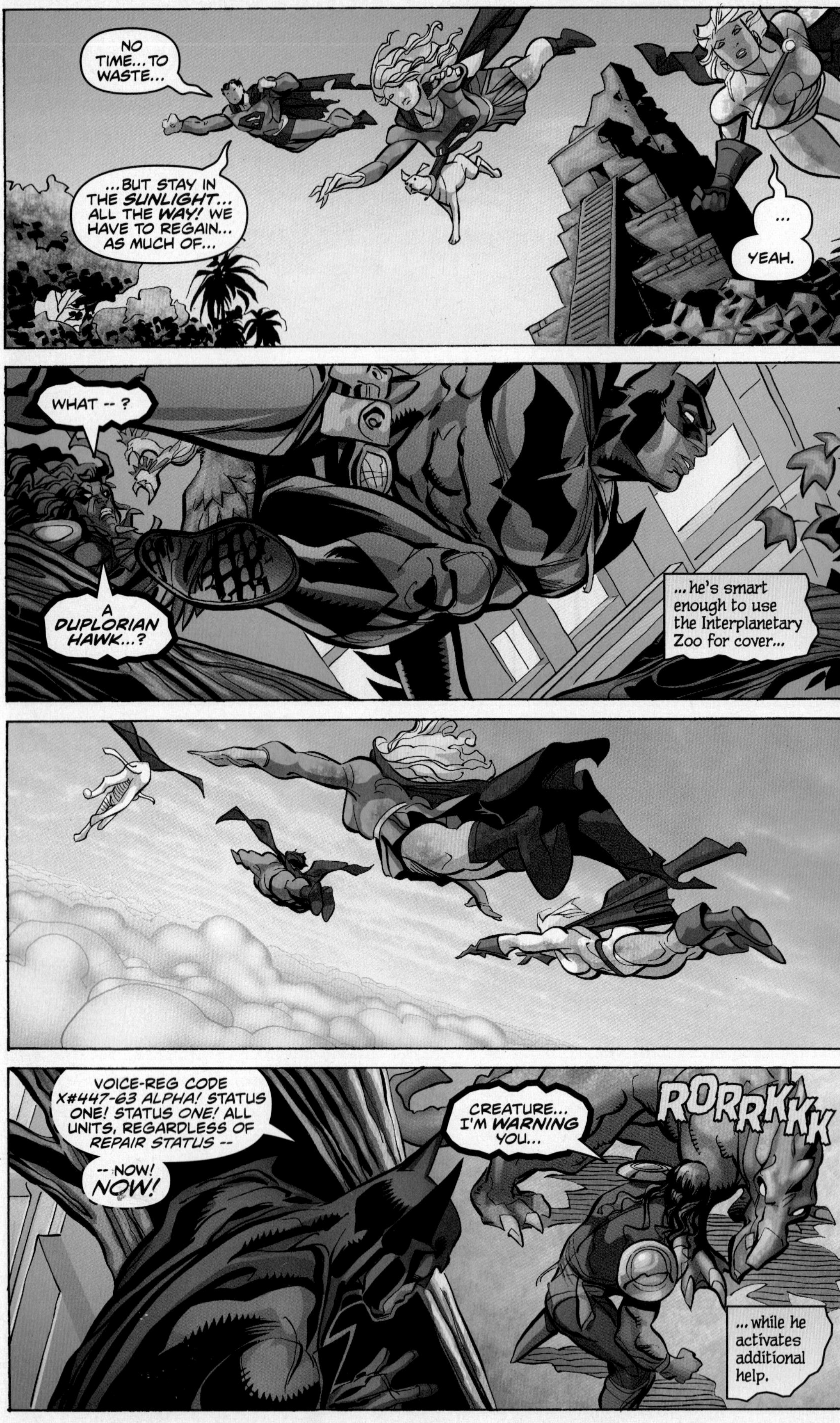
NO TIME... TO WASTE...
...BUT STAY IN THE SUNLIGHT... ALL THE WAY! WE HAVE TO REGAIN... AS MUCH OF...
...
YEAH.
WHAT -- ?
A DUPLORIAN HAWK...?
...he's smart enough to use the Interplanetary Zoo for cover...
VOICE-REG CODE X#447-63 ALPHA! STATUS ONE! STATUS ONE! ALL UNITS, REGARDLESS OF REPAIR STATUS --
-- NOW! NOW!
CREATURE... I'M WARNING YOU...
RORRKKK
...while he activates additional help.

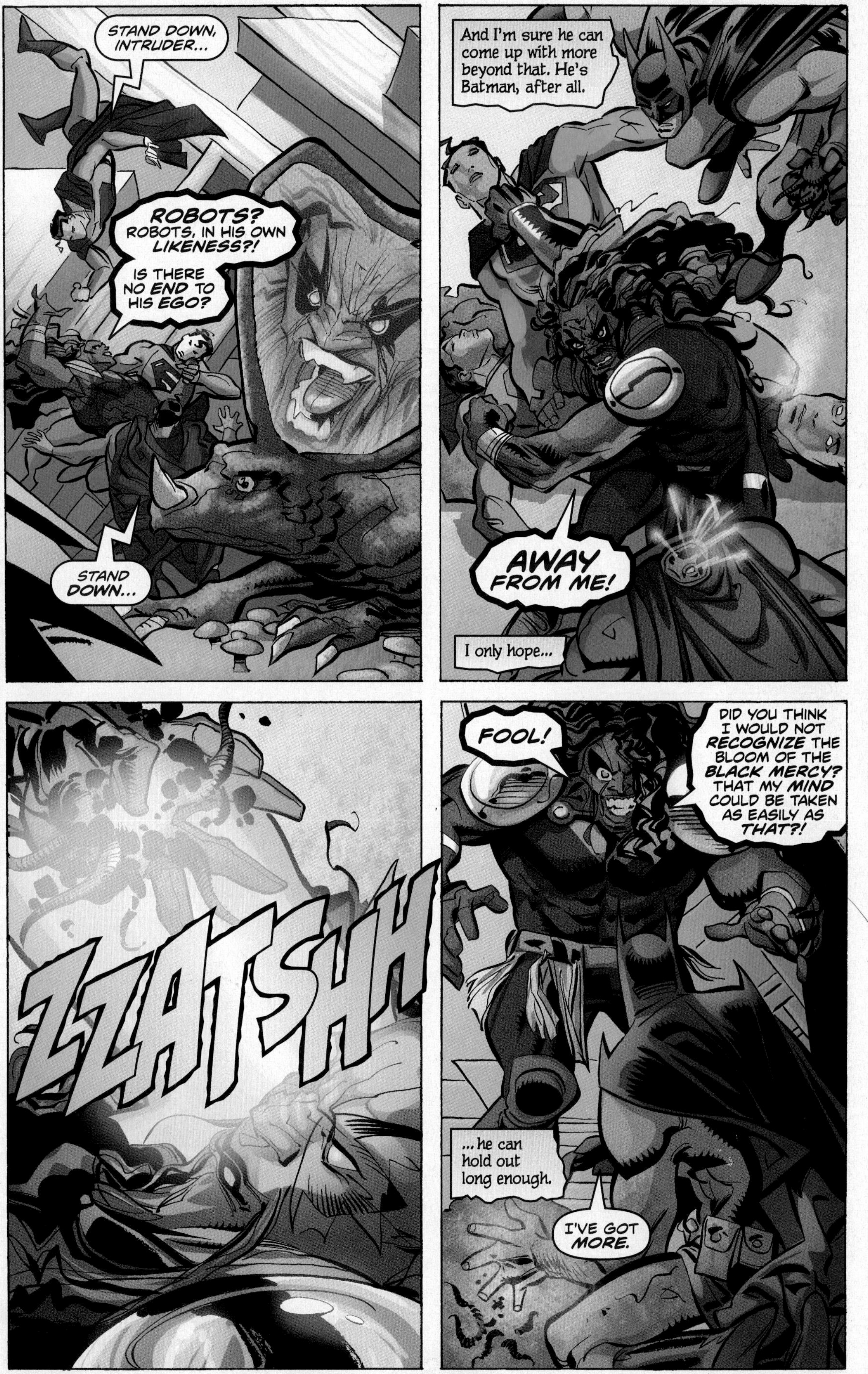
STAND DOWN, INTRUDER...
ROBOTS? ROBOTS, IN HIS OWN LIKENESS?!
IS THERE NO END TO HIS EGO?
STAND DOWN...
And I'm sure he can come up with more beyond that. He's Batman, after all.
AWAY FROM ME!
I only hope...
ZZATSHH
FOOL!
DID YOU THINK I WOULD NOT RECOGNIZE THE BLOOM OF THE BLACK MERCY? THAT MY MIND COULD BE TAKEN AS EASILY AS THAT?!
...he can hold out long enough.
I'VE GOT MORE.

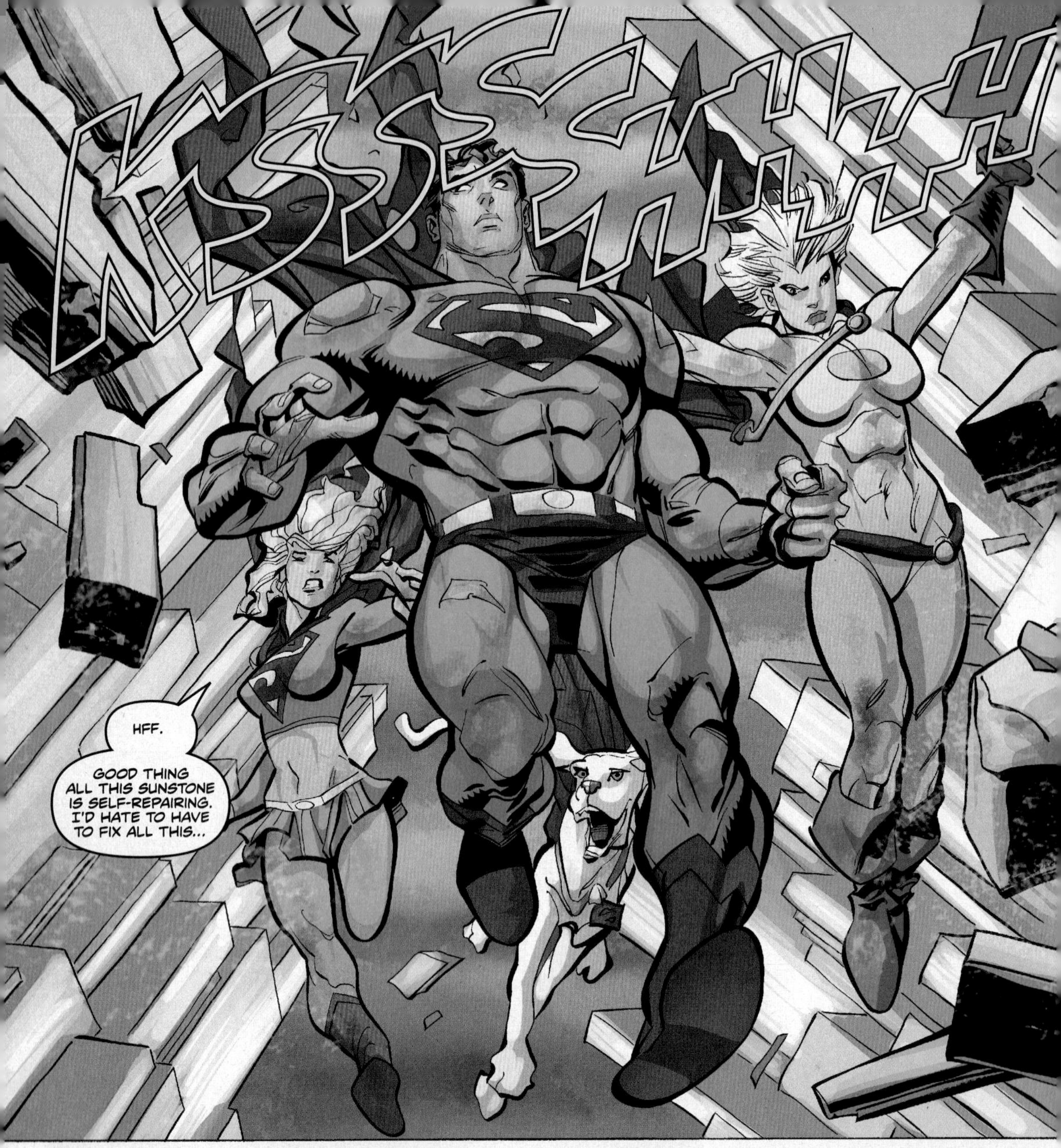
HFF.
GOOD THING ALL THIS SUNSTONE IS SELF-REPAIRING. I'D HATE TO HAVE TO FIX ALL THIS...

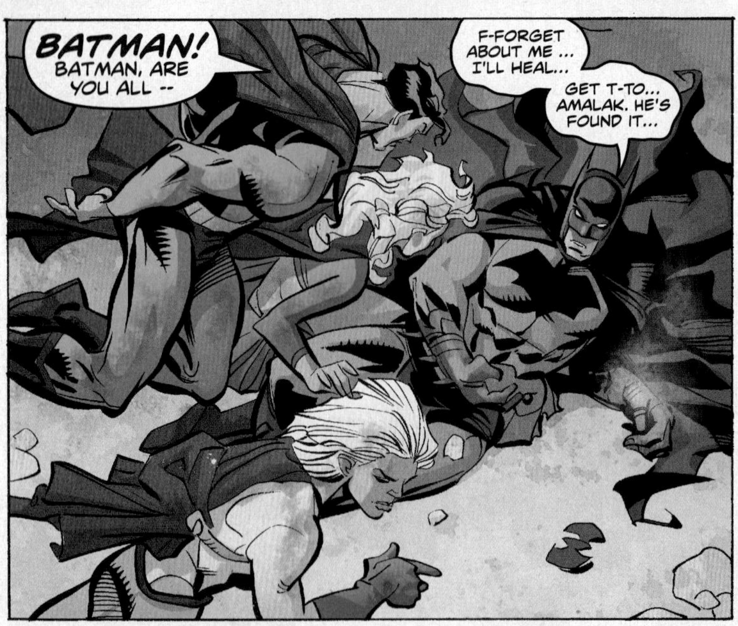
BATMAN! BATMAN, ARE YOU ALL --
F-FORGET ABOUT ME ... I'LL HEAL...
GET T-TO... AMALAK. HE'S FOUND IT...

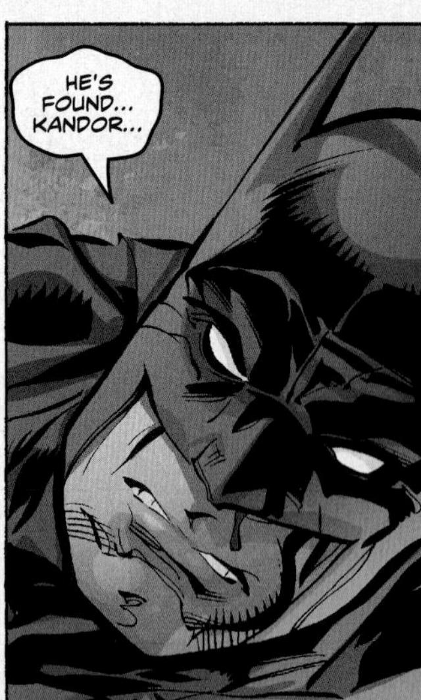
HE'S FOUND... KANDOR...

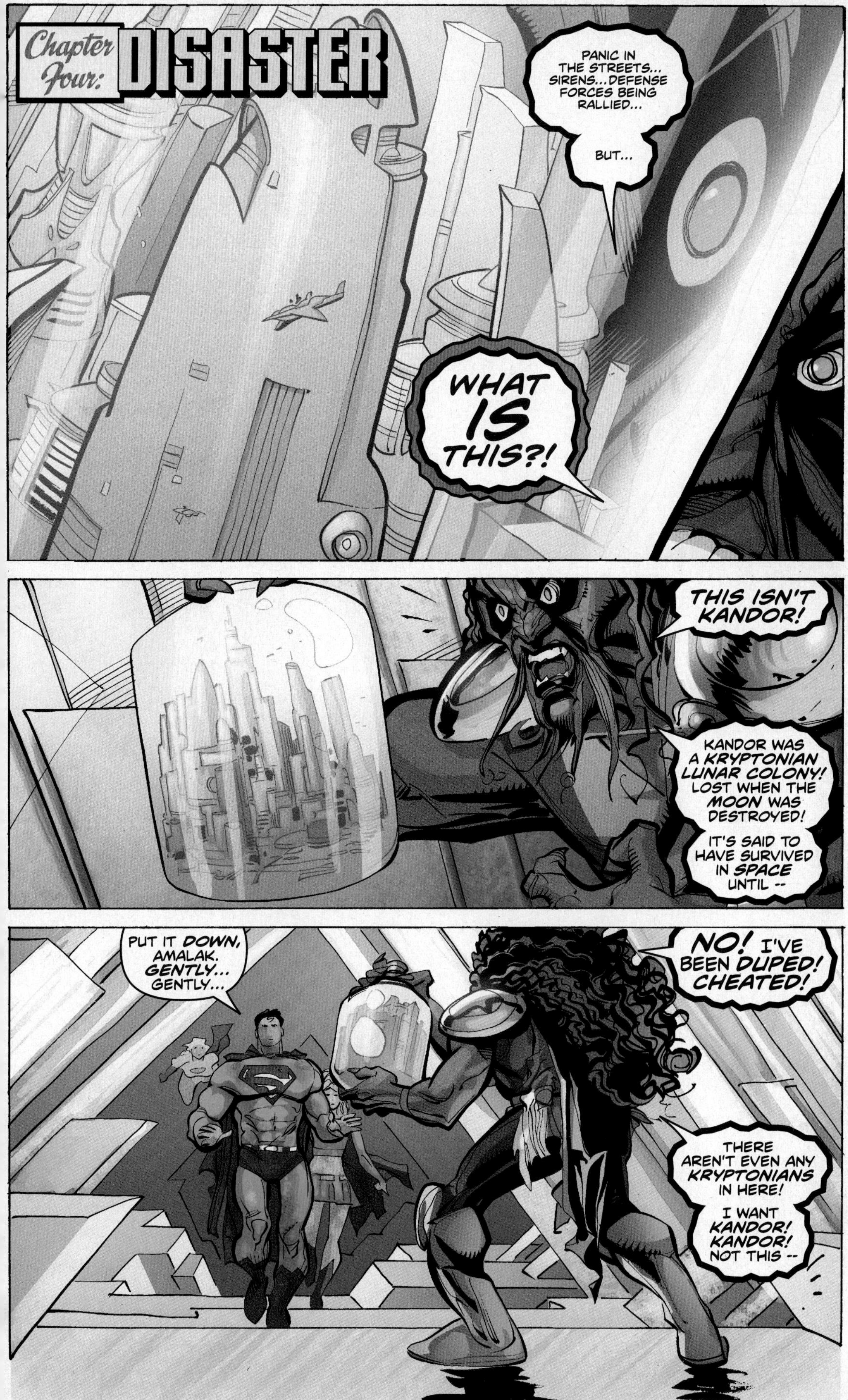
Chapter Four: DISASTER
PANIC IN THE STREETS... SIRENS...DEFENSE FORCES BEING RALLIED...
BUT...
WHAT IS THIS?!
THIS ISN'T KANDOR!
KANDOR WAS A KRYPTONIAN LUNAR COLONY! LOST WHEN THE MOON WAS DESTROYED!
IT'S SAID TO HAVE SURVIVED IN SPACE UNTIL --
PUT IT DOWN, AMALAK. GENTLY... GENTLY...
NO! I'VE BEEN DUPED! CHEATED!
THERE AREN'T EVEN ANY KRYPTONIANS IN HERE!
I WANT KANDOR! KANDOR! NOT THIS --

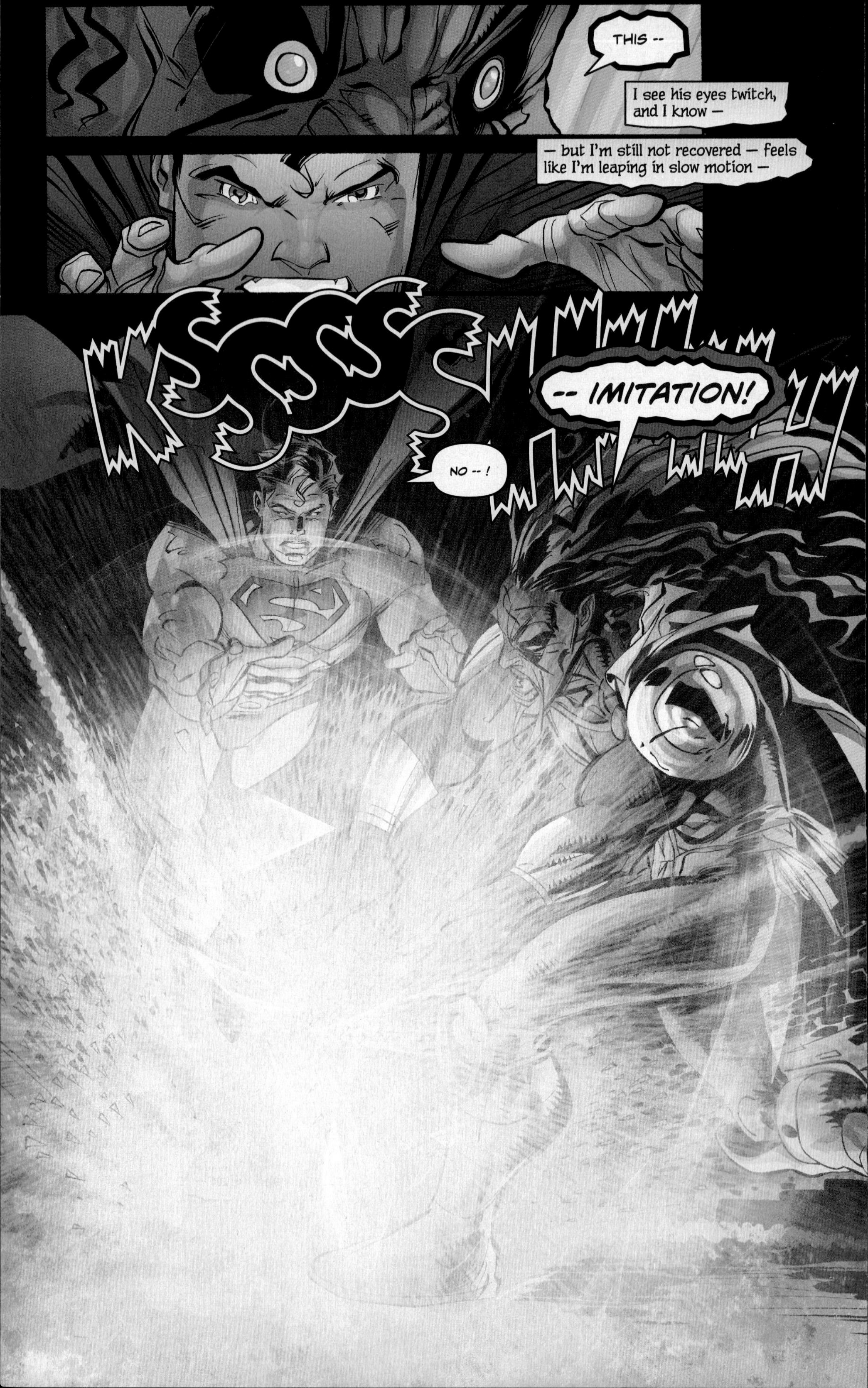
THIS --
I see his eyes twitch, and I know —
— but I'm still not recovered — feels like I'm leaping in slow motion —
KSSSSHHHHHHHHHH
-- IMITATION!
NO -- !

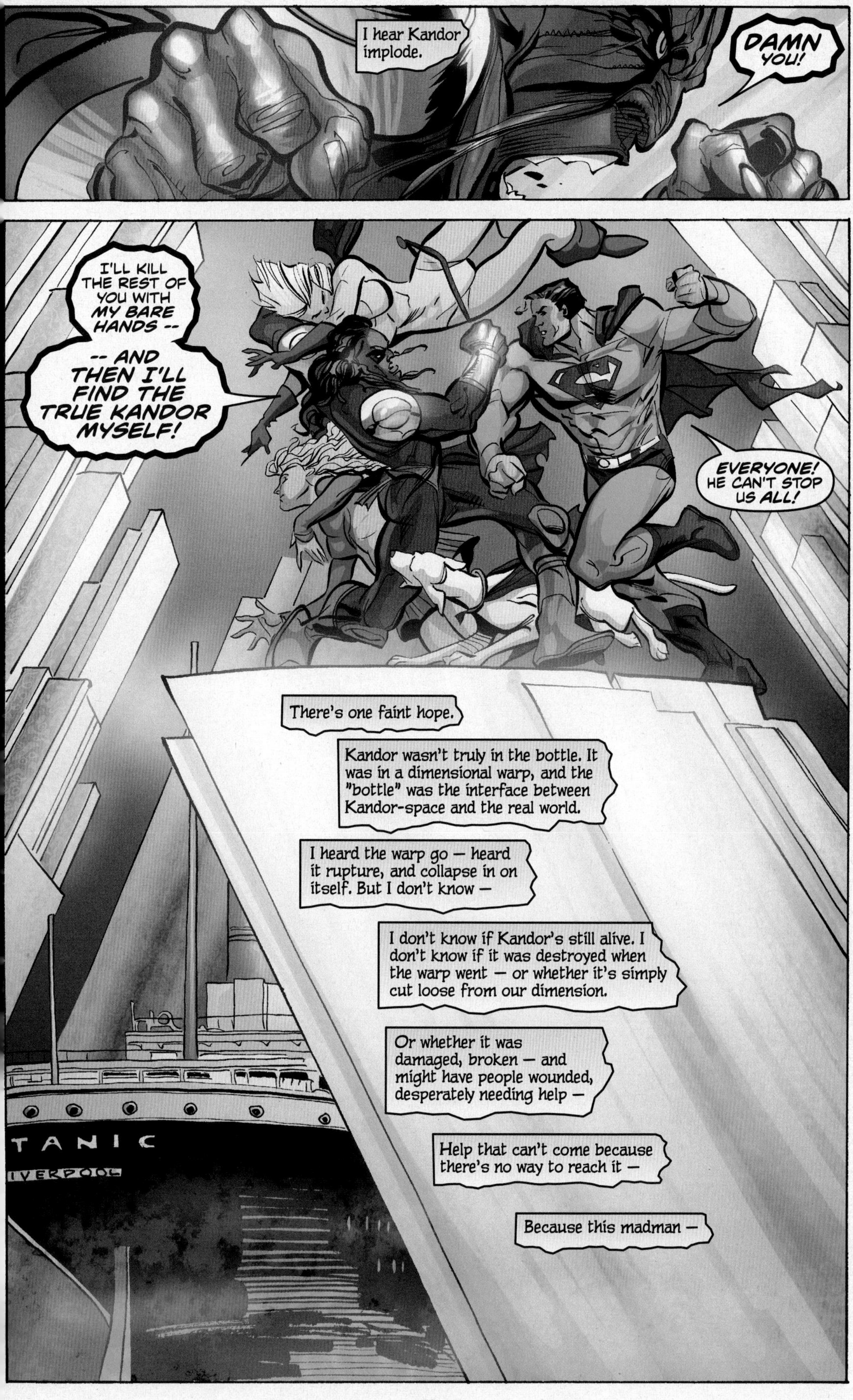

I hear Kandor implode.
DAMN YOU!
I'LL KILL THE REST OF YOU WITH MY BARE HANDS --
-- AND THEN I'LL FIND THE TRUE KANDOR MYSELF!
EVERYONE! HE CAN'T STOP US ALL!
There's one faint hope.
Kandor wasn't truly in the bottle. It was in a dimensional warp, and the "bottle" was the interface between Kandor-space and the real world.
I heard the warp go — heard it rupture, and collapse in on itself. But I don't know —
I don't know if Kandor's still alive. I don't know if it was destroyed when the warp went — or whether it's simply cut loose from our dimension.
Or whether it was damaged, broken — and might have people wounded, desperately needing help —
Help that can't come because there's no way to reach it —
Because this madman —
TANIC
IVERPOOL

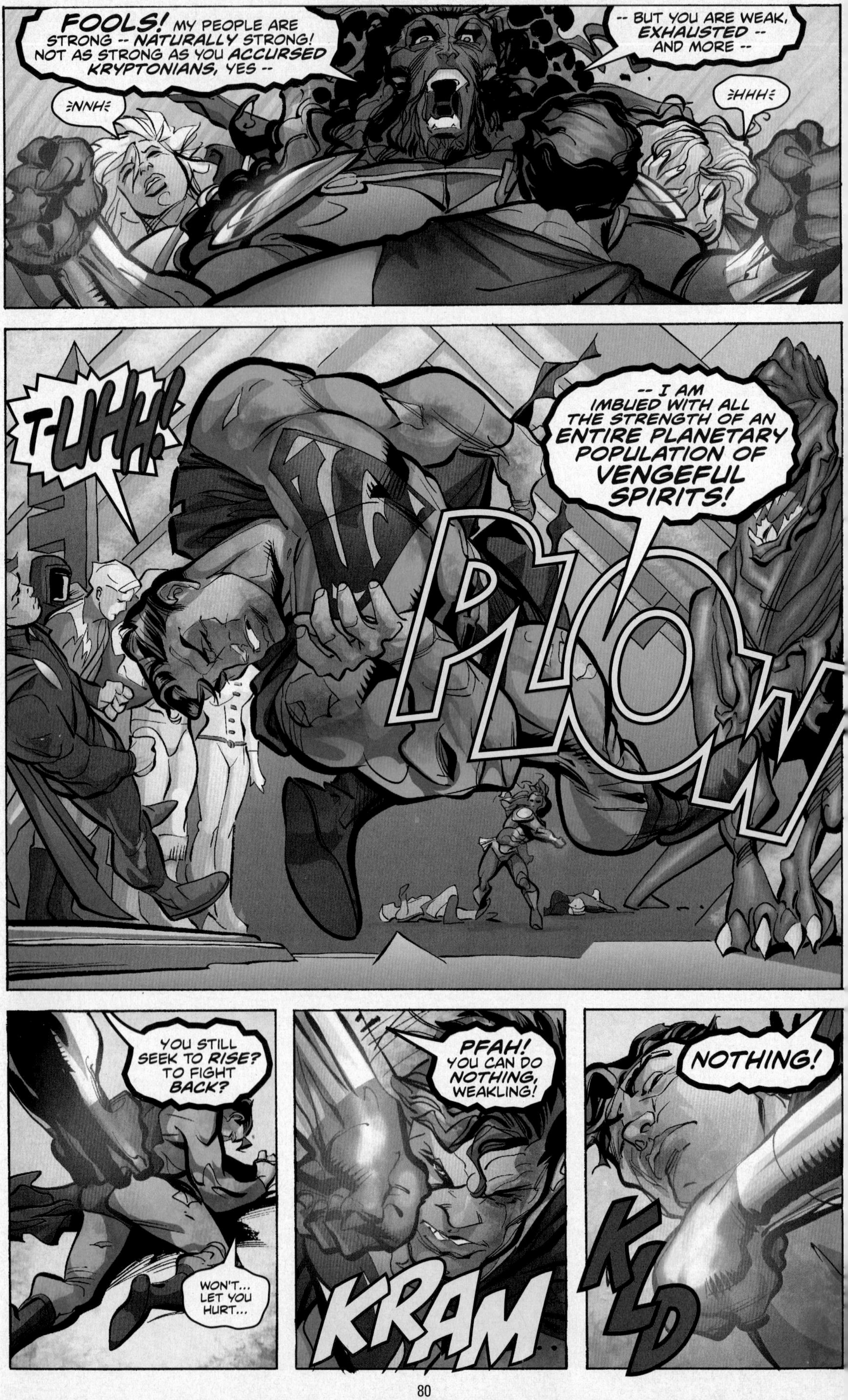

FOOLS! MY PEOPLE ARE STRONG -- NATURALLY STRONG! NOT AS STRONG AS YOU ACCURSED KRYPTONIANS, YES --
-- BUT YOU ARE WEAK, EXHAUSTED -- AND MORE --
NNH
HHH
T-UHH!
-- I AM IMBUED WITH ALL THE STRENGTH OF AN ENTIRE PLANETARY POPULATION OF VENGEFUL SPIRITS!
PLOW
YOU STILL SEEK TO RISE? TO FIGHT BACK?
WON'T... LET YOU HURT...
PFAH! YOU CAN DO NOTHING, WEAKLING!
KRAM
NOTHING!
KLD

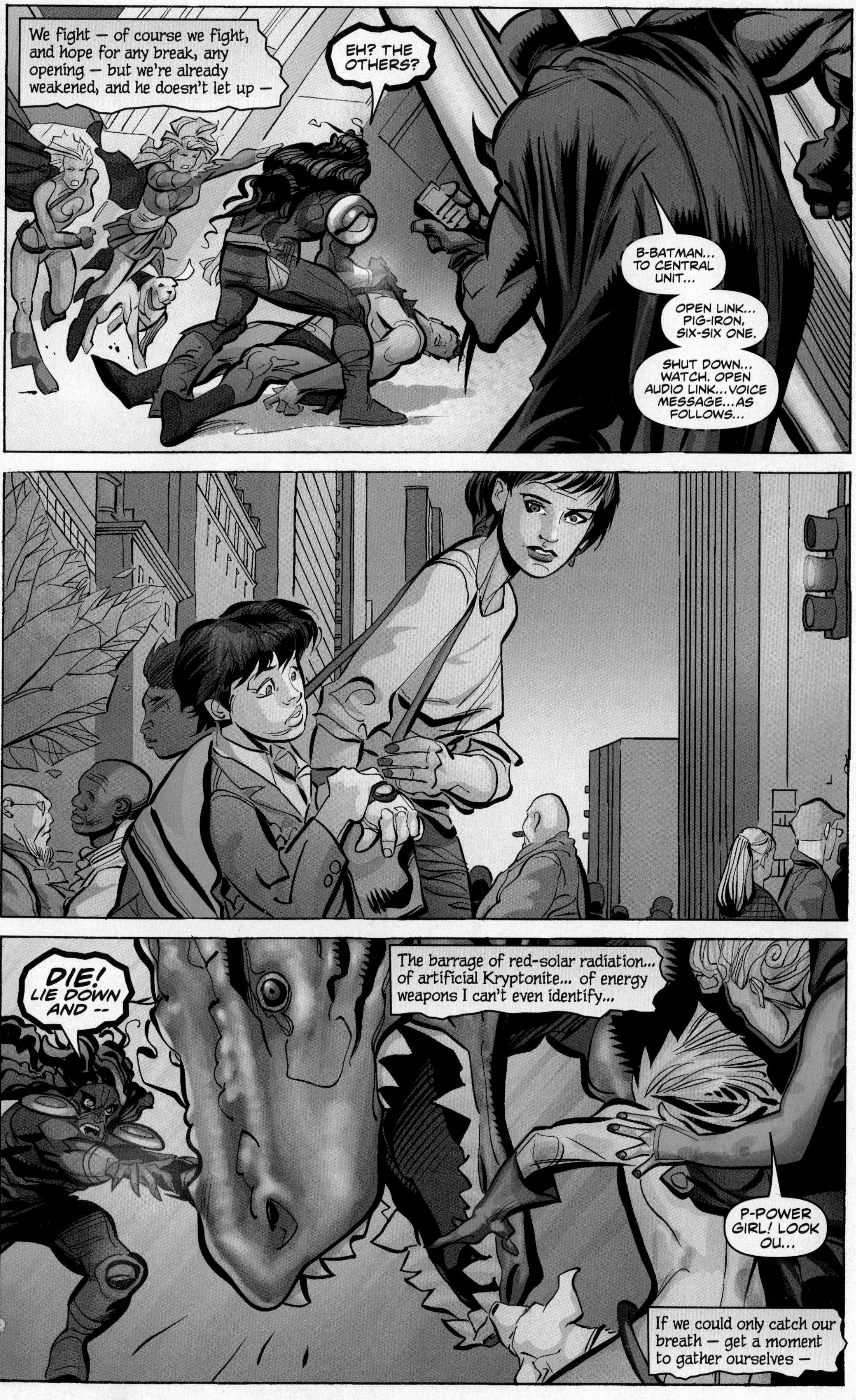

We fight — of course we fight, and hope for any break, any opening — but we're already weakened, and he doesn't let up —
EH? THE OTHERS?
B-BATMAN... TO CENTRAL UNIT...
OPEN LINK... PIG-IRON, SIX-SIX ONE.
SHUT DOWN... WATCH. OPEN AUDIO LINK...VOICE MESSAGE...AS FOLLOWS...
DIE! LIE DOWN AND --
The barrage of red-solar radiation... of artificial Kryptonite... of energy weapons I can't even identify...
P-POWER GIRL! LOOK OU...
If we could only catch our breath — get a moment to gather ourselves —

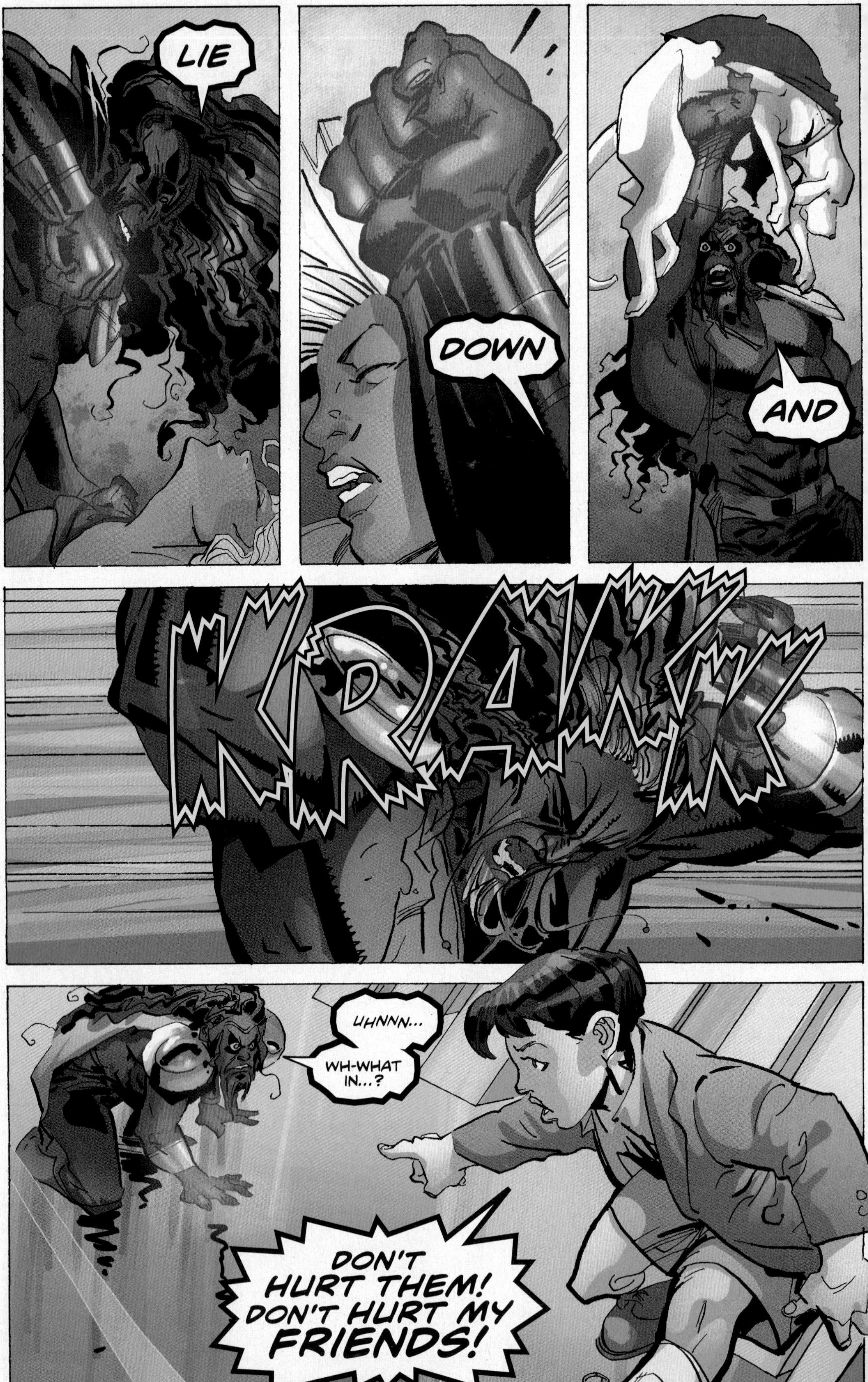
LIE
DOWN
AND
KRAAK
UHNNN...
WH-WHAT IN...?
DON'T HURT THEM! DON'T HURT MY FRIENDS!

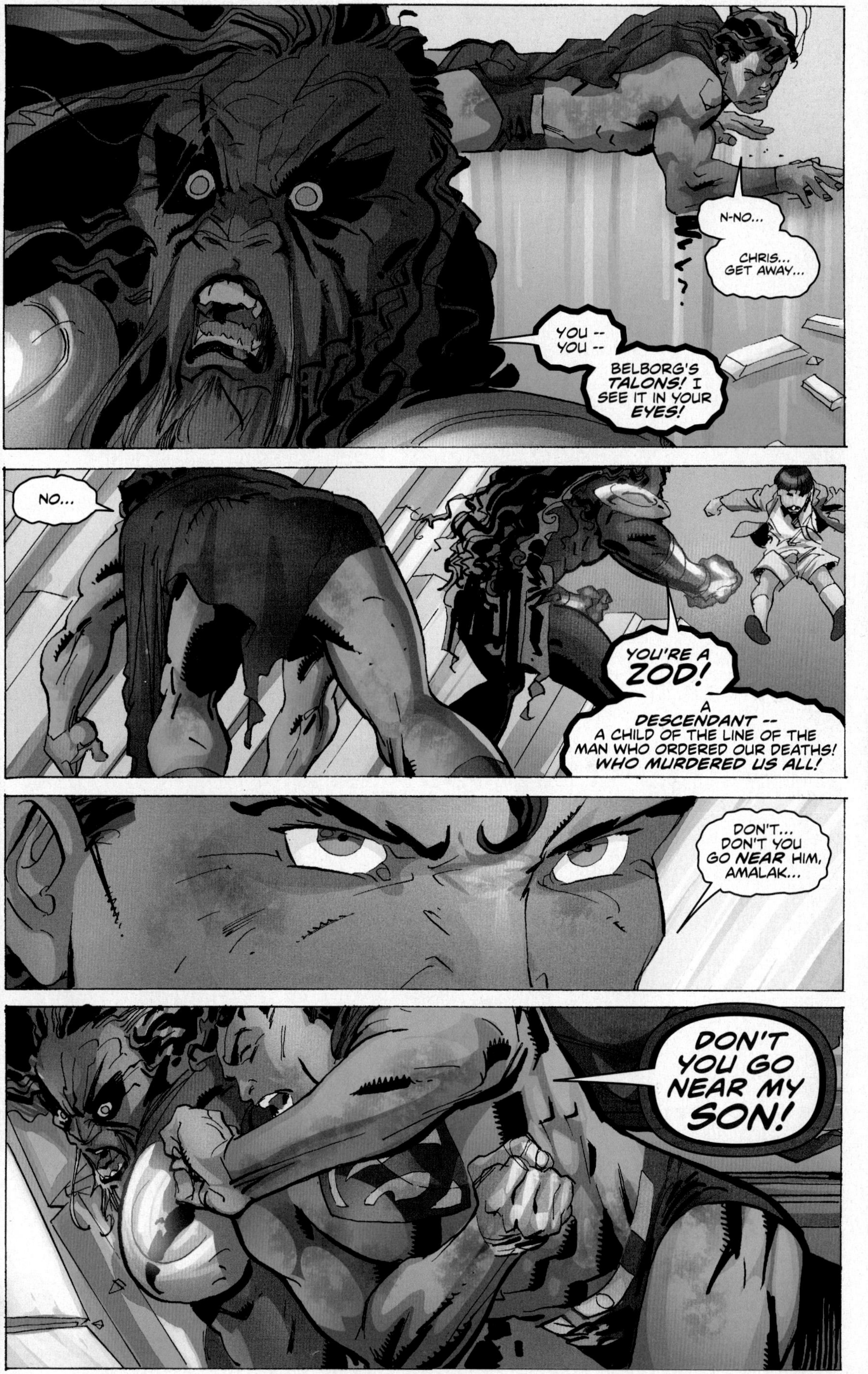
N-NO...
CHRIS... GET AWAY...
YOU -- YOU --
BELBORG'S TALONS! I SEE IT IN YOUR EYES!
NO...
YOU'RE A ZOD!
A DESCENDANT -- A CHILD OF THE LINE OF THE MAN WHO ORDERED OUR DEATHS! WHO MURDERED US ALL!
DON'T... DON'T YOU GO NEAR HIM, AMALAK...
DON'T YOU GO NEAR MY SON!

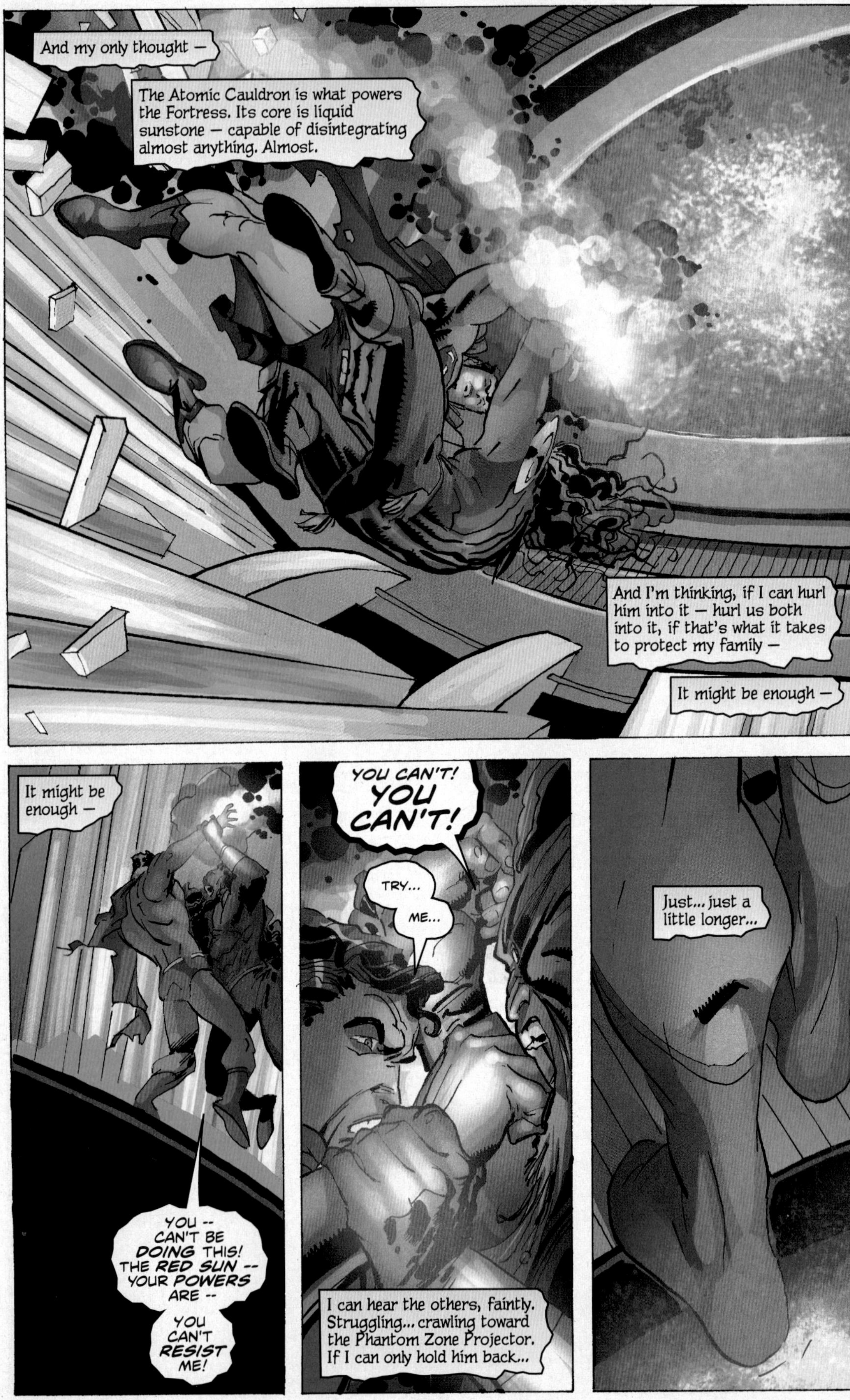

And my only thought —
The Atomic Cauldron is what powers the Fortress. Its core is liquid sunstone — capable of disintegrating almost anything. Almost.
And I'm thinking, if I can hurl him into it — hurl us both into it, if that's what it takes to protect my family —
It might be enough —
It might be enough —
YOU -- CAN'T BE DOING THIS! THE RED SUN -- YOUR POWERS ARE --
YOU CAN'T RESIST ME!
YOU CAN'T! YOU CAN'T!
TRY...
ME...
I can hear the others, faintly. Struggling... crawling toward the Phantom Zone Projector. If I can only hold him back...
Just... just a little longer...

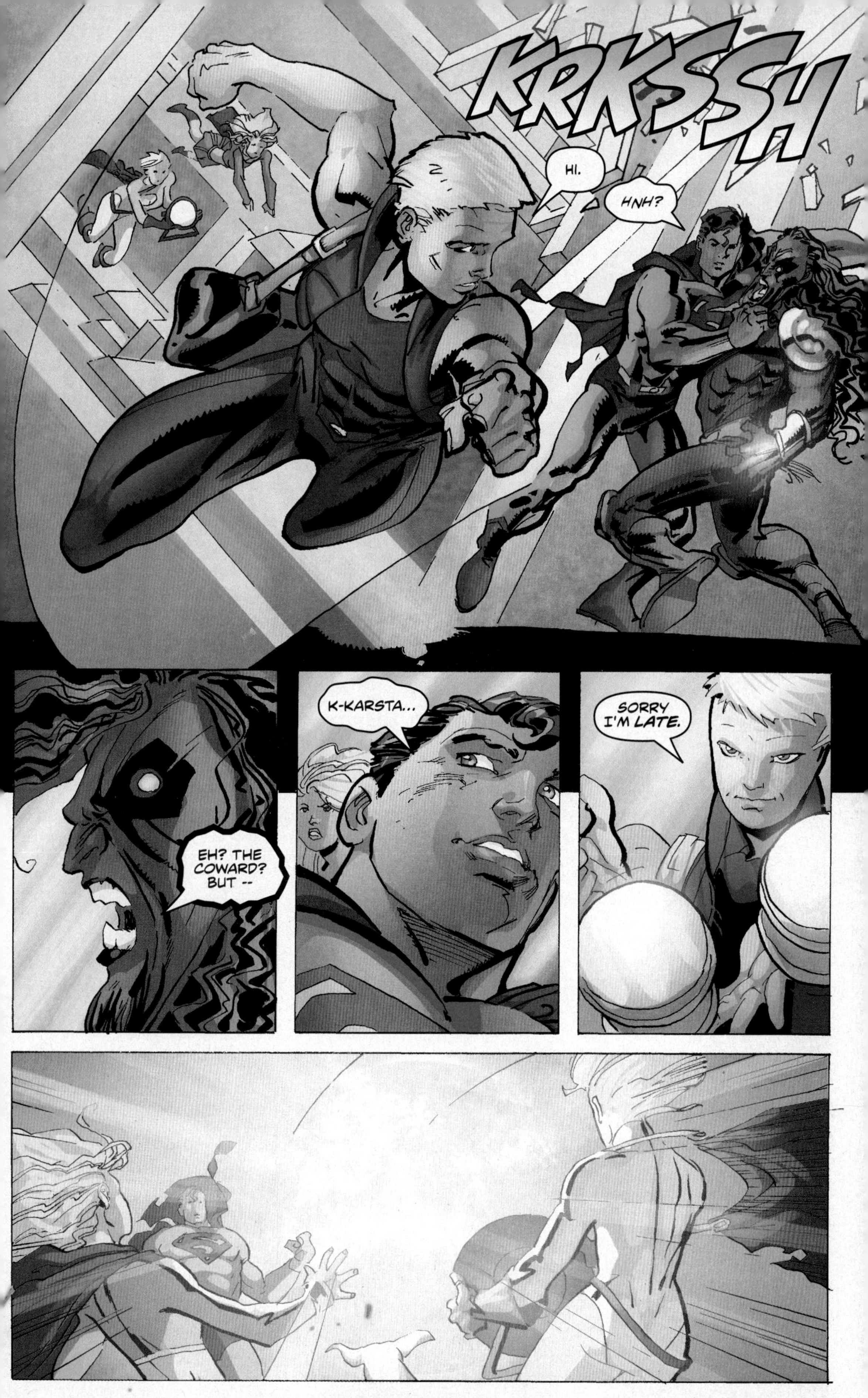
KRKSSH
HI.
HNH?
EH? THE COWARD? BUT --
K-KARSTA...
SORRY I'M LATE.

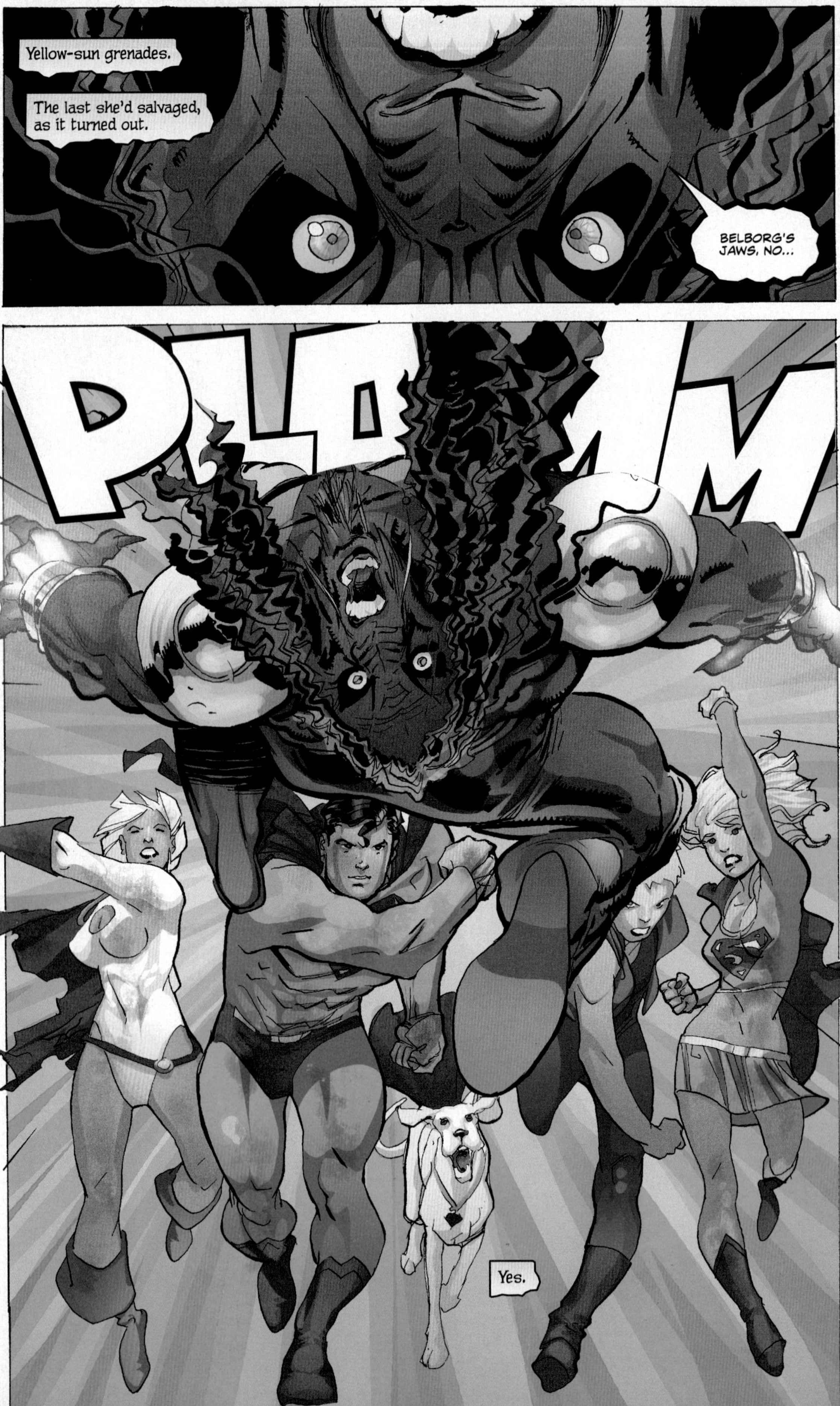
Yellow-sun grenades.
The last she'd salvaged, as it turned out.
BELBORG'S JAWS, NO...
Yes.

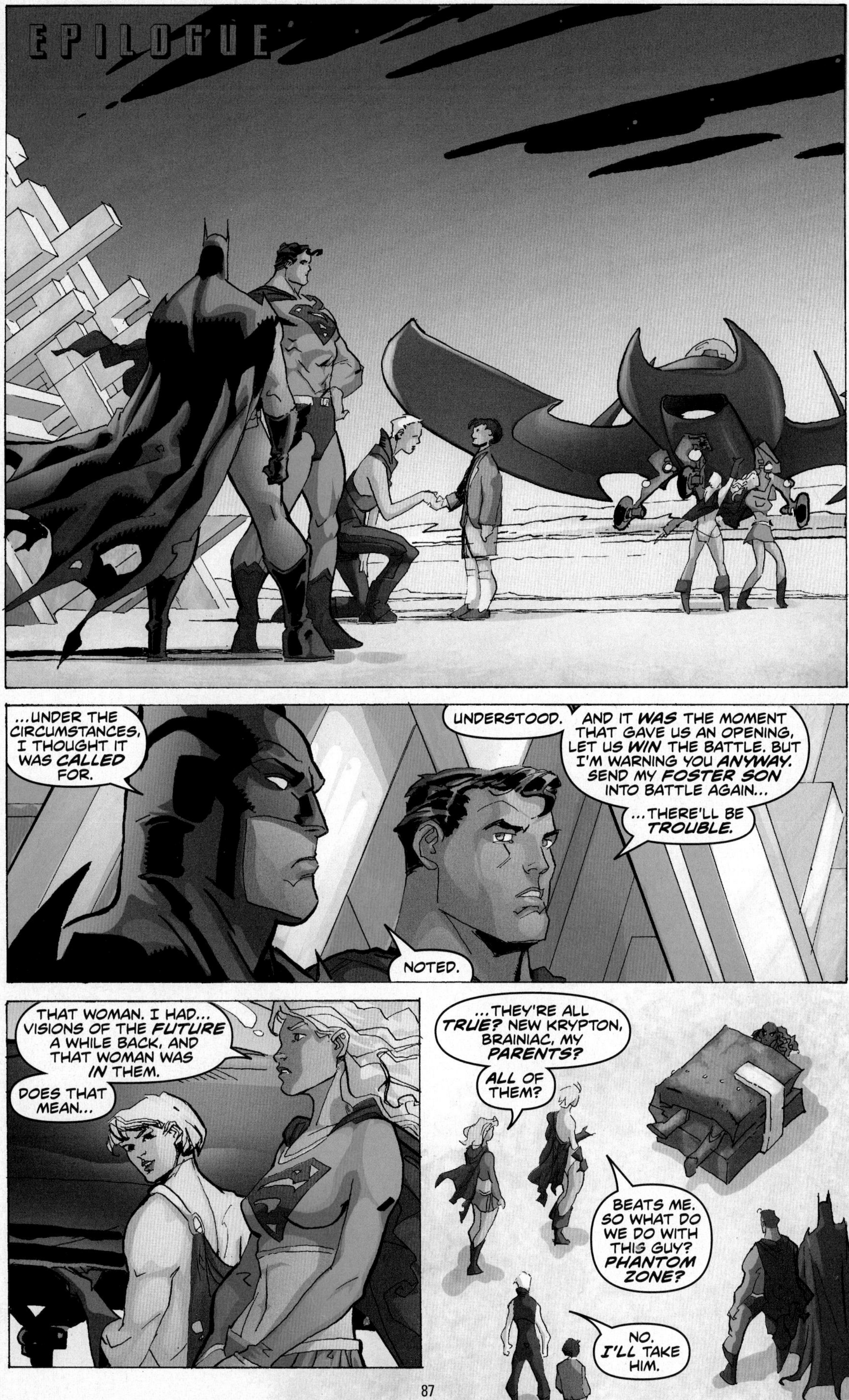
EPILOGUE
...UNDER THE CIRCUMSTANCES, I THOUGHT IT WAS CALLED FOR.
UNDERSTOOD.
AND IT WAS THE MOMENT THAT GAVE US AN OPENING, LET US WIN THE BATTLE. BUT I'M WARNING YOU ANYWAY. SEND MY FOSTER SON INTO BATTLE AGAIN...
...THERE'LL BE TROUBLE.
NOTED.
THAT WOMAN. I HAD... VISIONS OF THE FUTURE A WHILE BACK, AND THAT WOMAN WAS IN THEM.
DOES THAT MEAN...
...THEY'RE ALL TRUE? NEW KRYPTON, BRAINIAC, MY PARENTS?
ALL OF THEM?
BEATS ME. SO WHAT DO WE DO WITH THIS GUY? PHANTOM ZONE?
NO. I'LL TAKE HIM.

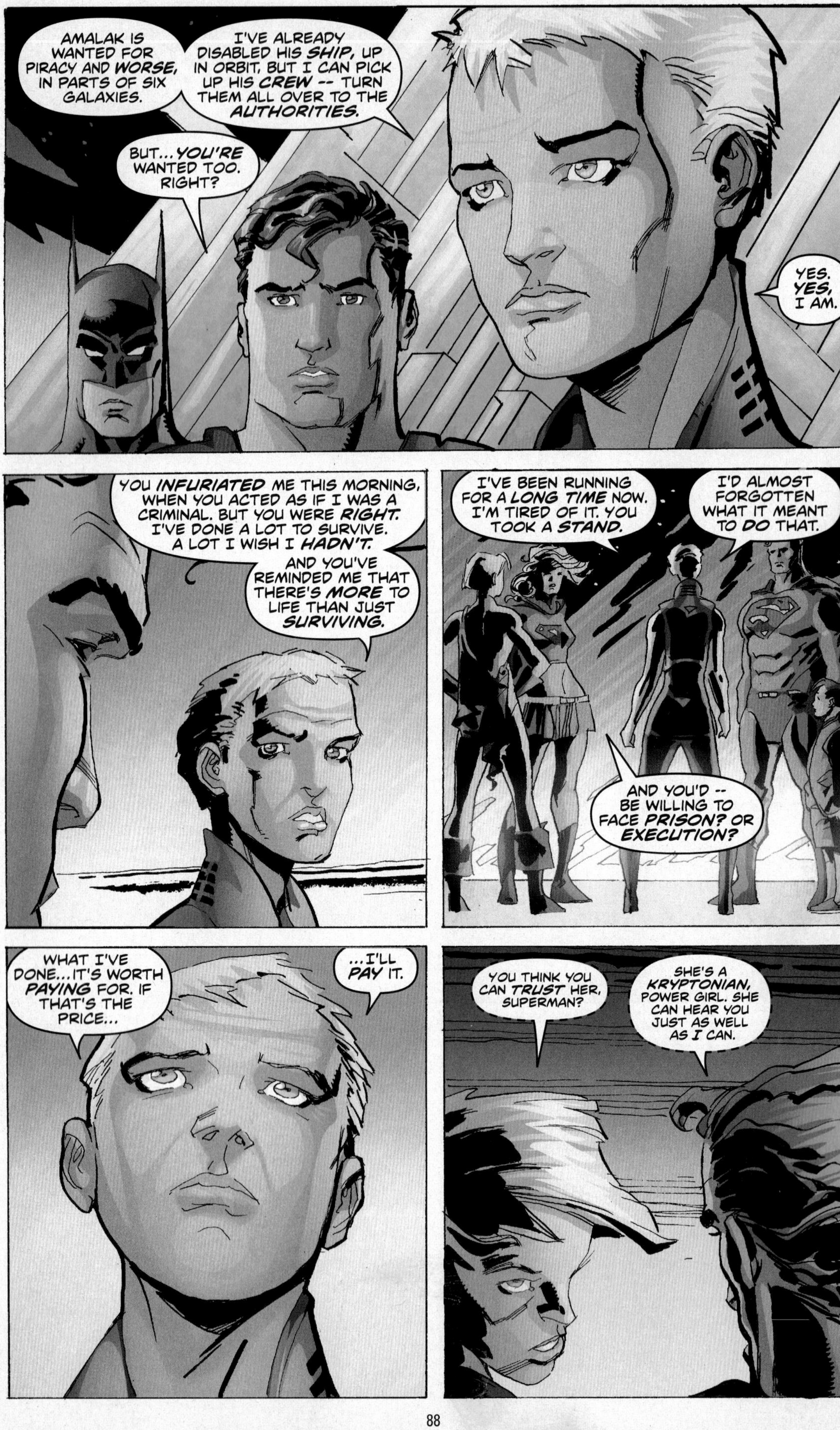

AMALAK IS WANTED FOR PIRACY AND WORSE, IN PARTS OF SIX GALAXIES.
I'VE ALREADY DISABLED HIS SHIP, UP IN ORBIT, BUT I CAN PICK UP HIS CREW -- TURN THEM ALL OVER TO THE AUTHORITIES.
BUT...YOU'RE WANTED TOO. RIGHT?
YES. YES, I AM.
YOU INFURIATED ME THIS MORNING, WHEN YOU ACTED AS IF I WAS A CRIMINAL. BUT YOU WERE RIGHT. I'VE DONE A LOT TO SURVIVE. A LOT I WISH I HADN'T.
AND YOU'VE REMINDED ME THAT THERE'S MORE TO LIFE THAN JUST SURVIVING.
I'VE BEEN RUNNING FOR A LONG TIME NOW. I'M TIRED OF IT. YOU TOOK A STAND.
I'D ALMOST FORGOTTEN WHAT IT MEANT TO DO THAT.
AND YOU'D -- BE WILLING TO FACE PRISON? OR EXECUTION?
WHAT I'VE DONE...IT'S WORTH PAYING FOR. IF THAT'S THE PRICE...
...I'LL PAY IT.
YOU THINK YOU CAN TRUST HER, SUPERMAN?
SHE'S A KRYPTONIAN, POWER GIRL. SHE CAN HEAR YOU JUST AS WELL AS I CAN.

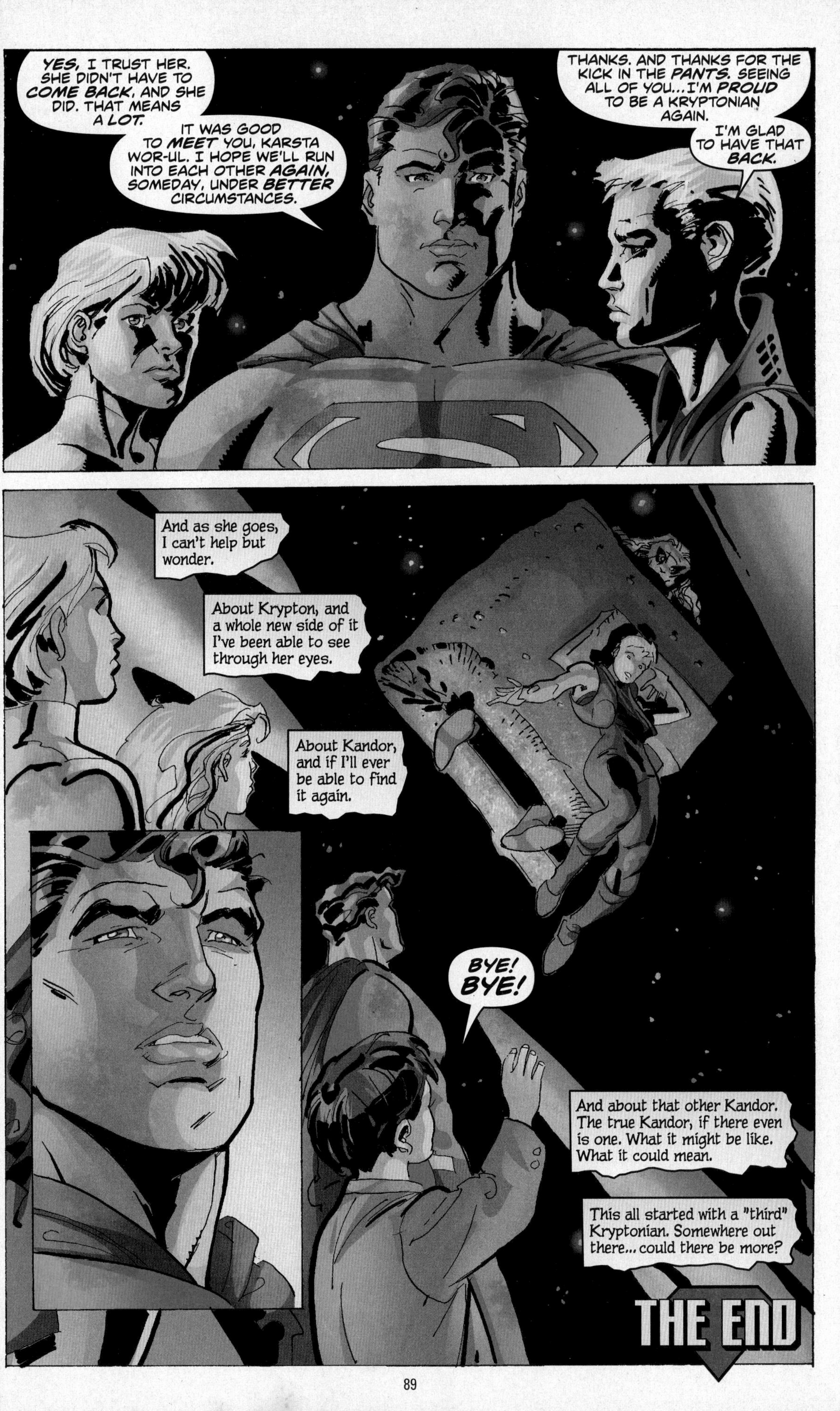
YES, I TRUST HER. SHE DIDN'T HAVE TO COME BACK, AND SHE DID. THAT MEANS A LOT.
IT WAS GOOD TO MEET YOU, KARSTA WOR-UL. I HOPE WE'LL RUN INTO EACH OTHER AGAIN, SOMEDAY, UNDER BETTER CIRCUMSTANCES.
THANKS. AND THANKS FOR THE KICK IN THE PANTS. SEEING ALL OF YOU... I'M PROUD TO BE A KRYPTONIAN AGAIN.
I'M GLAD TO HAVE THAT BACK.
And as she goes, I can't help but wonder.
About Krypton, and a whole new side of it I've been able to see through her eyes.
About Kandor, and if I'll ever be able to find it again.
BYE! BYE!
And about that other Kandor. The true Kandor, if there even is one. What it might be like. What it could mean.
This all started with a "third" Kryptonian. Somewhere out there... could there be more?
THE END

THE BEST DAY

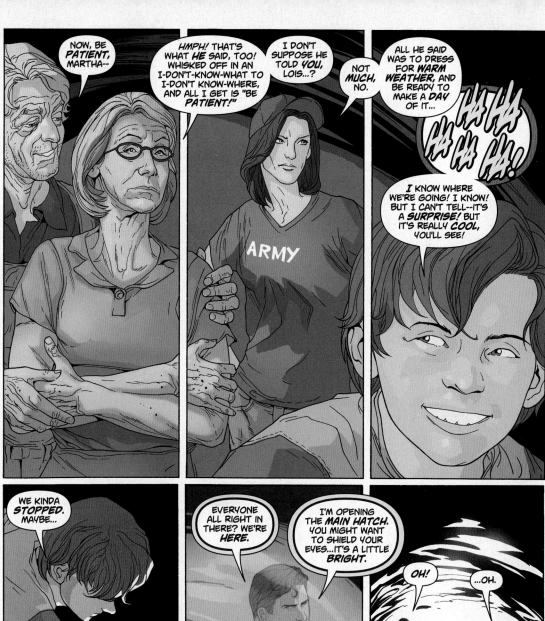

NOW, BE *PATIENT,* MARTHA--

HMPH! THAT'S WHAT *HE* SAID, TOO! WHISKED OFF IN AN I-DON'T-KNOW-WHAT TO I-DON'T-KNOW-WHERE, AND ALL I GET IS *"BE PATIENT!"*

I DON'T SUPPOSE HE TOLD *YOU,* LOIS...?

NOT *MUCH,* NO.

ALL HE SAID WAS TO DRESS FOR *WARM WEATHER,* AND BE READY TO MAKE A *DAY* OF IT...

HA HA, HA HA HA!

I KNOW WHERE WE'RE GOING! I KNOW! BUT I CAN'T TELL--IT'S A *SURPRISE!* BUT IT'S REALLY *COOL,* YOU'LL SEE!

WE KINDA *STOPPED.* MAYBE...

HMMM

EVERYONE ALL RIGHT IN THERE? WE'RE *HERE.*

I'M OPENING THE *MAIN HATCH.* YOU MIGHT WANT TO SHIELD YOUR EYES...IT'S A LITTLE *BRIGHT.*

OH!

...OH.

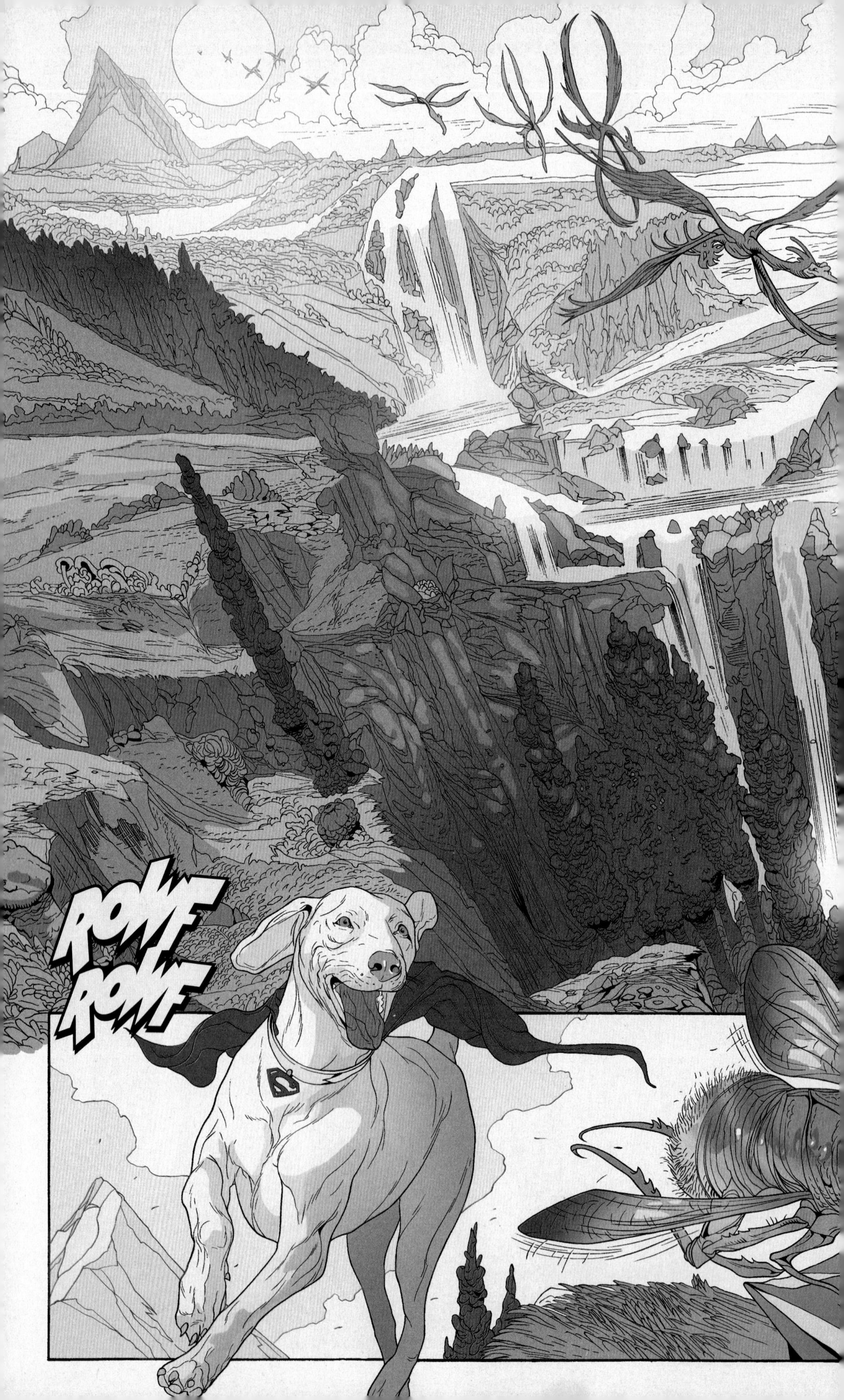
ROWF
ROWF

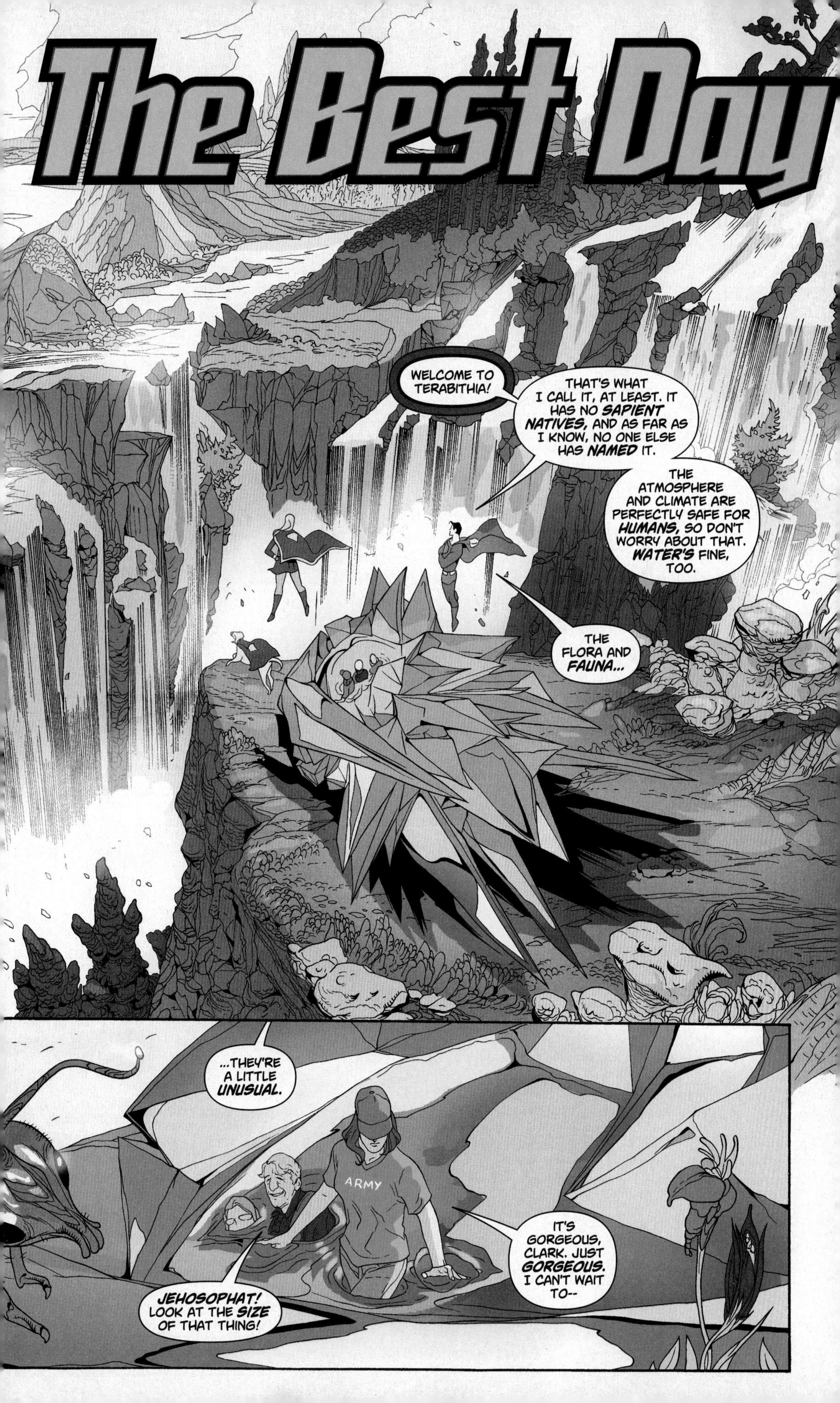
The Best Day
WELCOME TO TERABITHIA!
THAT'S WHAT I CALL IT, AT LEAST. IT HAS NO SAPIENT NATIVES, AND AS FAR AS I KNOW, NO ONE ELSE HAS NAMED IT.
THE ATMOSPHERE AND CLIMATE ARE PERFECTLY SAFE FOR HUMANS, SO DON'T WORRY ABOUT THAT. WATER'S FINE, TOO.
THE FLORA AND FAUNA...
...THEY'RE A LITTLE UNUSUAL.
ARMY
IT'S GORGEOUS, CLARK. JUST GORGEOUS. I CAN'T WAIT TO--
JEHOSOPHAT! LOOK AT THE SIZE OF THAT THING!

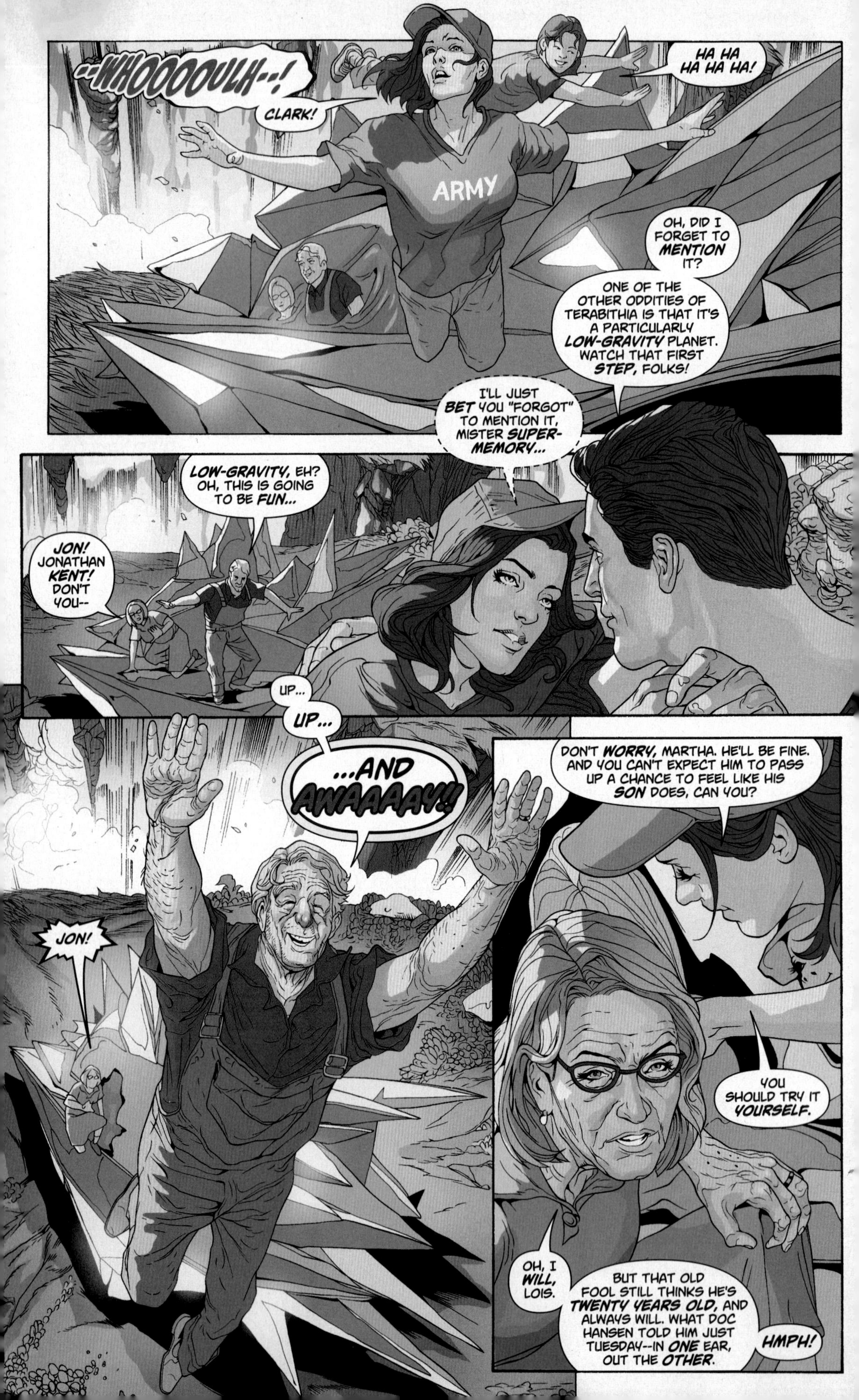
--WHOOOOOULH--!
CLARK!
HA HA HA HA HA!
OH, DID I FORGET TO MENTION IT?
ONE OF THE OTHER ODDITIES OF TERABITHIA IS THAT IT'S A PARTICULARLY LOW-GRAVITY PLANET. WATCH THAT FIRST STEP, FOLKS!
I'LL JUST BET YOU "FORGOT" TO MENTION IT, MISTER SUPER-MEMORY...
LOW-GRAVITY, EH? OH, THIS IS GOING TO BE FUN...
JON! JONATHAN KENT! DON'T YOU--
UP...
UP...
...AND AWAAAAAY!!
JON!
DON'T WORRY, MARTHA. HE'LL BE FINE. AND YOU CAN'T EXPECT HIM TO PASS UP A CHANCE TO FEEL LIKE HIS SON DOES, CAN YOU?
YOU SHOULD TRY IT YOURSELF.
OH, I WILL, LOIS.
BUT THAT OLD FOOL STILL THINKS HE'S TWENTY YEARS OLD, AND ALWAYS WILL. WHAT DOC HANSEN TOLD HIM JUST TUESDAY--IN ONE EAR, OUT THE OTHER.
HMPH!

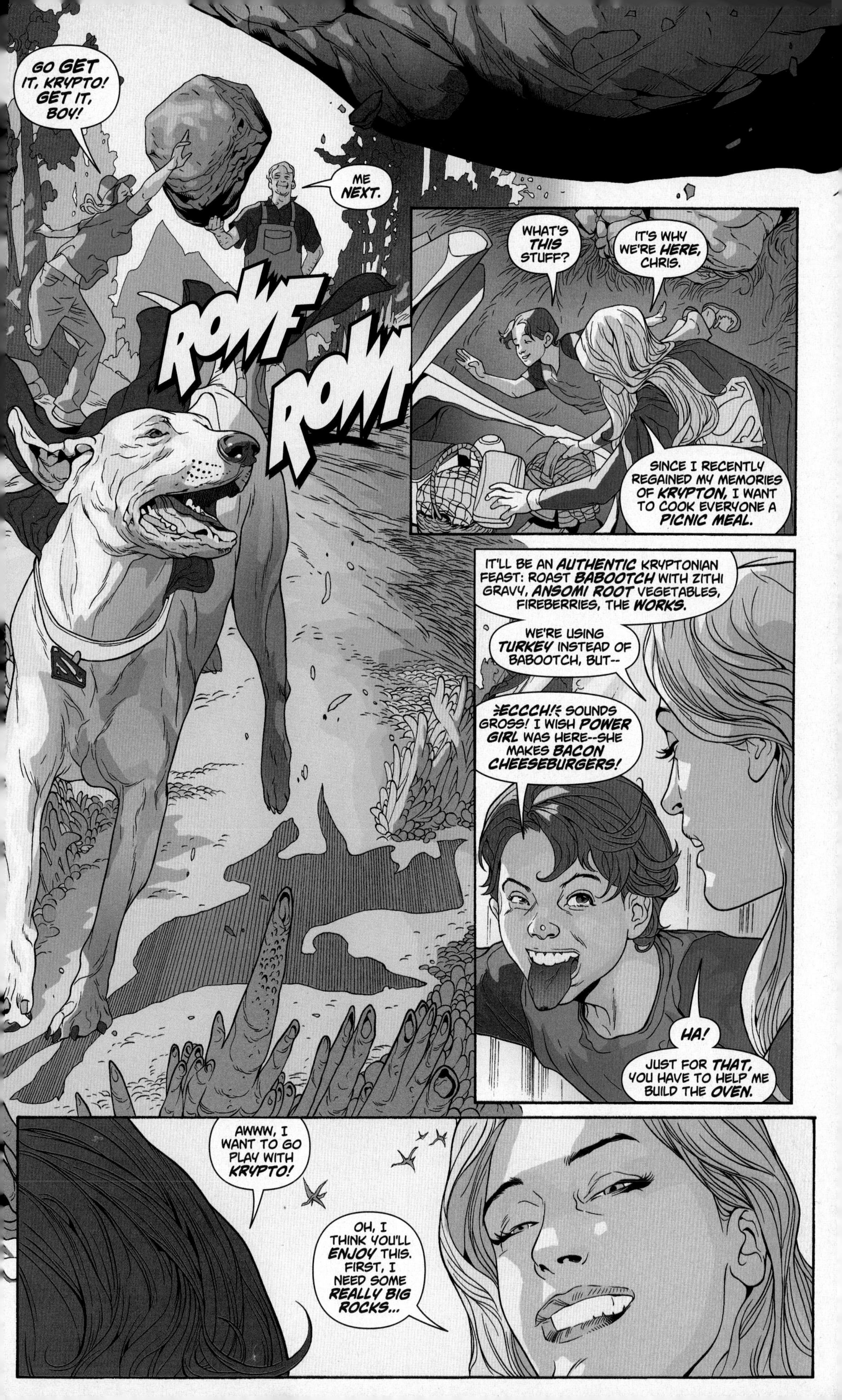
GO GET IT, KRYPTO! GET IT, BOY!
ME NEXT.
ROWF
ROWF
WHAT'S THIS STUFF?
IT'S WHY WE'RE HERE, CHRIS.
SINCE I RECENTLY REGAINED MY MEMORIES OF KRYPTON, I WANT TO COOK EVERYONE A PICNIC MEAL.
IT'LL BE AN AUTHENTIC KRYPTONIAN FEAST: ROAST BABOOTCH WITH ZITHI GRAVY, ANSOMI ROOT VEGETABLES, FIREBERRIES, THE WORKS.
WE'RE USING TURKEY INSTEAD OF BABOOTCH, BUT--
ECCCH! SOUNDS GROSS! I WISH POWER GIRL WAS HERE--SHE MAKES BACON CHEESEBURGERS!
HA!
JUST FOR THAT, YOU HAVE TO HELP ME BUILD THE OVEN.
AWWW, I WANT TO GO PLAY WITH KRYPTO!
OH, I THINK YOU'LL ENJOY THIS. FIRST, I NEED SOME REALLY BIG ROCKS...

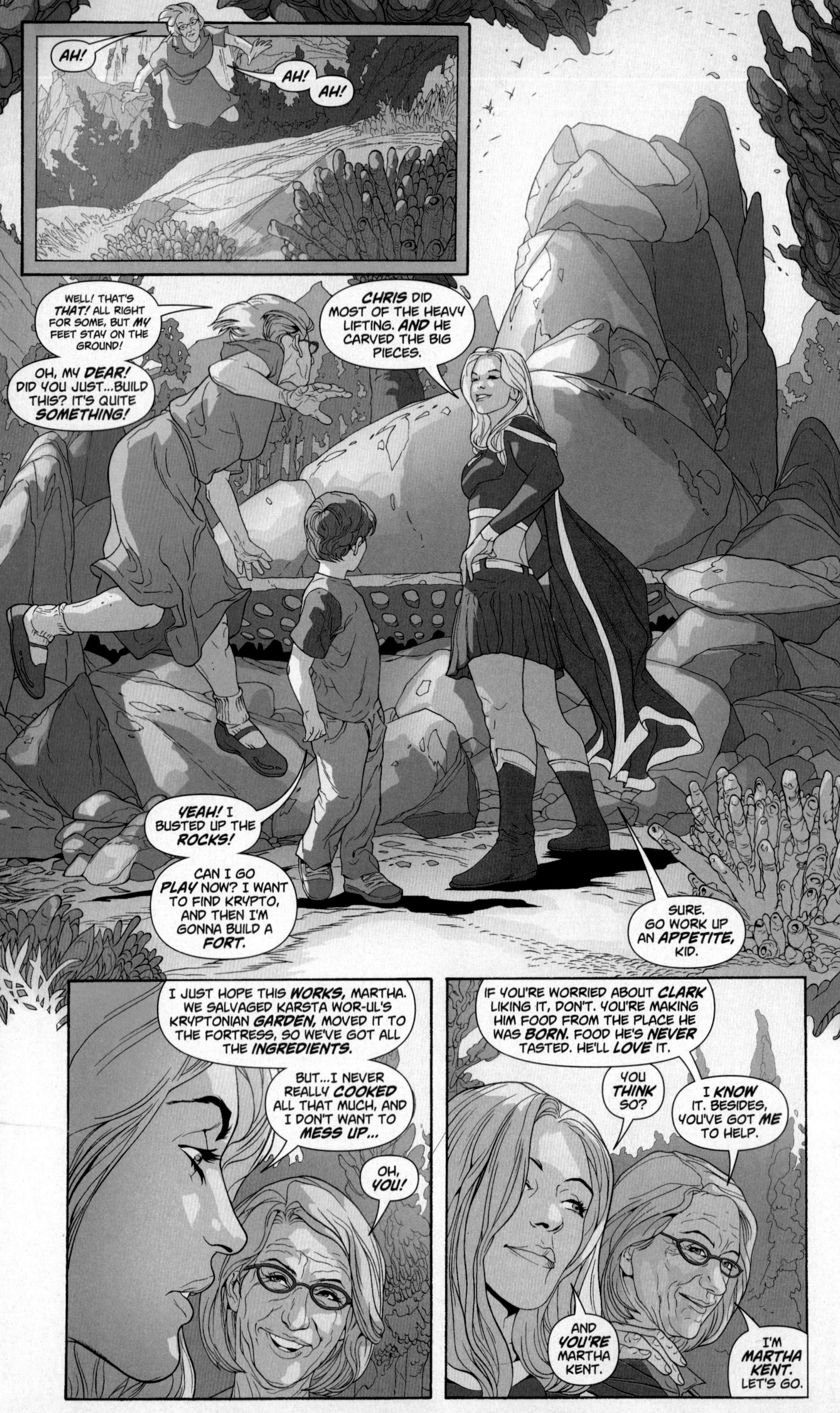
AH!
AH! AH!
WELL! THAT'S THAT! ALL RIGHT FOR SOME, BUT MY FEET STAY ON THE GROUND!
OH, MY DEAR! DID YOU JUST...BUILD THIS? IT'S QUITE SOMETHING!
CHRIS DID MOST OF THE HEAVY LIFTING. AND HE CARVED THE BIG PIECES.
YEAH! I BUSTED UP THE ROCKS!
CAN I GO PLAY NOW? I WANT TO FIND KRYPTO, AND THEN I'M GONNA BUILD A FORT.
SURE. GO WORK UP AN APPETITE, KID.
I JUST HOPE THIS WORKS, MARTHA. WE SALVAGED KARSTA WOR-UL'S KRYPTONIAN GARDEN, MOVED IT TO THE FORTRESS, SO WE'VE GOT ALL THE INGREDIENTS.
BUT...I NEVER REALLY COOKED ALL THAT MUCH, AND I DON'T WANT TO MESS UP...
OH, YOU!
IF YOU'RE WORRIED ABOUT CLARK LIKING IT, DON'T. YOU'RE MAKING HIM FOOD FROM THE PLACE HE WAS BORN. FOOD HE'S NEVER TASTED. HE'LL LOVE IT.
YOU THINK SO?
I KNOW IT. BESIDES, YOU'VE GOT ME TO HELP.
AND YOU'RE MARTHA KENT.
I'M MARTHA KENT. LET'S GO.

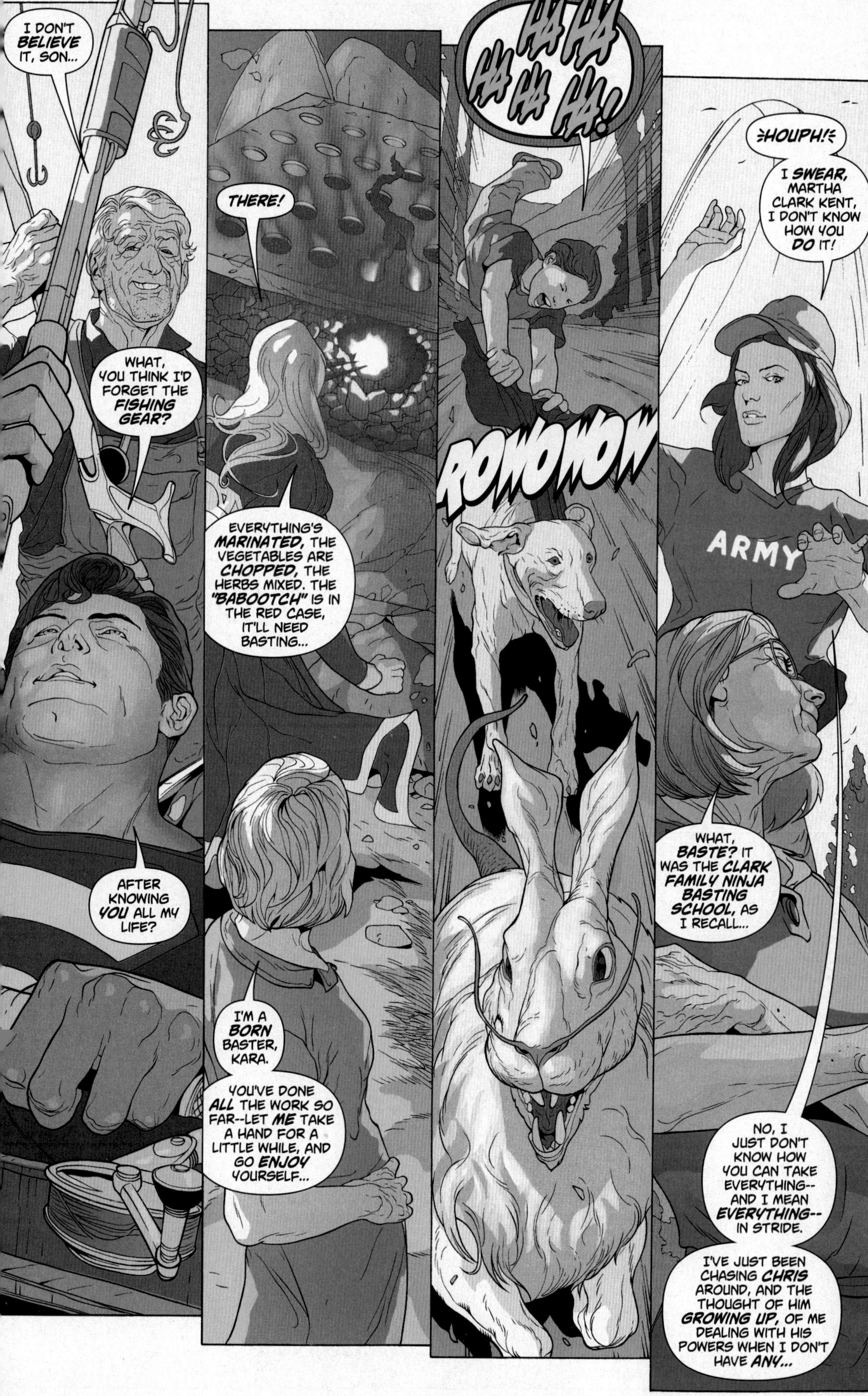
I DON'T BELIEVE IT, SON...
WHAT, YOU THINK I'D FORGET THE FISHING GEAR?
AFTER KNOWING YOU ALL MY LIFE?
THERE!
EVERYTHING'S MARINATED, THE VEGETABLES ARE CHOPPED, THE HERBS MIXED. THE "BABOOTCH" IS IN THE RED CASE, IT'LL NEED BASTING...
I'M A BORN BASTER, KARA.
YOU'VE DONE ALL THE WORK SO FAR--LET ME TAKE A HAND FOR A LITTLE WHILE, AND GO ENJOY YOURSELF...
HA HA HA HA HA!
ROWOWOW
HOUPH!
I SWEAR, MARTHA CLARK KENT, I DON'T KNOW HOW YOU DO IT!
ARMY
WHAT, BASTE? IT WAS THE CLARK FAMILY NINJA BASTING SCHOOL, AS I RECALL...
NO, I JUST DON'T KNOW HOW YOU CAN TAKE EVERYTHING--AND I MEAN EVERYTHING--IN STRIDE.
I'VE JUST BEEN CHASING CHRIS AROUND, AND THE THOUGHT OF HIM GROWING UP, OF ME DEALING WITH HIS POWERS WHEN I DON'T HAVE ANY...

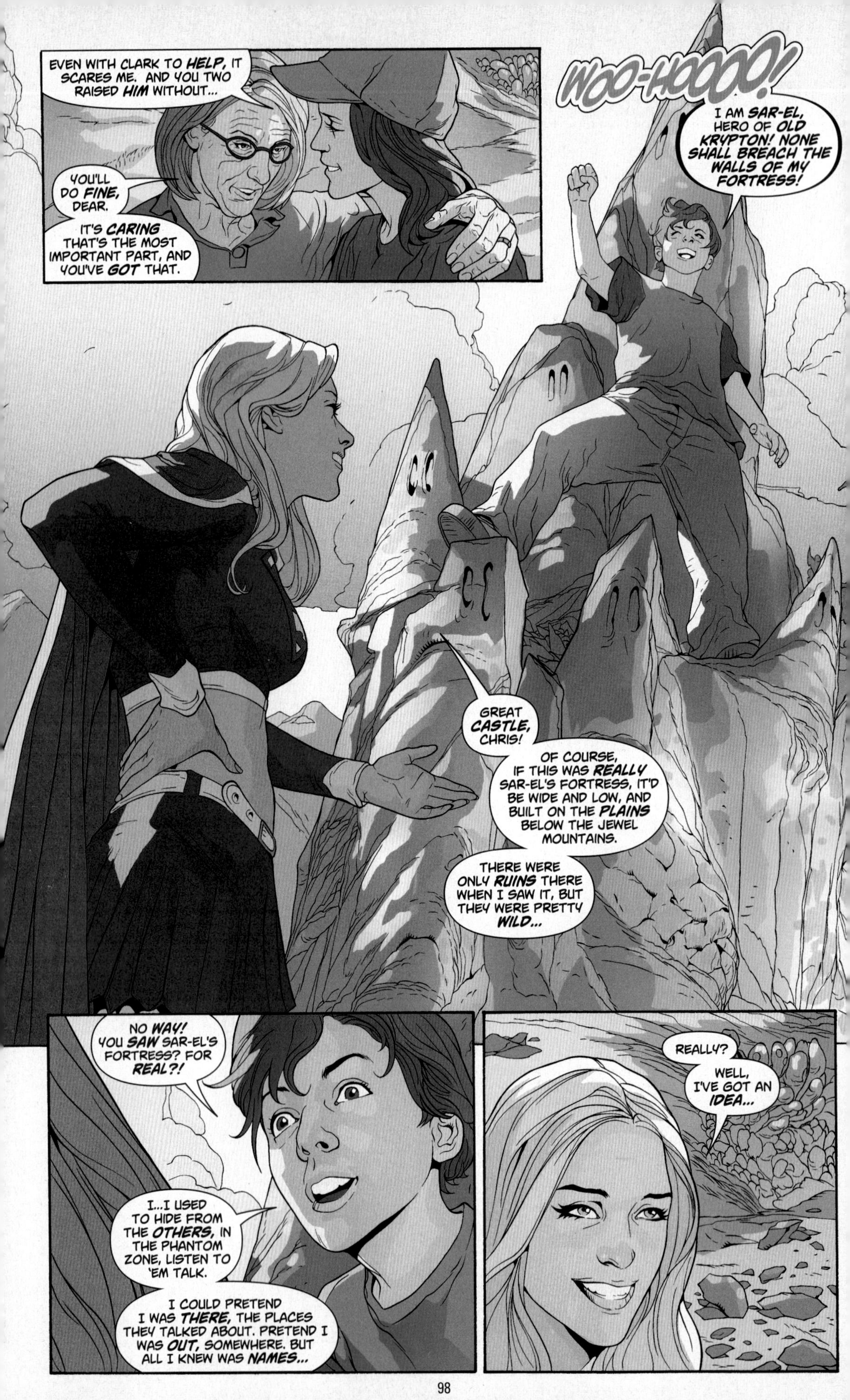
EVEN WITH CLARK TO HELP, IT SCARES ME. AND YOU TWO RAISED HIM WITHOUT...
YOU'LL DO FINE, DEAR.
IT'S CARING THAT'S THE MOST IMPORTANT PART, AND YOU'VE GOT THAT.
WOO-HOOOO!
I AM SAR-EL, HERO OF OLD KRYPTON! NONE SHALL BREACH THE WALLS OF MY FORTRESS!
GREAT CASTLE, CHRIS!
OF COURSE, IF THIS WAS REALLY SAR-EL'S FORTRESS, IT'D BE WIDE AND LOW, AND BUILT ON THE PLAINS BELOW THE JEWEL MOUNTAINS.
THERE WERE ONLY RUINS THERE WHEN I SAW IT, BUT THEY WERE PRETTY WILD...
NO WAY! YOU SAW SAR-EL'S FORTRESS? FOR REAL?!
I...I USED TO HIDE FROM THE OTHERS, IN THE PHANTOM ZONE, LISTEN TO 'EM TALK.
I COULD PRETEND I WAS THERE, THE PLACES THEY TALKED ABOUT. PRETEND I WAS OUT, SOMEWHERE. BUT ALL I KNEW WAS NAMES...
REALLY?
WELL, I'VE GOT AN IDEA...

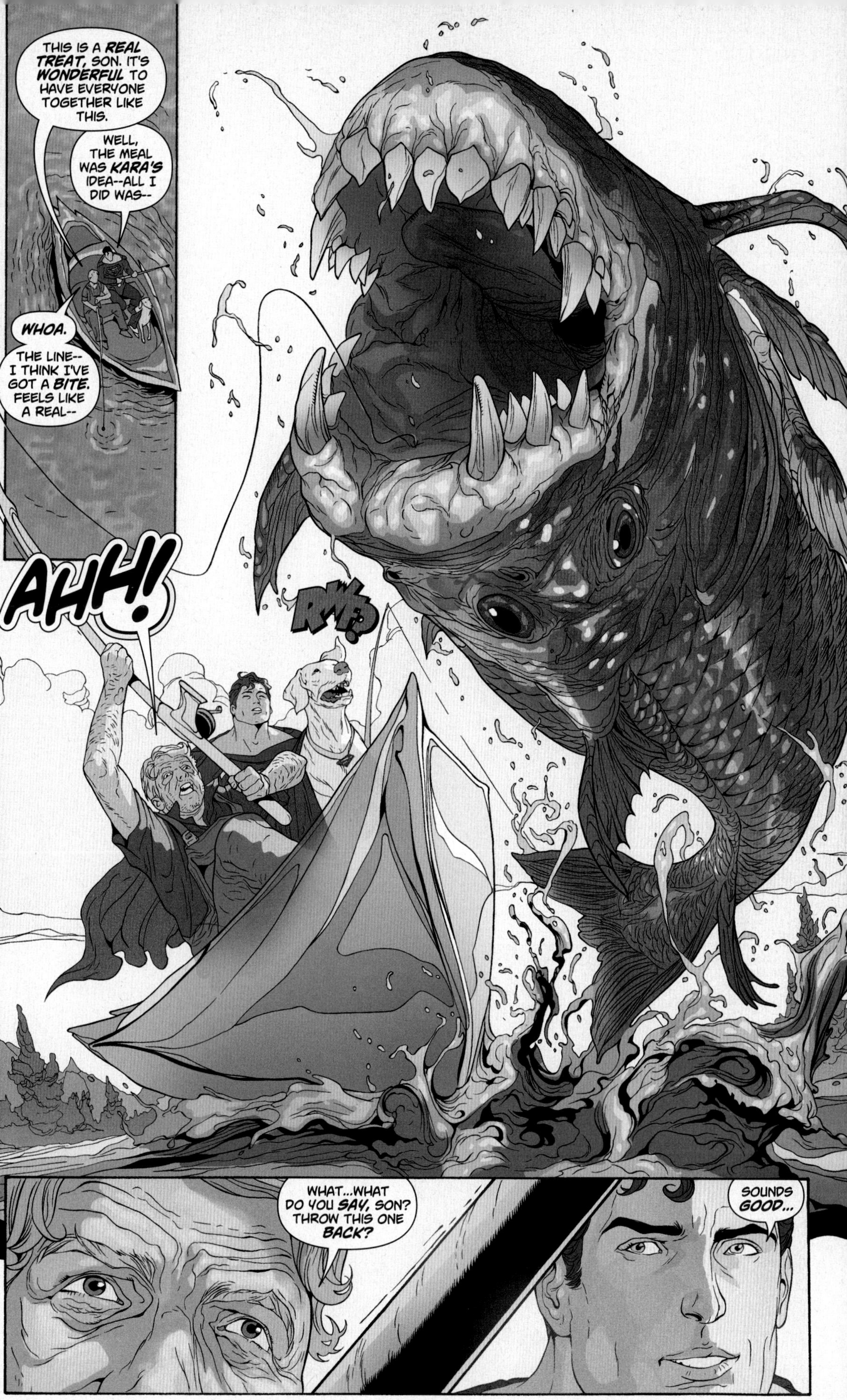
THIS IS A REAL TREAT, SON. IT'S WONDERFUL TO HAVE EVERYONE TOGETHER LIKE THIS.
WELL, THE MEAL WAS KARA'S IDEA--ALL I DID WAS--
WHOA.
THE LINE-- I THINK I'VE GOT A BITE. FEELS LIKE A REAL--
AHH!
RWF?
WHAT...WHAT DO YOU SAY, SON? THROW THIS ONE BACK?
SOUNDS GOOD...

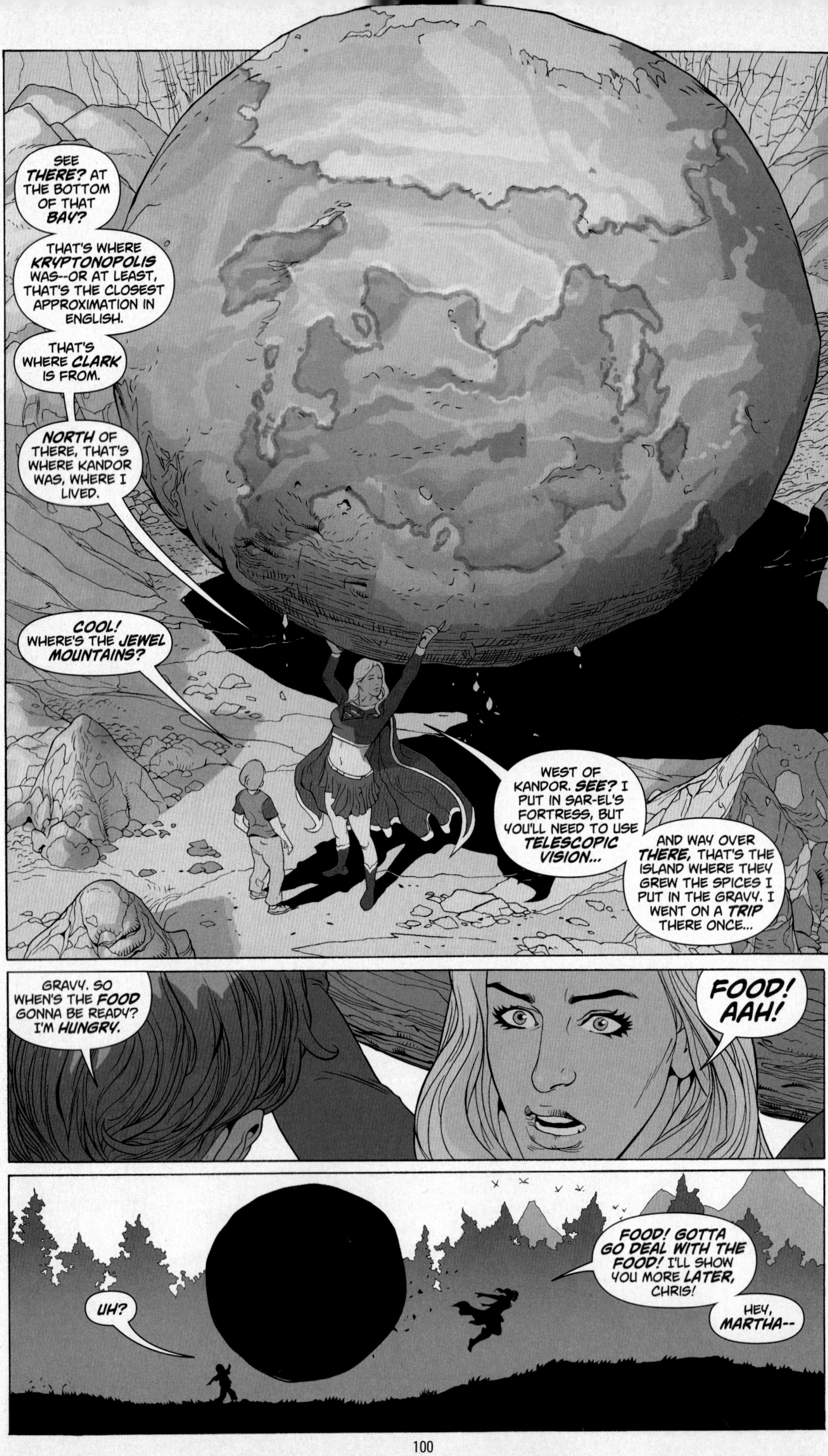

SEE THERE? AT THE BOTTOM OF THAT BAY?
THAT'S WHERE KRYPTONOPOLIS WAS--OR AT LEAST, THAT'S THE CLOSEST APPROXIMATION IN ENGLISH.
THAT'S WHERE CLARK IS FROM.
NORTH OF THERE, THAT'S WHERE KANDOR WAS, WHERE I LIVED.
COOL! WHERE'S THE JEWEL MOUNTAINS?
WEST OF KANDOR. SEE? I PUT IN SAR-EL'S FORTRESS, BUT YOU'LL NEED TO USE TELESCOPIC VISION...
AND WAY OVER THERE, THAT'S THE ISLAND WHERE THEY GREW THE SPICES I PUT IN THE GRAVY. I WENT ON A TRIP THERE ONCE...
GRAVY. SO WHEN'S THE FOOD GONNA BE READY? I'M HUNGRY.
FOOD! AAH!
UH?
FOOD! GOTTA GO DEAL WITH THE FOOD! I'LL SHOW YOU MORE LATER, CHRIS!
HEY, MARTHA--

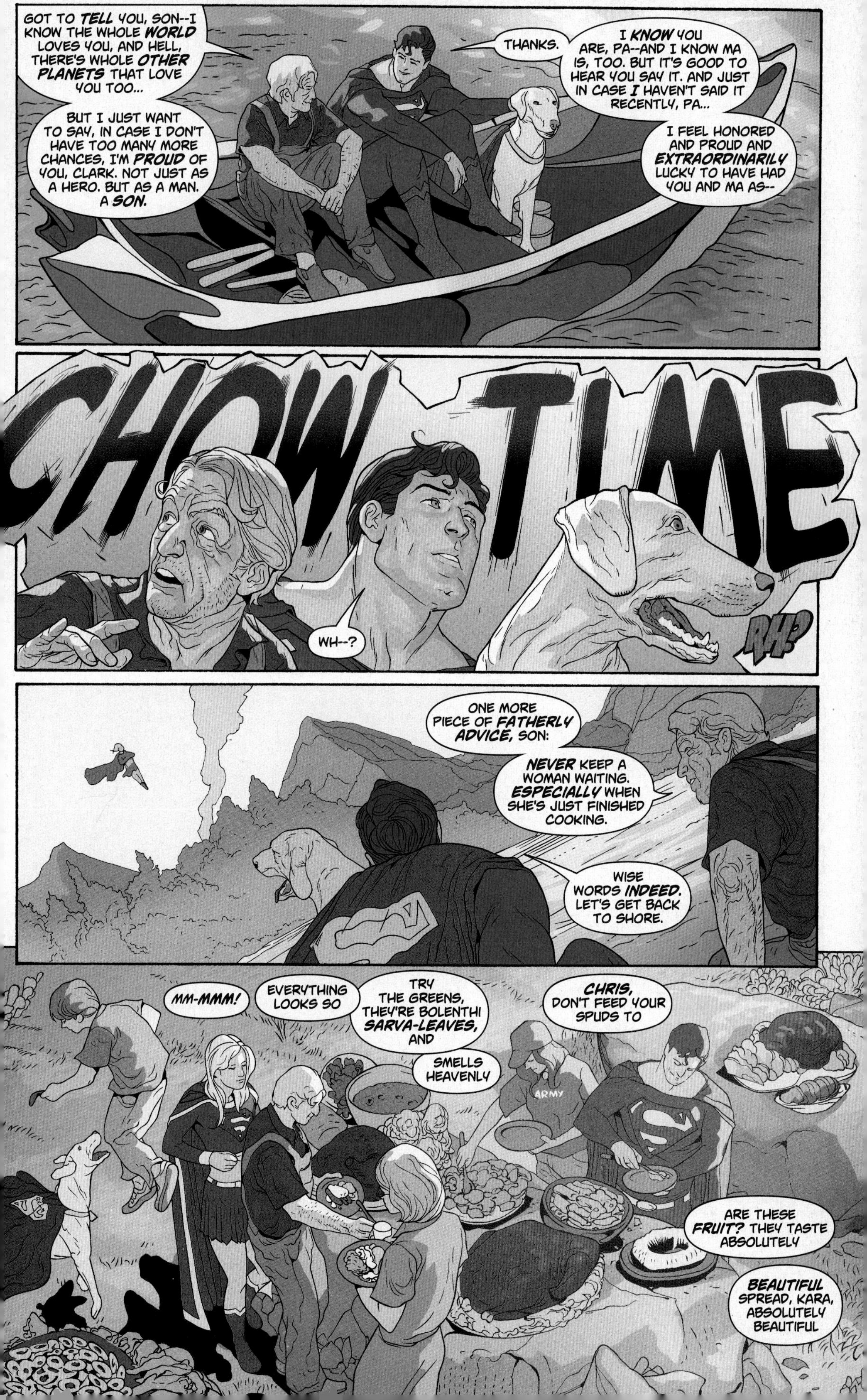
GOT TO TELL YOU, SON--I KNOW THE WHOLE WORLD LOVES YOU, AND HELL, THERE'S WHOLE OTHER PLANETS THAT LOVE YOU TOO...
BUT I JUST WANT TO SAY, IN CASE I DON'T HAVE TOO MANY MORE CHANCES, I'M PROUD OF YOU, CLARK. NOT JUST AS A HERO. BUT AS A MAN. A SON.
THANKS.
I KNOW YOU ARE, PA--AND I KNOW MA IS, TOO. BUT IT'S GOOD TO HEAR YOU SAY IT. AND JUST IN CASE I HAVEN'T SAID IT RECENTLY, PA...
I FEEL HONORED AND PROUD AND EXTRAORDINARILY LUCKY TO HAVE HAD YOU AND MA AS--
CHOW TIME
WH--?
RAH?
ONE MORE PIECE OF FATHERLY ADVICE, SON:
NEVER KEEP A WOMAN WAITING. ESPECIALLY WHEN SHE'S JUST FINISHED COOKING.
WISE WORDS INDEED. LET'S GET BACK TO SHORE.
MM-MMM!
EVERYTHING LOOKS SO
TRY THE GREENS, THEY'RE BOLENTHI SARVA-LEAVES, AND
SMELLS HEAVENLY
CHRIS, DON'T FEED YOUR SPUDS TO
ARMY
ARE THESE FRUIT? THEY TASTE ABSOLUTELY
BEAUTIFUL SPREAD, KARA, ABSOLUTELY BEAUTIFUL

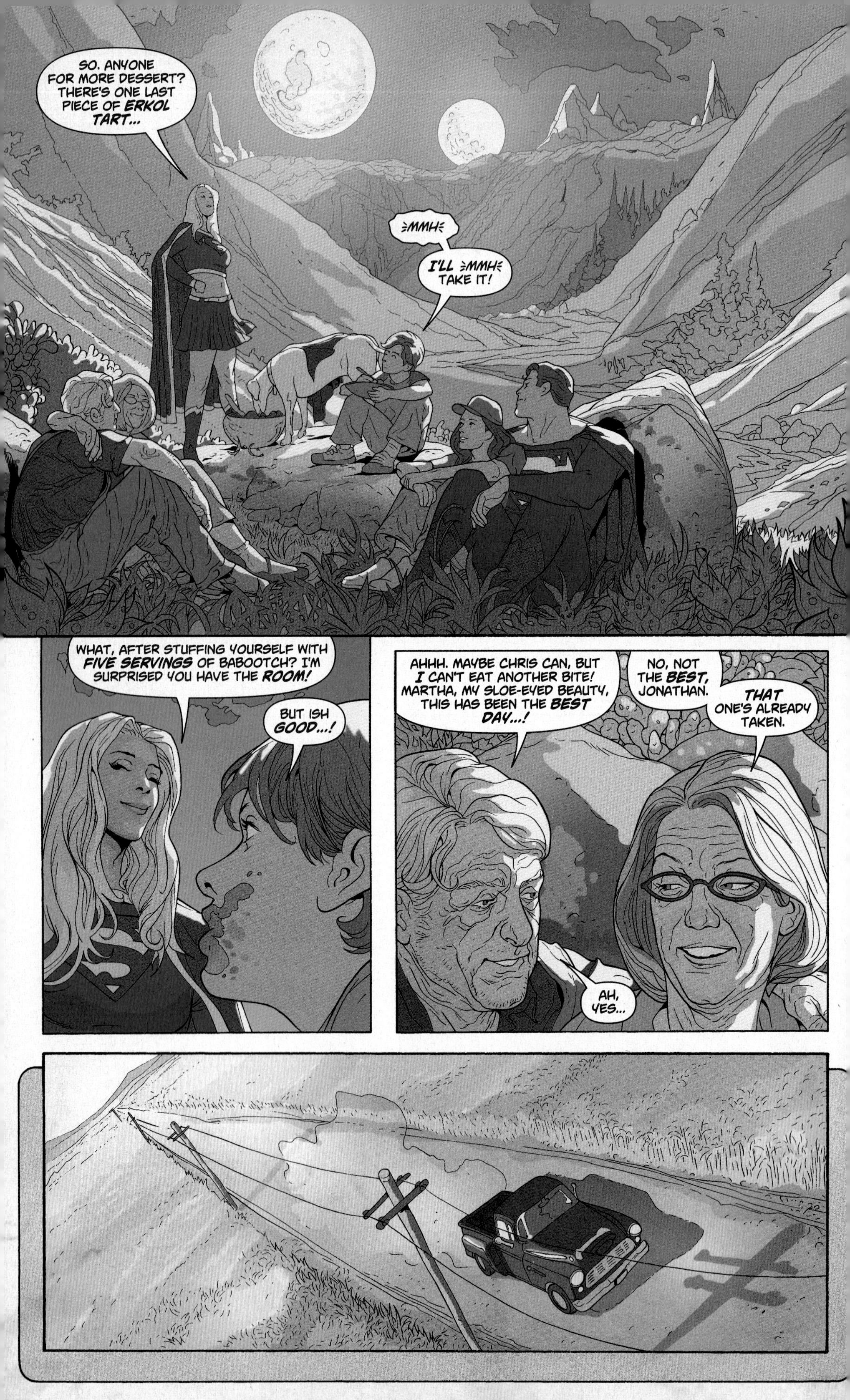

SO. ANYONE FOR MORE DESSERT? THERE'S ONE LAST PIECE OF ERKOL TART...
MMH
I'LL MMH TAKE IT!
WHAT, AFTER STUFFING YOURSELF WITH FIVE SERVINGS OF BABOOTCH? I'M SURPRISED YOU HAVE THE ROOM!
BUT ISH GOOD...!
AHHH. MAYBE CHRIS CAN, BUT I CAN'T EAT ANOTHER BITE! MARTHA, MY SLOE-EYED BEAUTY, THIS HAS BEEN THE BEST DAY...!
NO, NOT THE BEST, JONATHAN.
THAT ONE'S ALREADY TAKEN.
AH, YES...

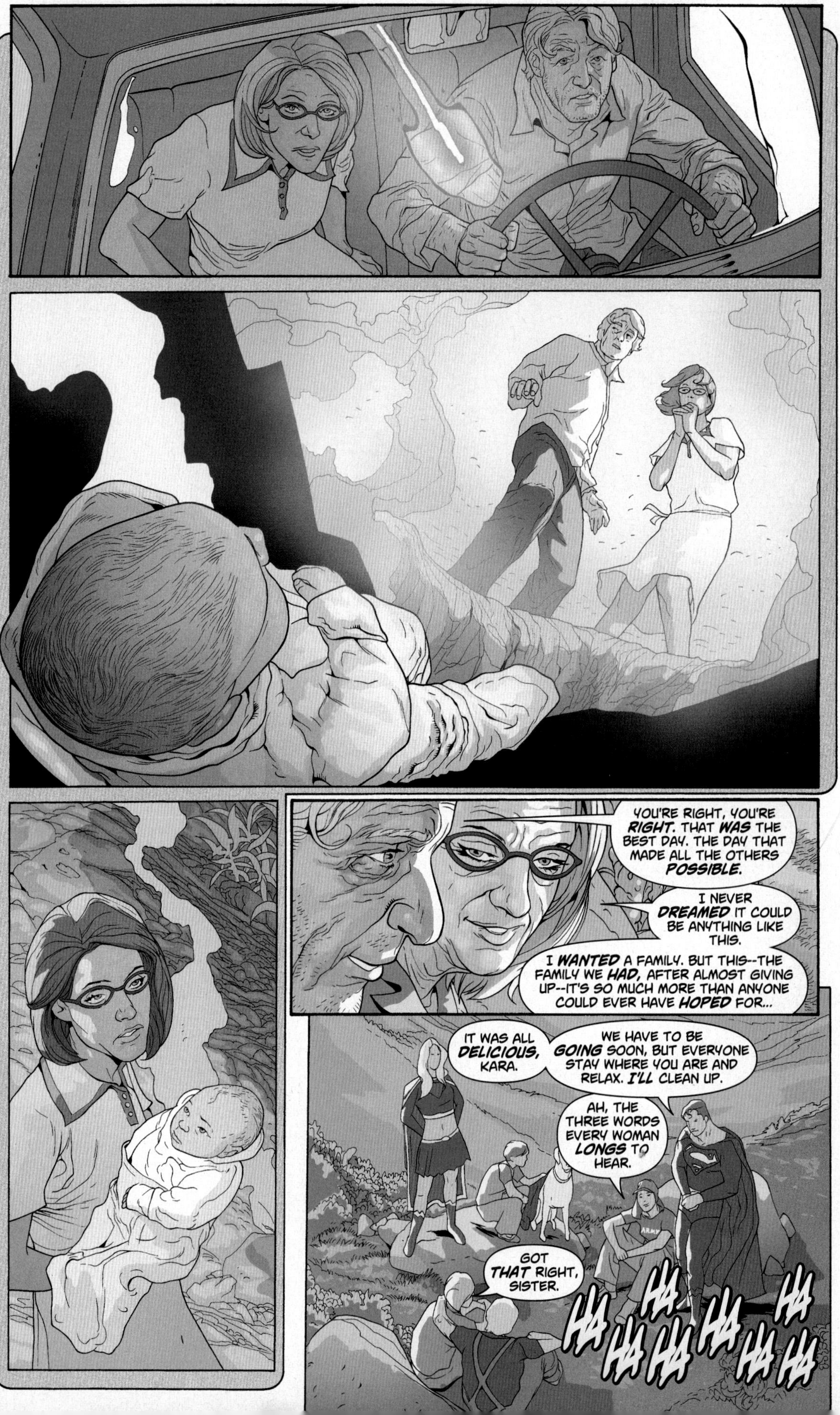
YOU'RE RIGHT, YOU'RE RIGHT. THAT WAS THE BEST DAY. THE DAY THAT MADE ALL THE OTHERS POSSIBLE.
I NEVER DREAMED IT COULD BE ANYTHING LIKE THIS.
I WANTED A FAMILY. BUT THIS--THE FAMILY WE HAD, AFTER ALMOST GIVING UP--IT'S SO MUCH MORE THAN ANYONE COULD EVER HAVE HOPED FOR...
IT WAS ALL DELICIOUS, KARA.
WE HAVE TO BE GOING SOON, BUT EVERYONE STAY WHERE YOU ARE AND RELAX. I'LL CLEAN UP.
AH, THE THREE WORDS EVERY WOMAN LONGS TO HEAR.
GOT THAT RIGHT, SISTER.
HA HA HA HA HA HA HA HA HA HA

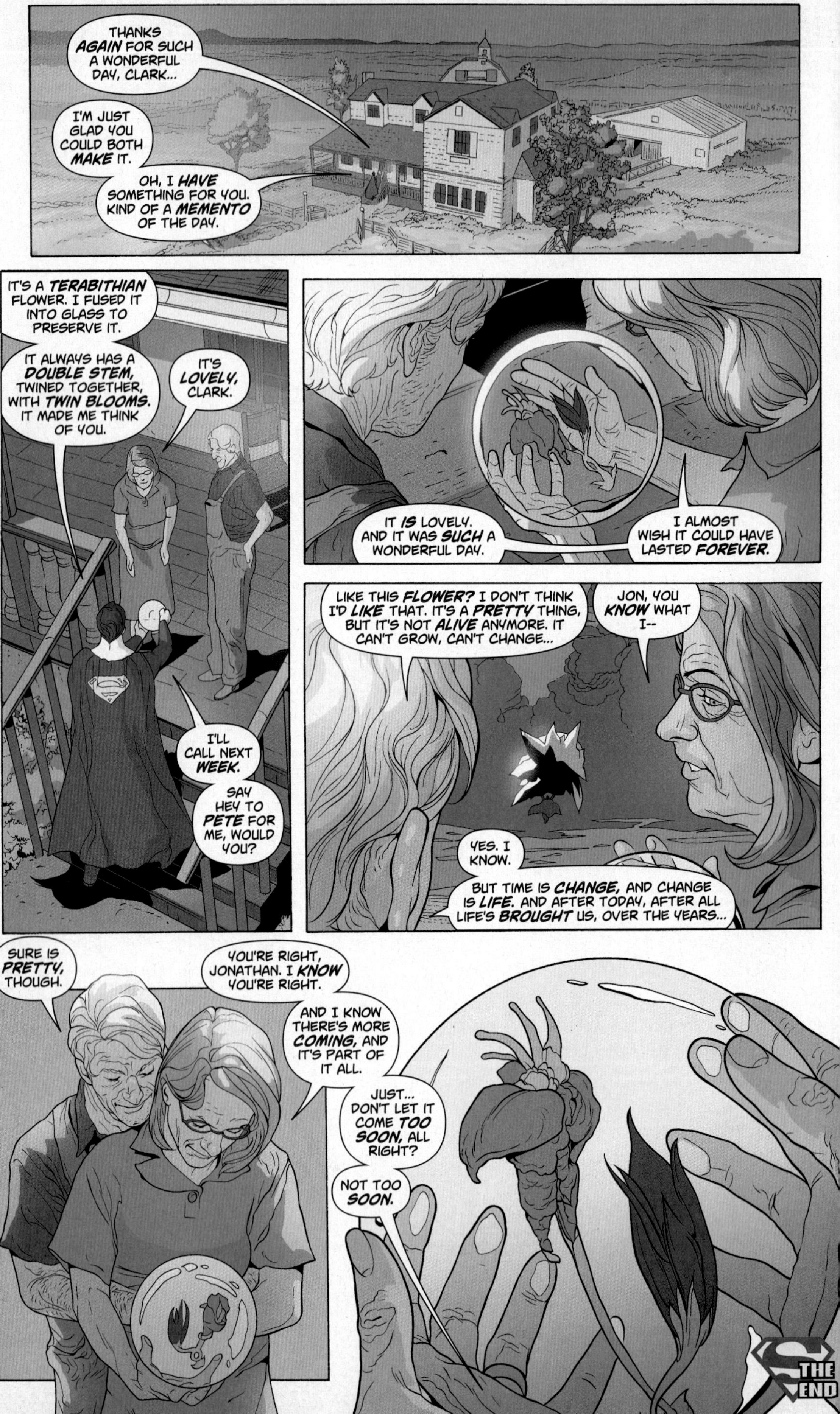
THANKS AGAIN FOR SUCH A WONDERFUL DAY, CLARK...
I'M JUST GLAD YOU COULD BOTH MAKE IT.
OH, I HAVE SOMETHING FOR YOU. KIND OF A MEMENTO OF THE DAY.
IT'S A TERABITHIAN FLOWER. I FUSED IT INTO GLASS TO PRESERVE IT.
IT ALWAYS HAS A DOUBLE STEM, TWINED TOGETHER, WITH TWIN BLOOMS. IT MADE ME THINK OF YOU.
IT'S LOVELY, CLARK.
I'LL CALL NEXT WEEK.
SAY HEY TO PETE FOR ME, WOULD YOU?
IT IS LOVELY. AND IT WAS SUCH A WONDERFUL DAY.
I ALMOST WISH IT COULD HAVE LASTED FOREVER.
LIKE THIS FLOWER? I DON'T THINK I'D LIKE THAT. IT'S A PRETTY THING, BUT IT'S NOT ALIVE ANYMORE. IT CAN'T GROW, CAN'T CHANGE...
JON, YOU KNOW WHAT I--
YES. I KNOW.
BUT TIME IS CHANGE, AND CHANGE IS LIFE. AND AFTER TODAY, AFTER ALL LIFE'S BROUGHT US, OVER THE YEARS...
SURE IS PRETTY, THOUGH.
YOU'RE RIGHT, JONATHAN. I KNOW YOU'RE RIGHT.
AND I KNOW THERE'S MORE COMING, AND IT'S PART OF IT ALL.
JUST... DON'T LET IT COME TOO SOON, ALL RIGHT?
NOT TOO SOON.
THE END

Cover art and color by Renato Guedes.

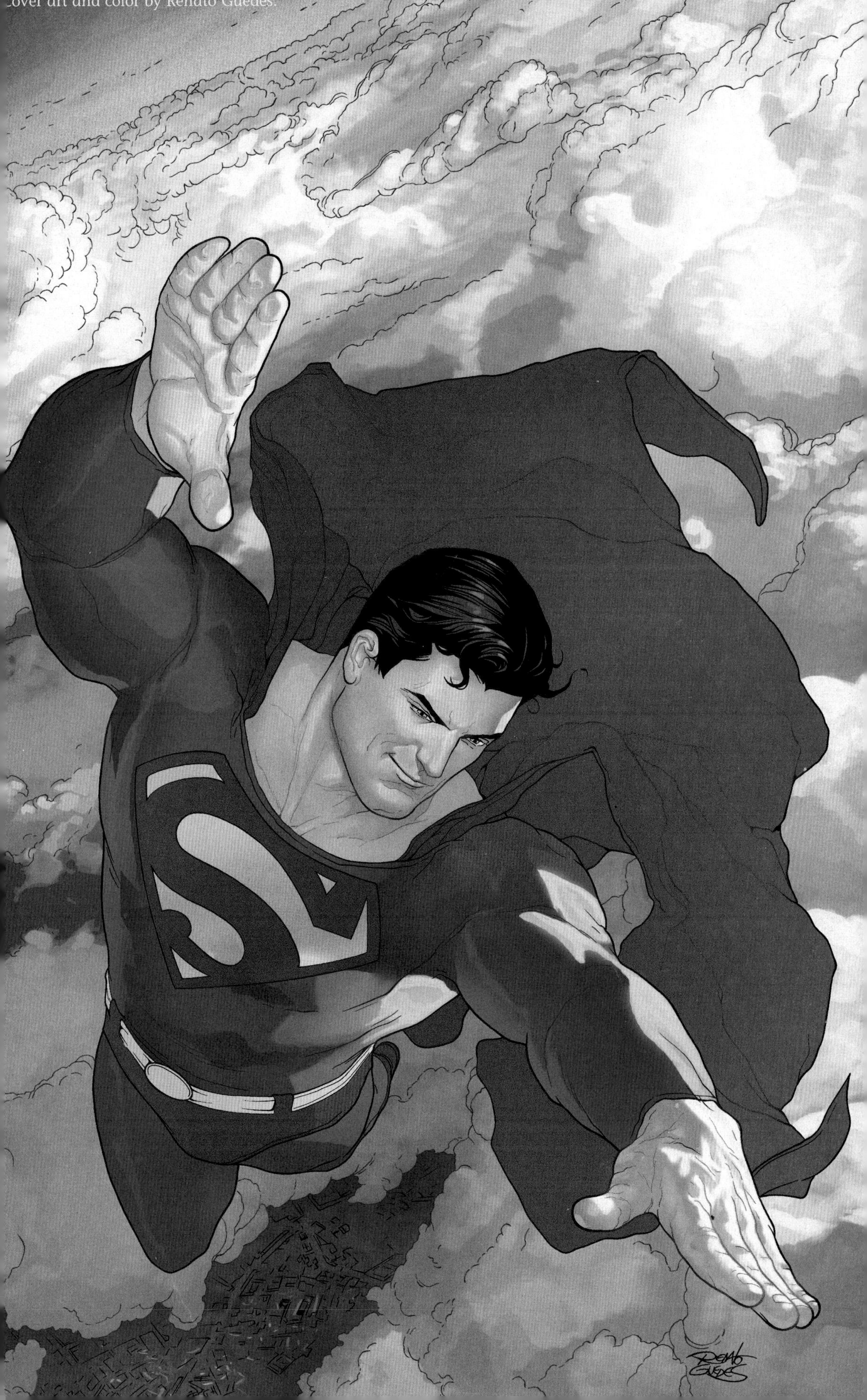

Cover art and color by Renato Guedes.

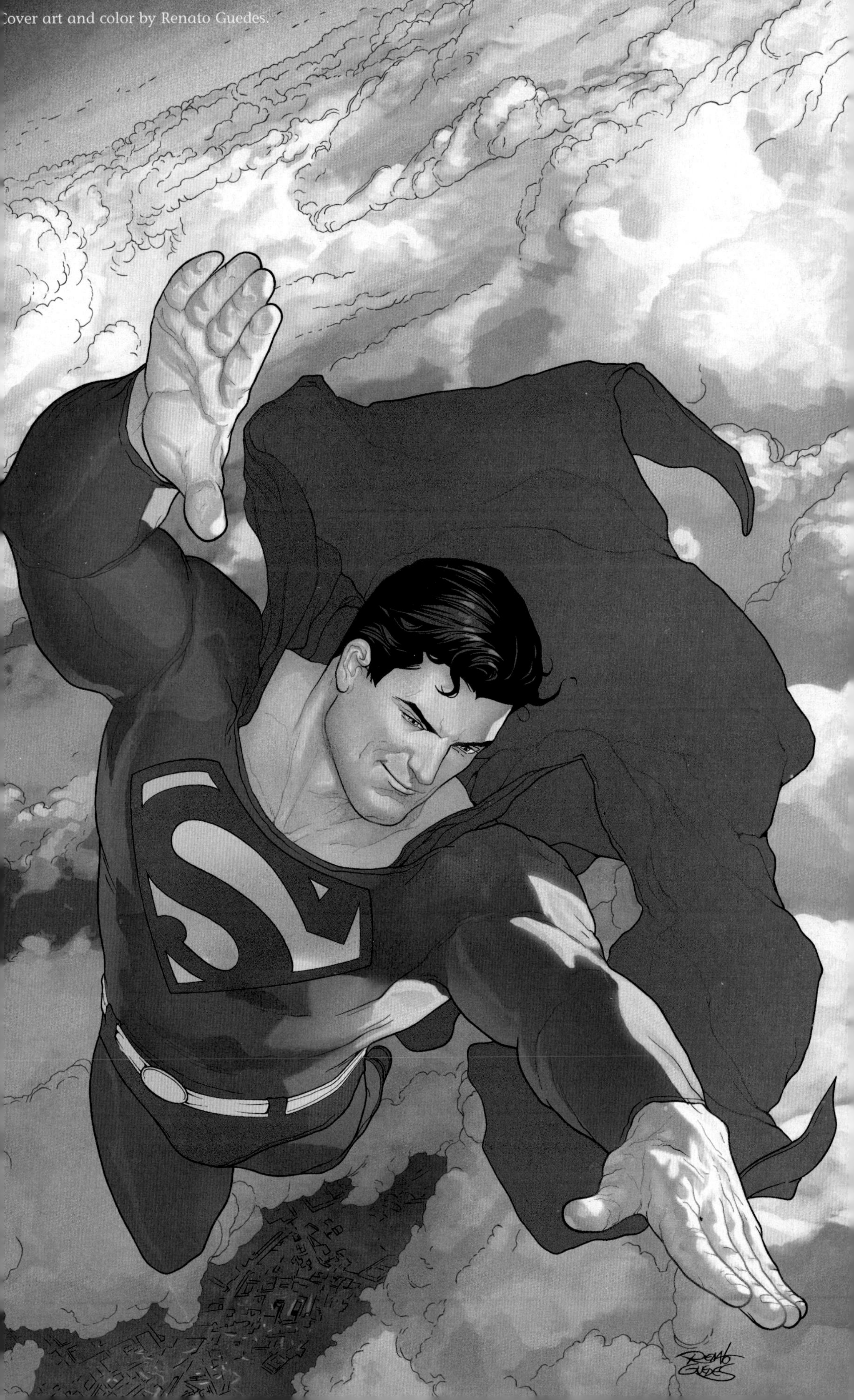

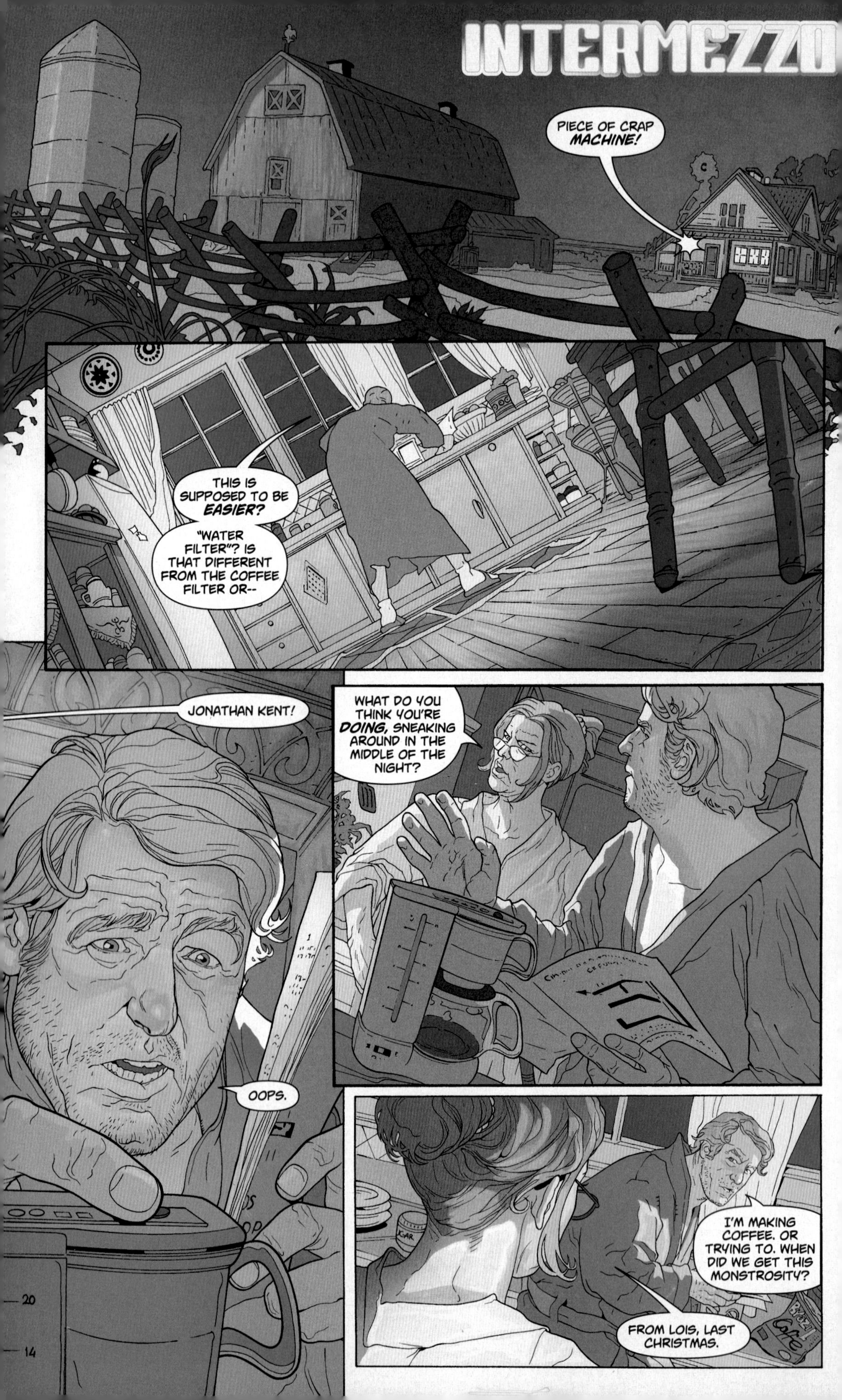
INTERMEZZO
PIECE OF CRAP MACHINE!
THIS IS SUPPOSED TO BE EASIER?
"WATER FILTER"? IS THAT DIFFERENT FROM THE COFFEE FILTER OR--
JONATHAN KENT!
WHAT DO YOU THINK YOU'RE DOING, SNEAKING AROUND IN THE MIDDLE OF THE NIGHT?
OOPS.
I'M MAKING COFFEE. OR TRYING TO. WHEN DID WE GET THIS MONSTROSITY?
FROM LOIS, LAST CHRISTMAS.

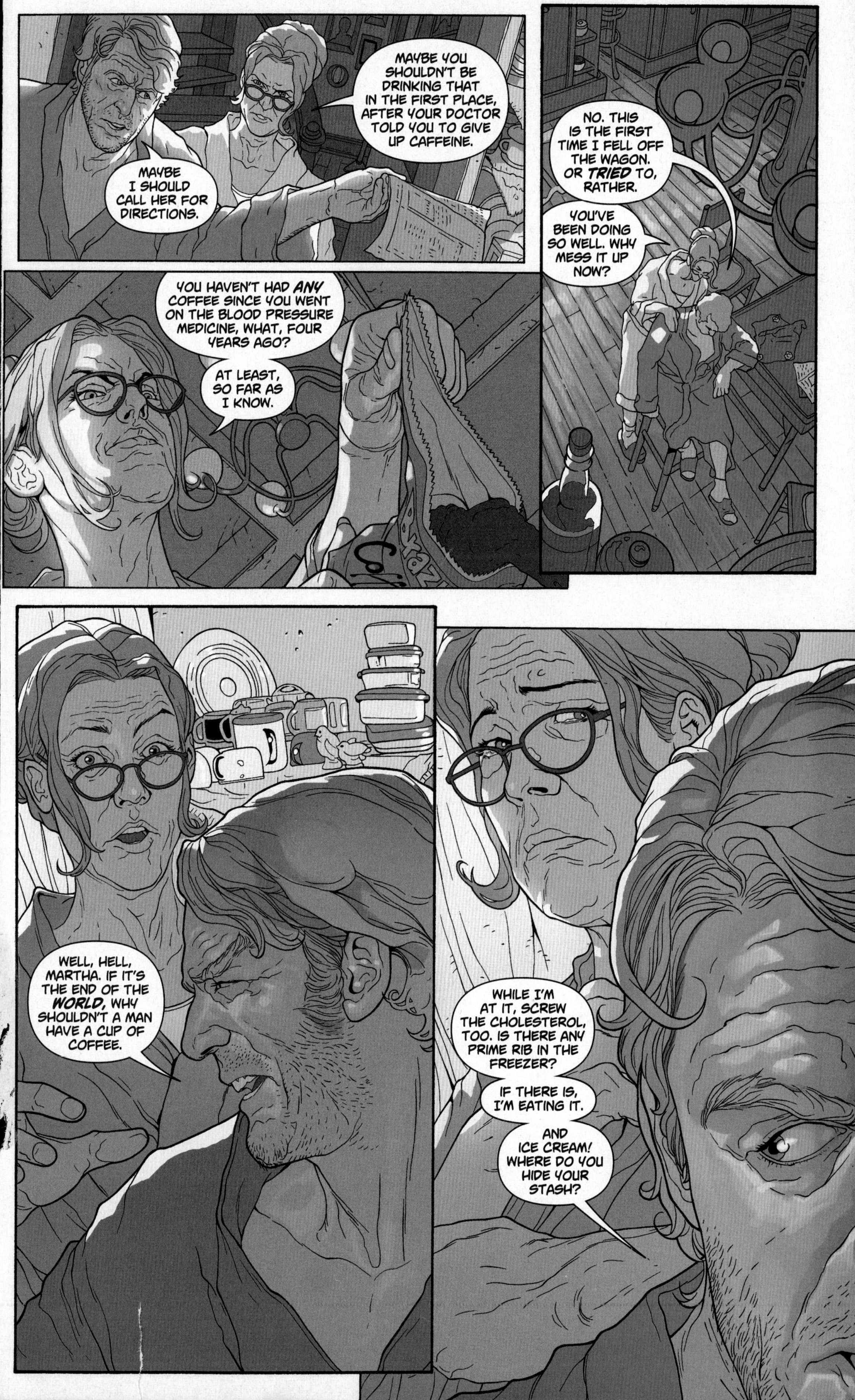
MAYBE YOU SHOULDN'T BE DRINKING THAT IN THE FIRST PLACE, AFTER YOUR DOCTOR TOLD YOU TO GIVE UP CAFFEINE.
MAYBE I SHOULD CALL HER FOR DIRECTIONS.
NO. THIS IS THE FIRST TIME I FELL OFF THE WAGON. OR *TRIED* TO, RATHER.
YOU'VE BEEN DOING SO WELL. WHY MESS IT UP NOW?
YOU HAVEN'T HAD *ANY* COFFEE SINCE YOU WENT ON THE BLOOD PRESSURE MEDICINE, WHAT, FOUR YEARS AGO?
AT LEAST, SO FAR AS I KNOW.
WELL, HELL, MARTHA. IF IT'S THE END OF THE *WORLD*, WHY SHOULDN'T A MAN HAVE A CUP OF COFFEE.
WHILE I'M AT IT, SCREW THE CHOLESTEROL, TOO. IS THERE ANY PRIME RIB IN THE FREEZER?
IF THERE IS, I'M EATING IT.
AND ICE CREAM! WHERE DO YOU HIDE YOUR STASH?

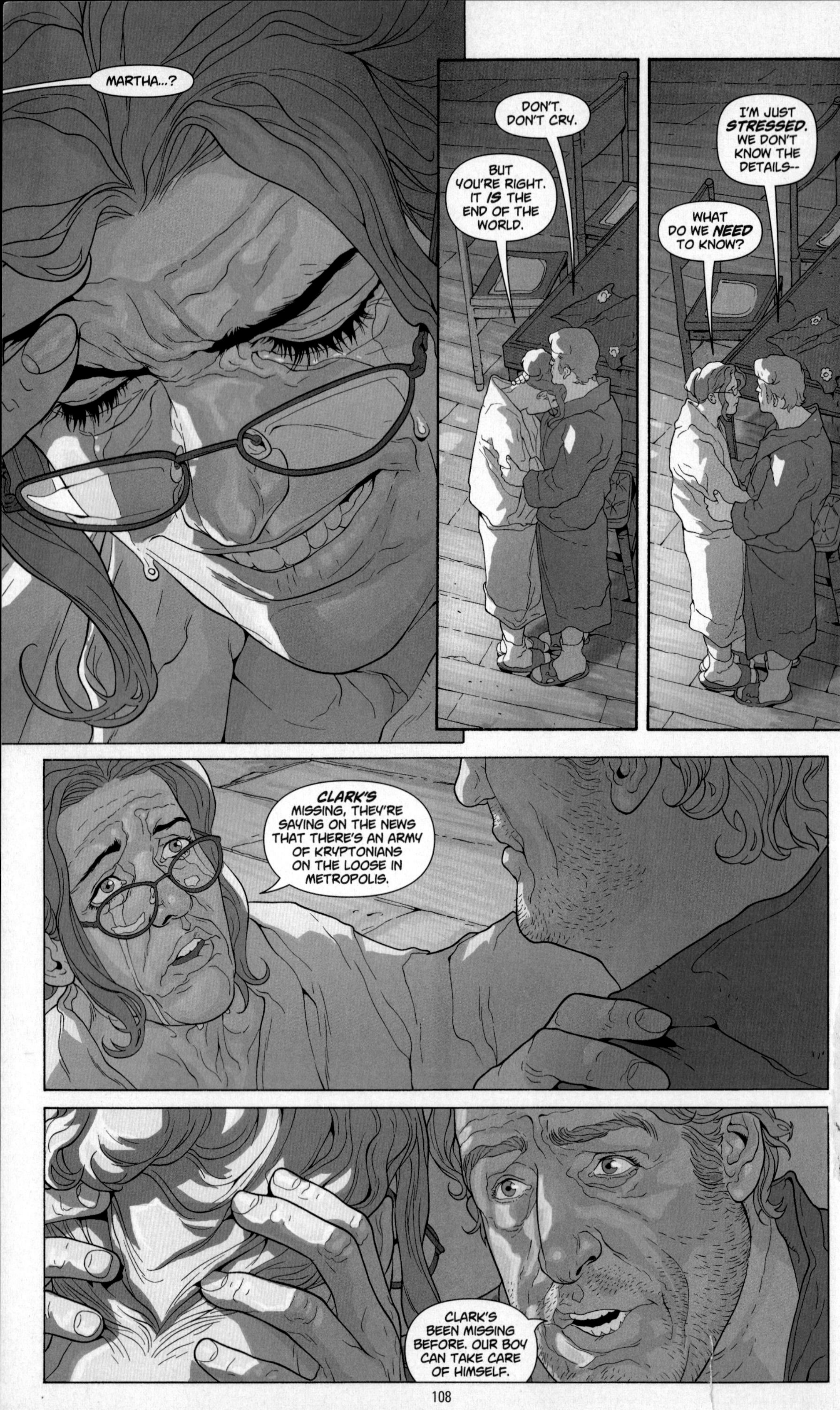
MARTHA...?
DON'T. DON'T CRY.
BUT YOU'RE RIGHT. IT IS THE END OF THE WORLD.
I'M JUST STRESSED. WE DON'T KNOW THE DETAILS--
WHAT DO WE NEED TO KNOW?
CLARK'S MISSING, THEY'RE SAYING ON THE NEWS THAT THERE'S AN ARMY OF KRYPTONIANS ON THE LOOSE IN METROPOLIS.
CLARK'S BEEN MISSING BEFORE. OUR BOY CAN TAKE CARE OF HIMSELF.

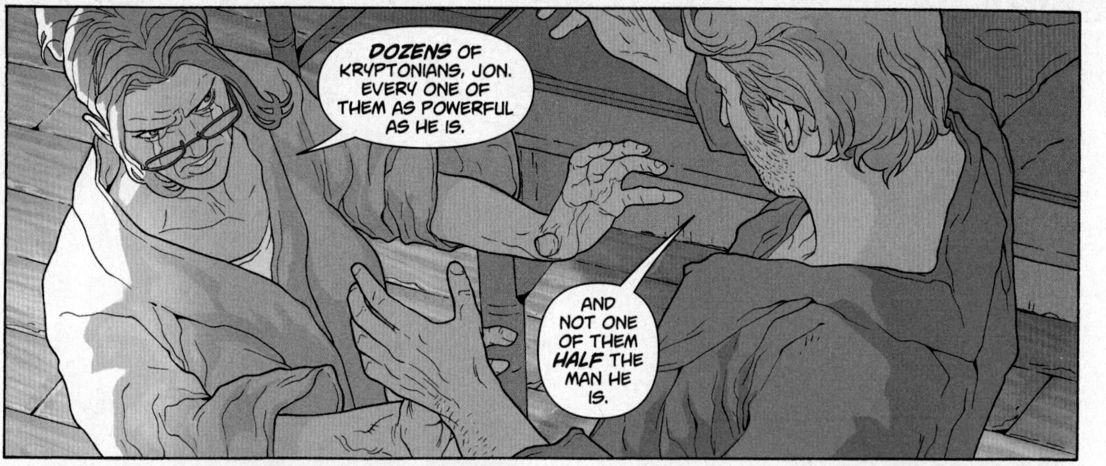
DOZENS OF KRYPTONIANS, JON. EVERY ONE OF THEM AS POWERFUL AS HE IS.
AND NOT ONE OF THEM HALF THE MAN HE IS.

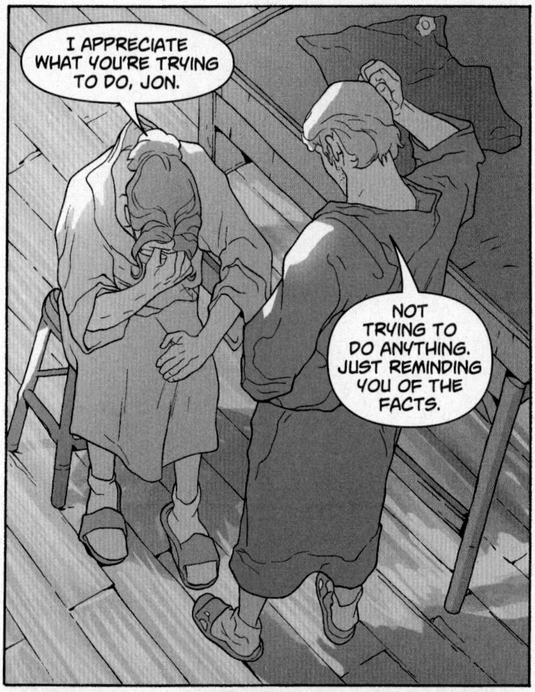
I APPRECIATE WHAT YOU'RE TRYING TO DO, JON.
NOT TRYING TO DO ANYTHING. JUST REMINDING YOU OF THE FACTS.

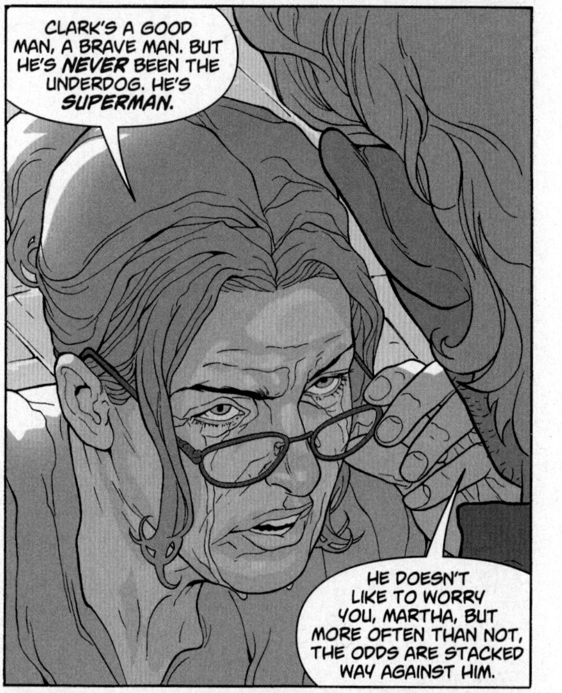
CLARK'S A GOOD MAN, A BRAVE MAN. BUT HE'S NEVER BEEN THE UNDERDOG. HE'S SUPERMAN.
HE DOESN'T LIKE TO WORRY YOU, MARTHA, BUT MORE OFTEN THAN NOT, THE ODDS ARE STACKED WAY AGAINST HIM.

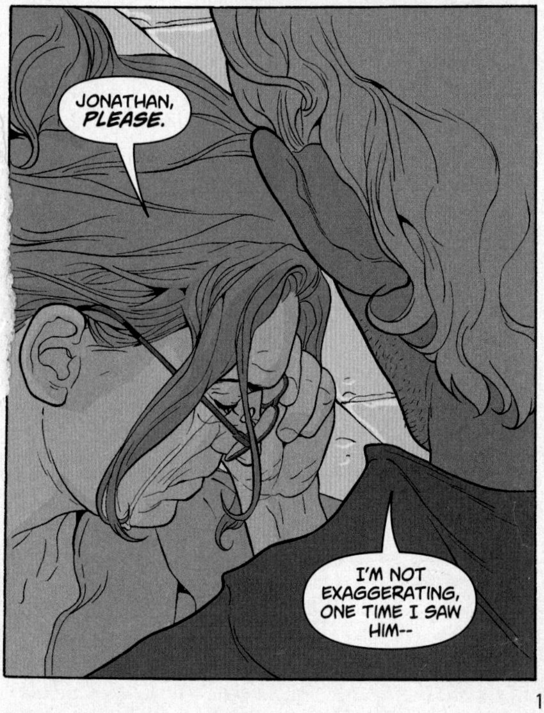
JONATHAN, PLEASE.
I'M NOT EXAGGERATING, ONE TIME I SAW HIM--

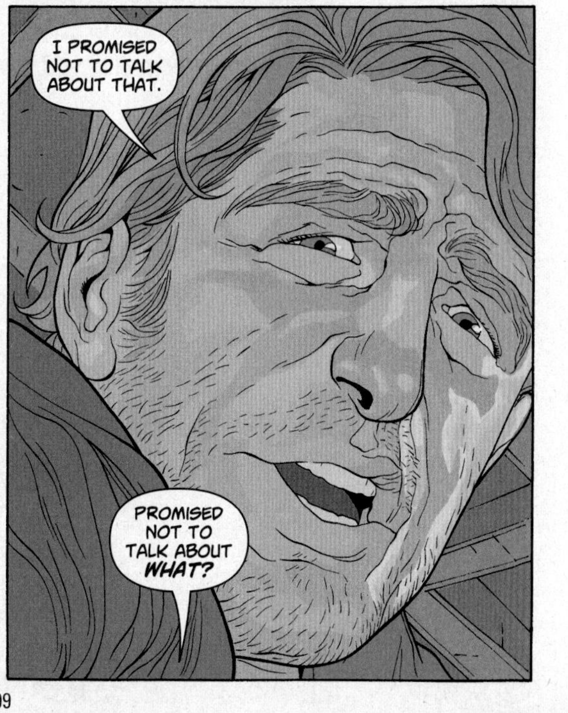
I PROMISED NOT TO TALK ABOUT THAT.
PROMISED NOT TO TALK ABOUT WHAT?

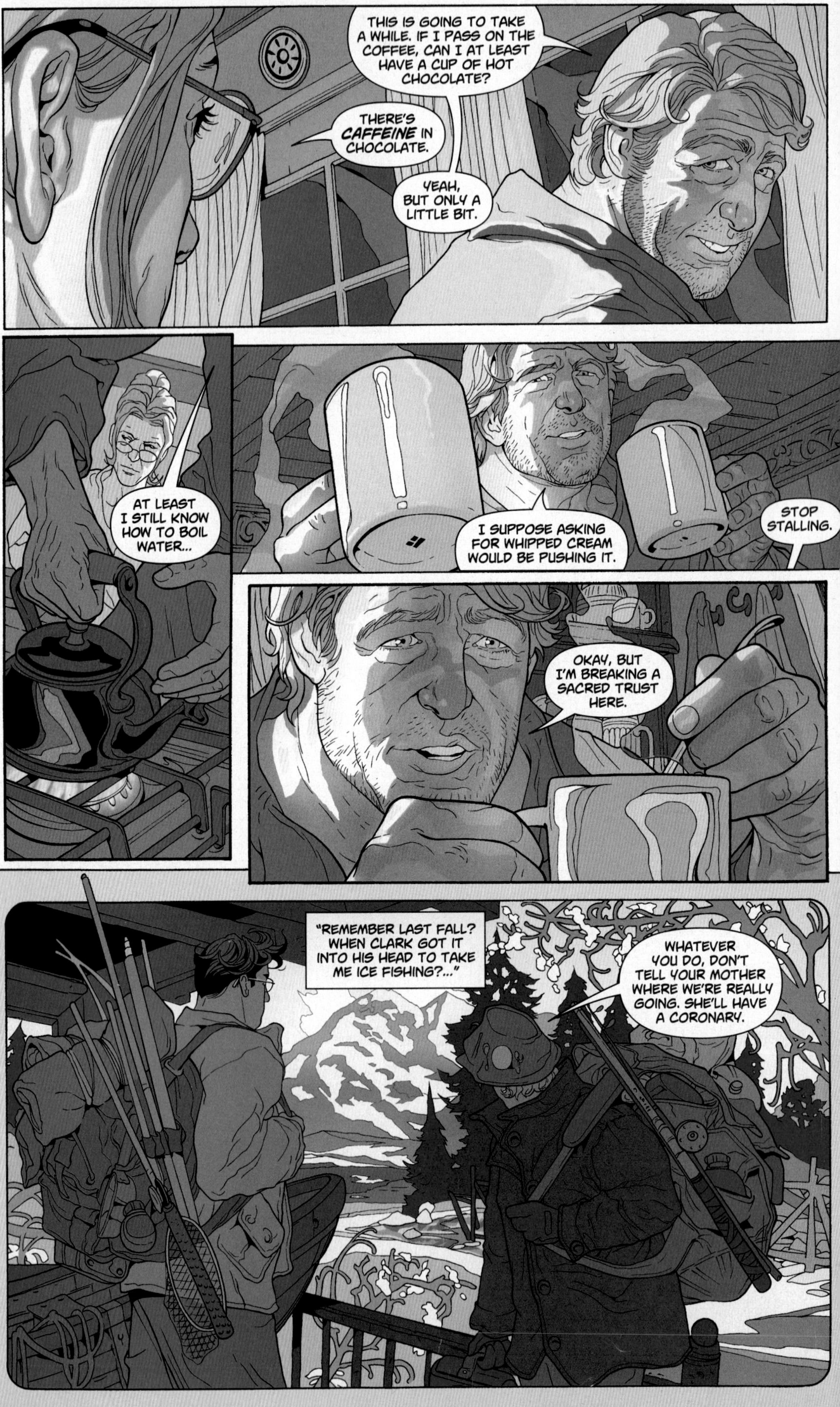
THIS IS GOING TO TAKE A WHILE. IF I PASS ON THE COFFEE, CAN I AT LEAST HAVE A CUP OF HOT CHOCOLATE?
THERE'S CAFFEINE IN CHOCOLATE.
YEAH, BUT ONLY A LITTLE BIT.
AT LEAST I STILL KNOW HOW TO BOIL WATER...
I SUPPOSE ASKING FOR WHIPPED CREAM WOULD BE PUSHING IT.
STOP STALLING.
OKAY, BUT I'M BREAKING A SACRED TRUST HERE.
"REMEMBER LAST FALL? WHEN CLARK GOT IT INTO HIS HEAD TO TAKE ME ICE FISHING?..."
WHATEVER YOU DO, DON'T TELL YOUR MOTHER WHERE WE'RE REALLY GOING. SHE'LL HAVE A CORONARY.

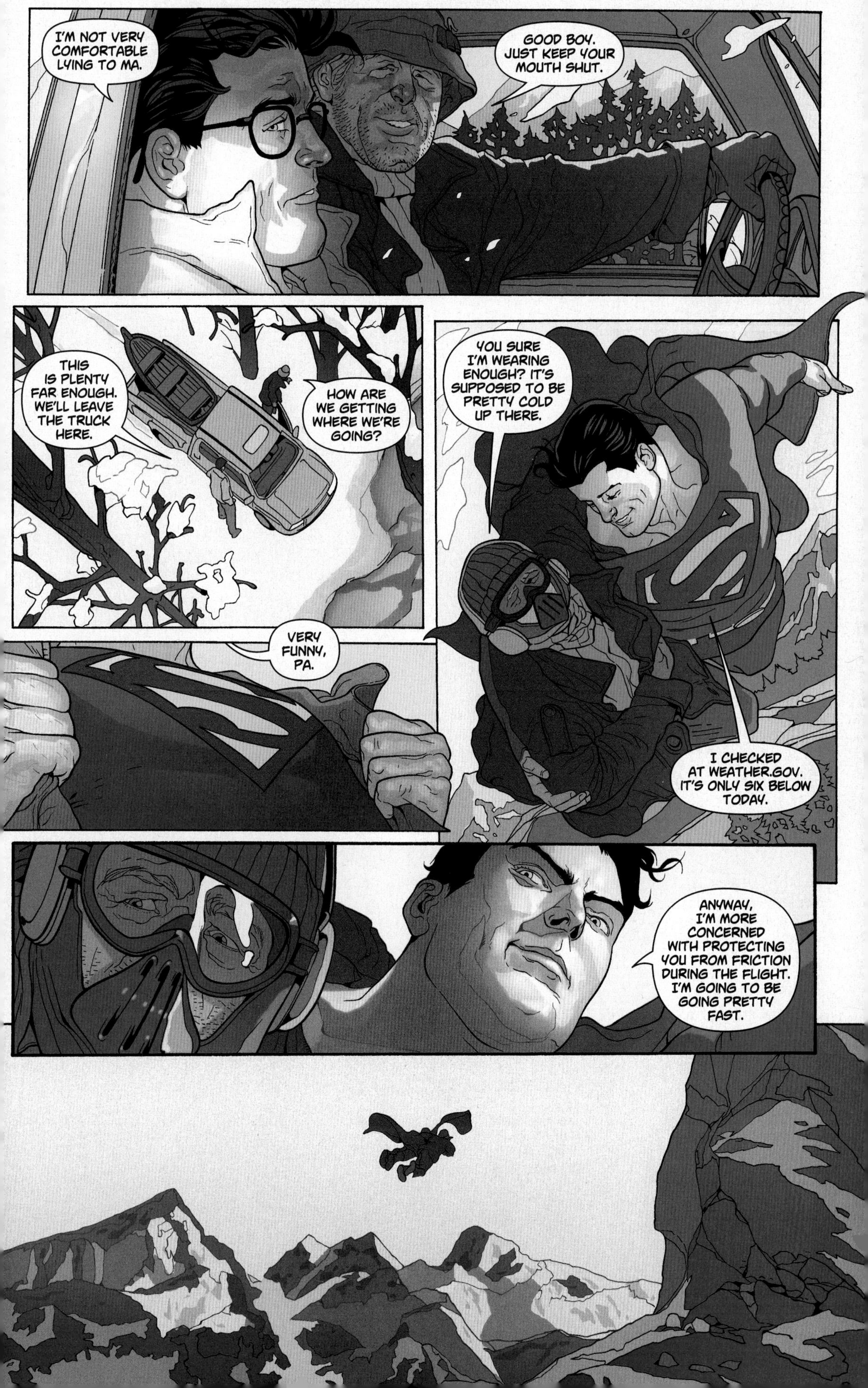

I'M NOT VERY COMFORTABLE LYING TO MA.
GOOD BOY. JUST KEEP YOUR MOUTH SHUT.
THIS IS PLENTY FAR ENOUGH. WE'LL LEAVE THE TRUCK HERE.
HOW ARE WE GETTING WHERE WE'RE GOING?
VERY FUNNY, PA.
YOU SURE I'M WEARING ENOUGH? IT'S SUPPOSED TO BE PRETTY COLD UP THERE.
I CHECKED AT WEATHER.GOV. IT'S ONLY SIX BELOW TODAY.
ANYWAY, I'M MORE CONCERNED WITH PROTECTING YOU FROM FRICTION DURING THE FLIGHT. I'M GOING TO BE GOING PRETTY FAST.

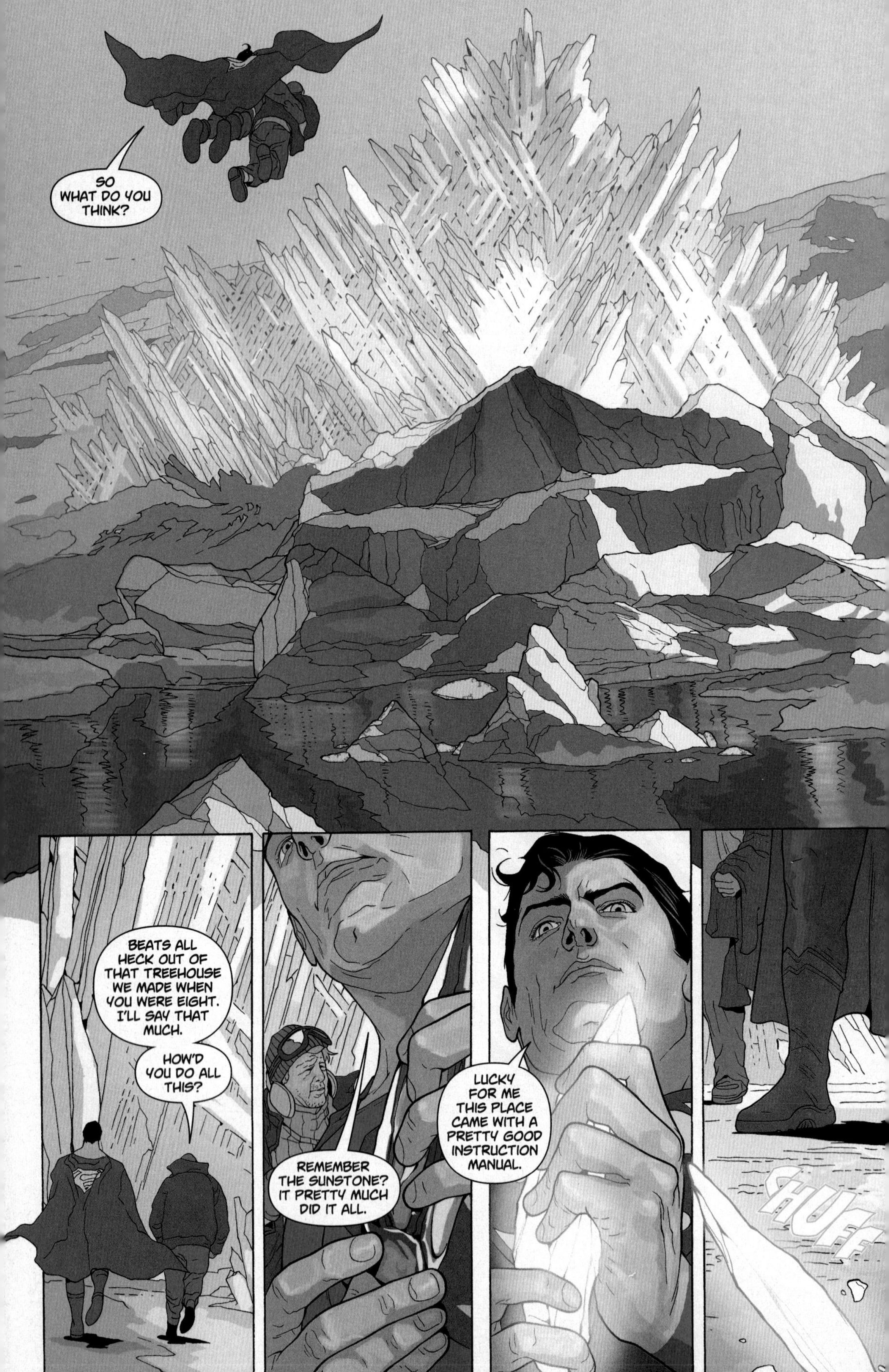
SO WHAT DO YOU THINK?
BEATS ALL HECK OUT OF THAT TREEHOUSE WE MADE WHEN YOU WERE EIGHT. I'LL SAY THAT MUCH.
HOW'D YOU DO ALL THIS?
REMEMBER THE SUNSTONE? IT PRETTY MUCH DID IT ALL.
LUCKY FOR ME THIS PLACE CAME WITH A PRETTY GOOD INSTRUCTION MANUAL.
CHUFF

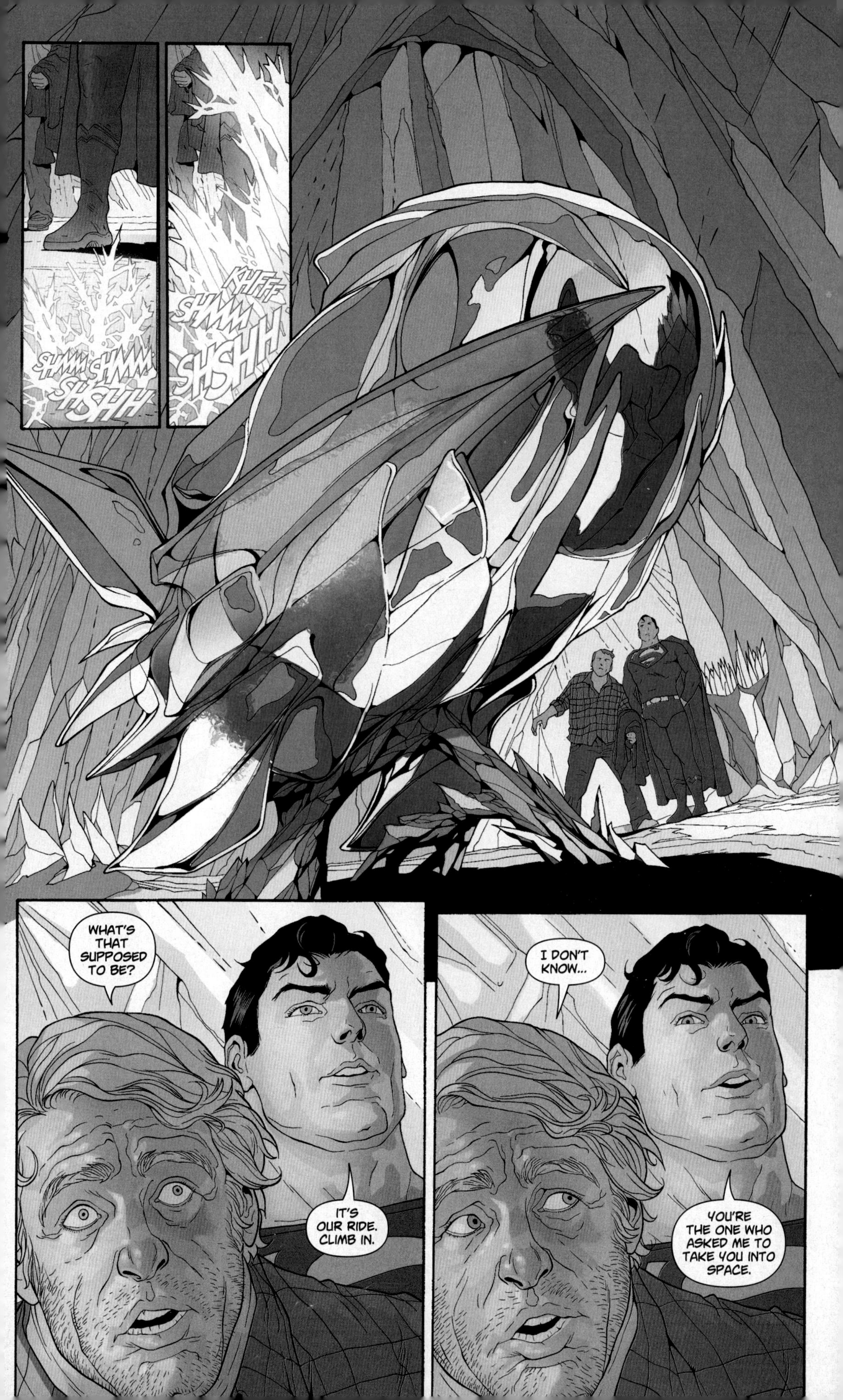
SHMM SHMM
SHSHH
KHFFF
SHMM
SHSHH
WHAT'S THAT SUPPOSED TO BE?
IT'S OUR RIDE. CLIMB IN.
I DON'T KNOW...
YOU'RE THE ONE WHO ASKED ME TO TAKE YOU INTO SPACE.

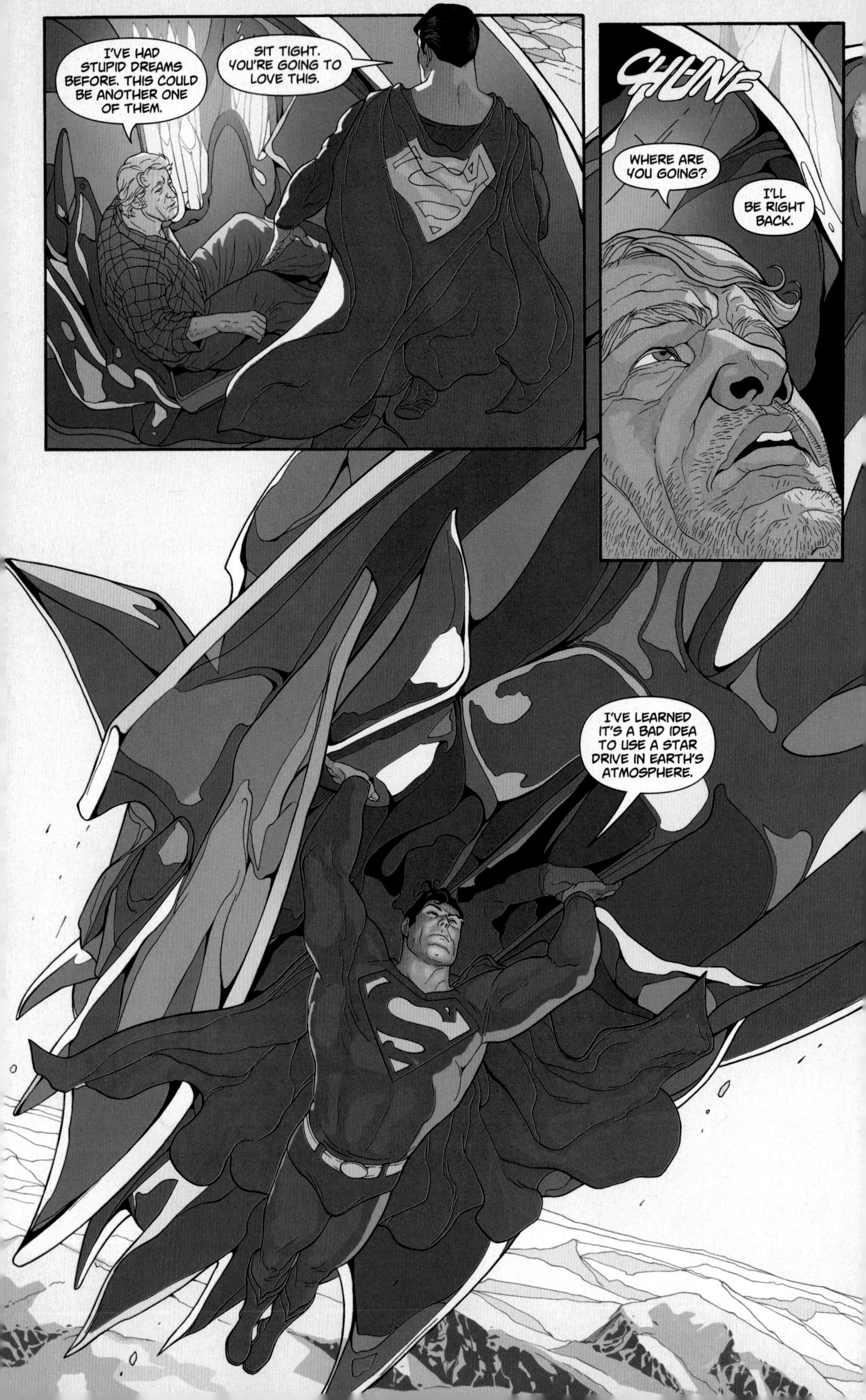
I'VE HAD STUPID DREAMS BEFORE. THIS COULD BE ANOTHER ONE OF THEM.
SIT TIGHT. YOU'RE GOING TO LOVE THIS.
CHUNF
WHERE ARE YOU GOING?
I'LL BE RIGHT BACK.
I'VE LEARNED IT'S A BAD IDEA TO USE A STAR DRIVE IN EARTH'S ATMOSPHERE.

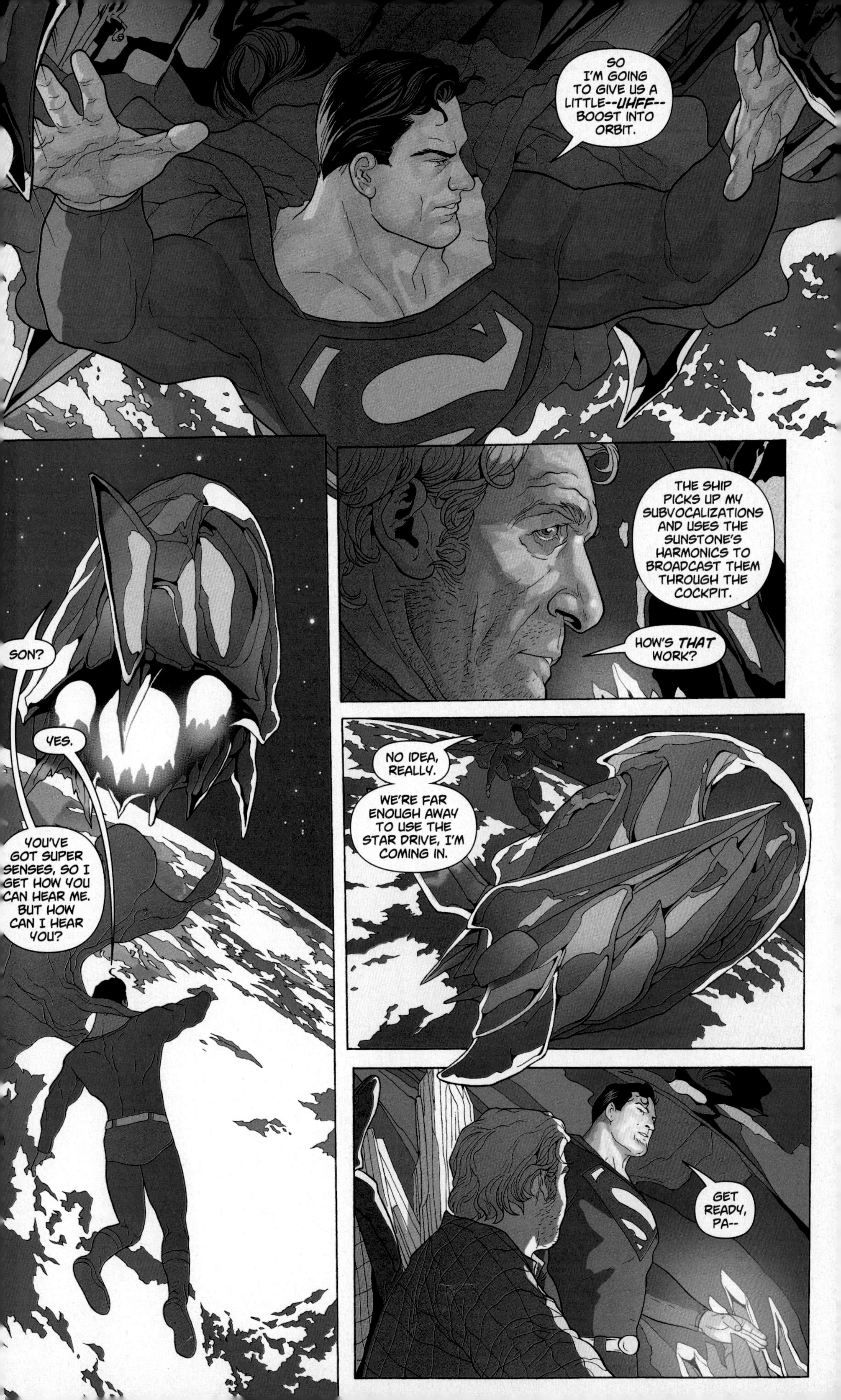
SO I'M GOING TO GIVE US A LITTLE--UHFF--BOOST INTO ORBIT.
SON?
YES.
YOU'VE GOT SUPER SENSES, SO I GET HOW YOU CAN HEAR ME. BUT HOW CAN I HEAR YOU?
THE SHIP PICKS UP MY SUBVOCALIZATIONS AND USES THE SUNSTONE'S HARMONICS TO BROADCAST THEM THROUGH THE COCKPIT.
HOW'S THAT WORK?
NO IDEA, REALLY.
WE'RE FAR ENOUGH AWAY TO USE THE STAR DRIVE, I'M COMING IN.
GET READY, PA--

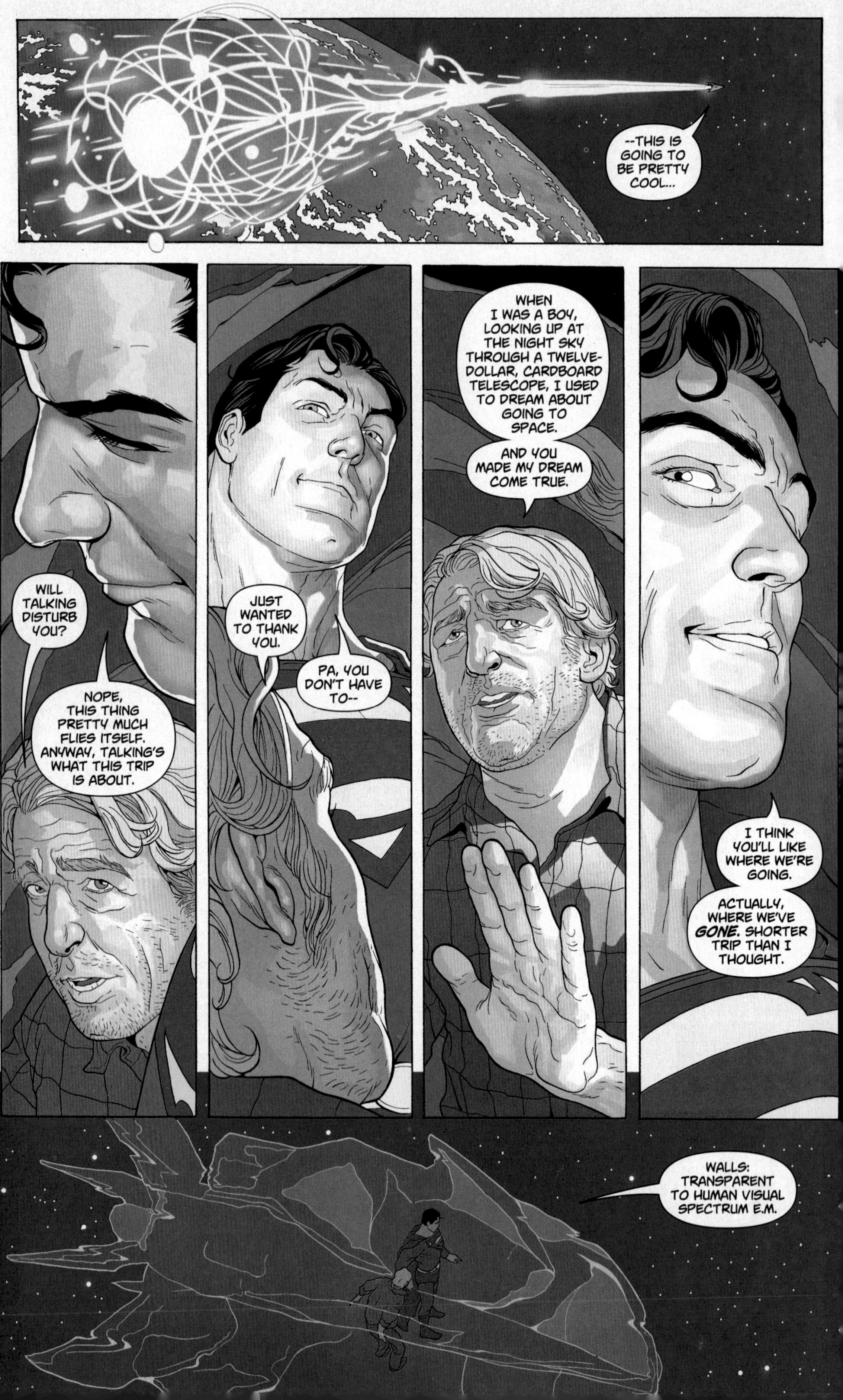
--THIS IS GOING TO BE PRETTY COOL...
WILL TALKING DISTURB YOU?
NOPE, THIS THING PRETTY MUCH FLIES ITSELF. ANYWAY, TALKING'S WHAT THIS TRIP IS ABOUT.
JUST WANTED TO THANK YOU.
PA, YOU DON'T HAVE TO--
WHEN I WAS A BOY, LOOKING UP AT THE NIGHT SKY THROUGH A TWELVE-DOLLAR, CARDBOARD TELESCOPE, I USED TO DREAM ABOUT GOING TO SPACE.
AND YOU MADE MY DREAM COME TRUE.
I THINK YOU'LL LIKE WHERE WE'RE GOING.
ACTUALLY, WHERE WE'VE GONE. SHORTER TRIP THAN I THOUGHT.
WALLS: TRANSPARENT TO HUMAN VISUAL SPECTRUM E.M.

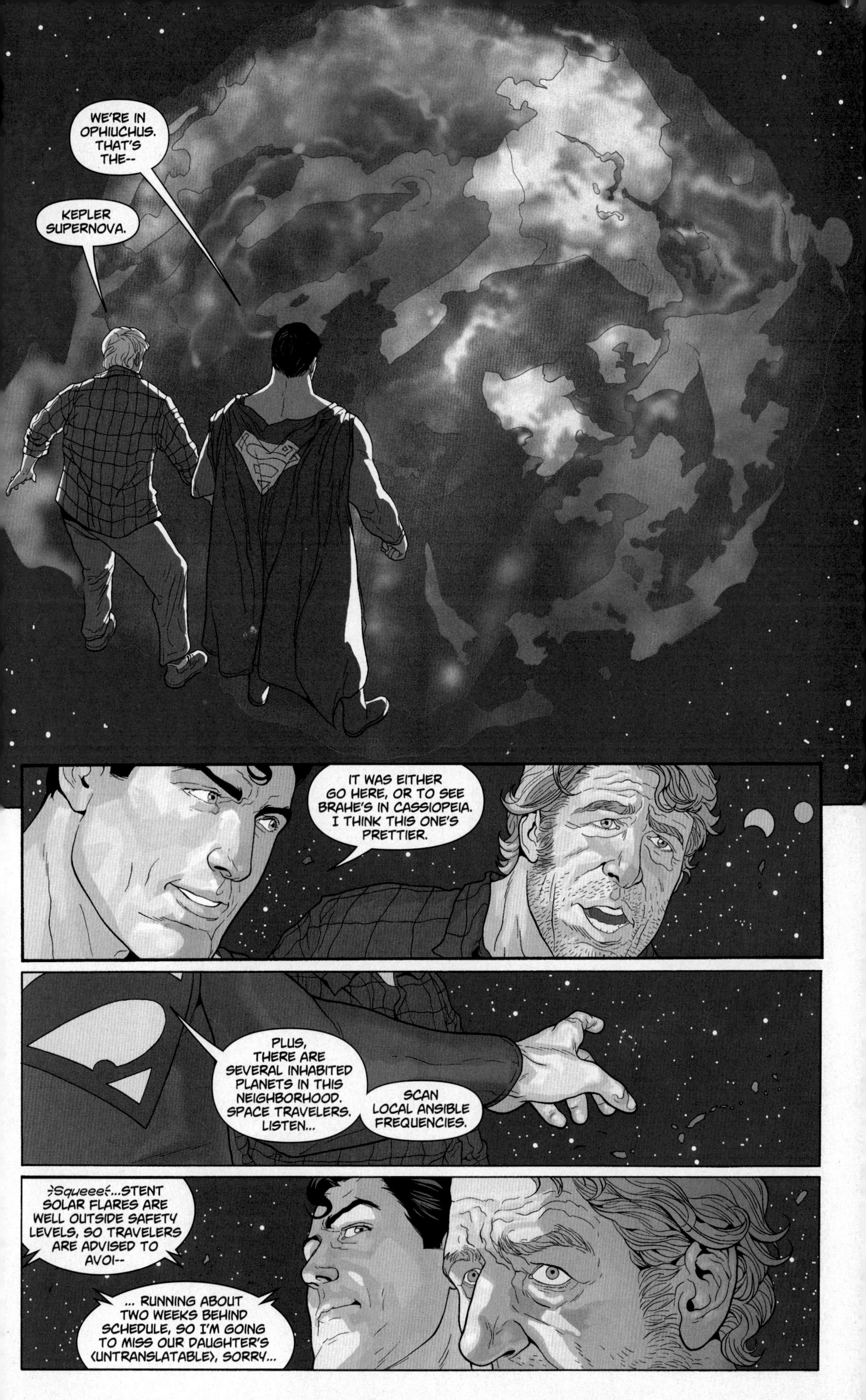

WE'RE IN OPHIUCHUS. THAT'S THE--
KEPLER SUPERNOVA.
IT WAS EITHER GO HERE, OR TO SEE BRAHE'S IN CASSIOPEIA. I THINK THIS ONE'S PRETTIER.
PLUS, THERE ARE SEVERAL INHABITED PLANETS IN THIS NEIGHBORHOOD. SPACE TRAVELERS. LISTEN...
SCAN LOCAL ANSIBLE FREQUENCIES.
Squeee...STENT SOLAR FLARES ARE WELL OUTSIDE SAFETY LEVELS, SO TRAVELERS ARE ADVISED TO AVOI--
... RUNNING ABOUT TWO WEEKS BEHIND SCHEDULE, SO I'M GOING TO MISS OUR DAUGHTER'S (UNTRANSLATABLE), SORRY...

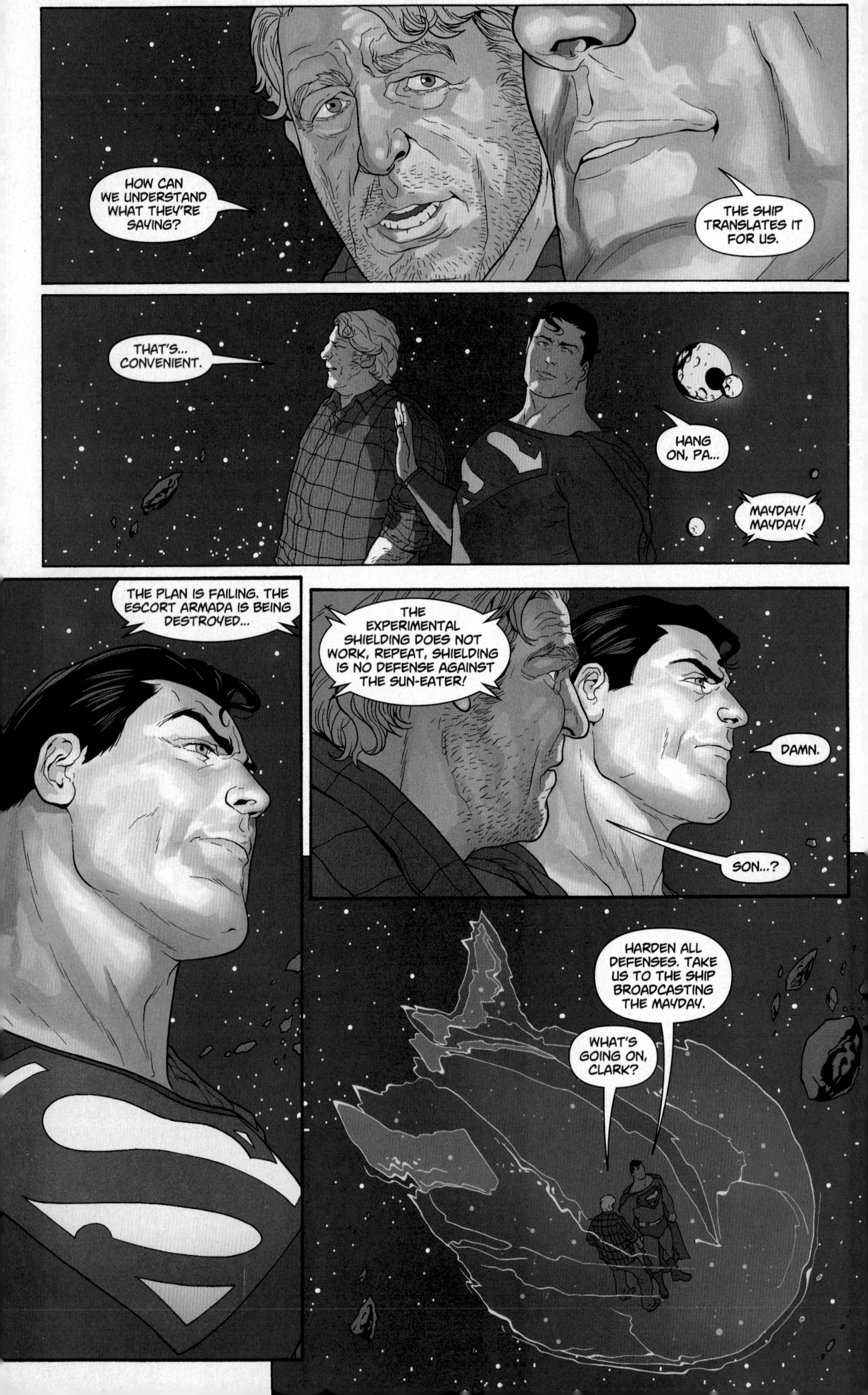
HOW CAN WE UNDERSTAND WHAT THEY'RE SAYING?
THE SHIP TRANSLATES IT FOR US.
THAT'S... CONVENIENT.
HANG ON, PA...
MAYDAY! MAYDAY!
THE PLAN IS FAILING. THE ESCORT ARMADA IS BEING DESTROYED...
THE EXPERIMENTAL SHIELDING DOES NOT WORK, REPEAT, SHIELDING IS NO DEFENSE AGAINST THE SUN-EATER!
DAMN.
SON...?
HARDEN ALL DEFENSES. TAKE US TO THE SHIP BROADCASTING THE MAYDAY.
WHAT'S GOING ON, CLARK?

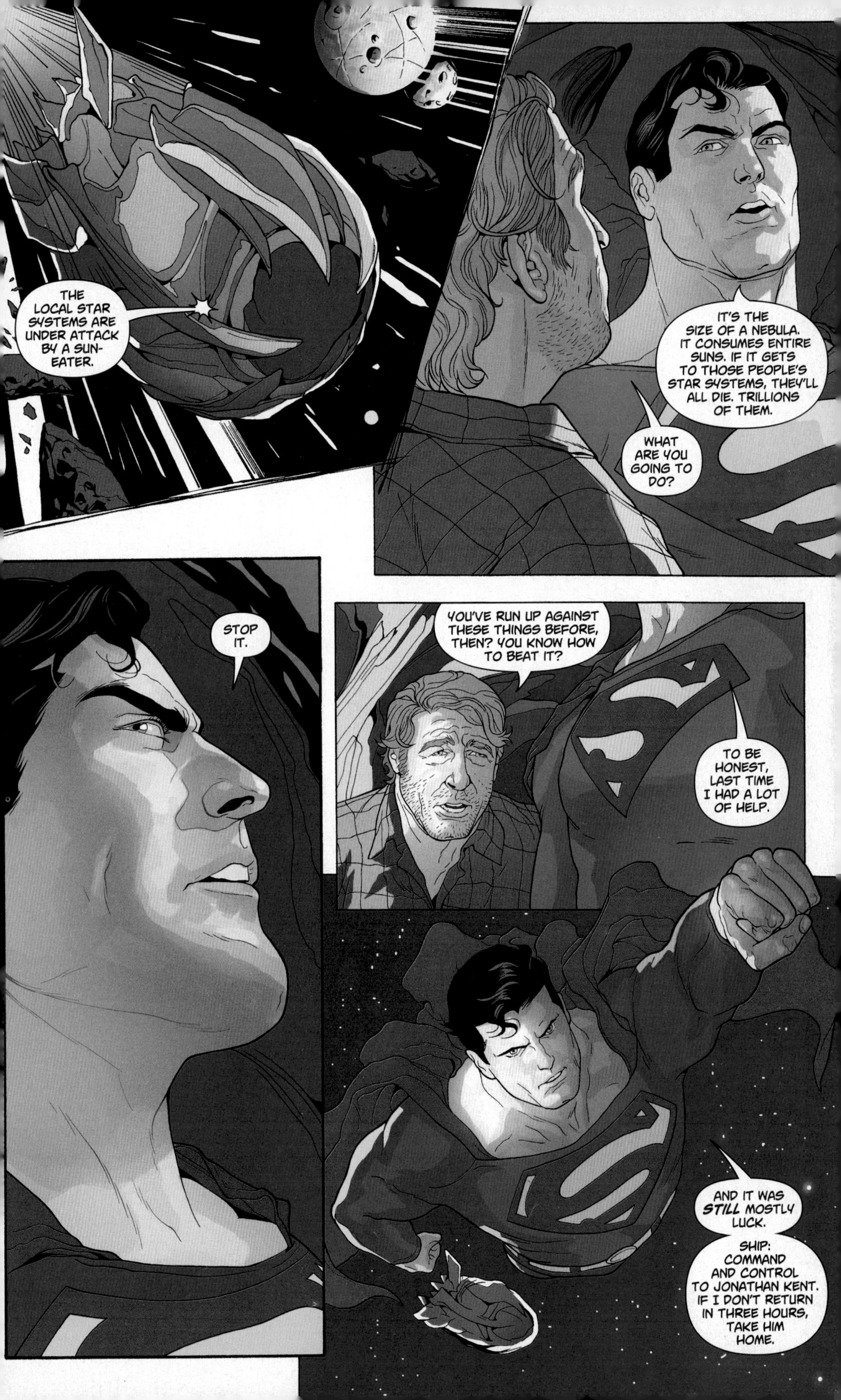
THE LOCAL STAR SYSTEMS ARE UNDER ATTACK BY A SUN-EATER.
IT'S THE SIZE OF A NEBULA. IT CONSUMES ENTIRE SUNS. IF IT GETS TO THOSE PEOPLE'S STAR SYSTEMS, THEY'LL ALL DIE. TRILLIONS OF THEM.
WHAT ARE YOU GOING TO DO?
STOP IT.
YOU'VE RUN UP AGAINST THESE THINGS BEFORE, THEN? YOU KNOW HOW TO BEAT IT?
TO BE HONEST, LAST TIME I HAD A LOT OF HELP.
AND IT WAS STILL MOSTLY LUCK.
SHIP: COMMAND AND CONTROL TO JONATHAN KENT. IF I DON'T RETURN IN THREE HOURS, TAKE HIM HOME.

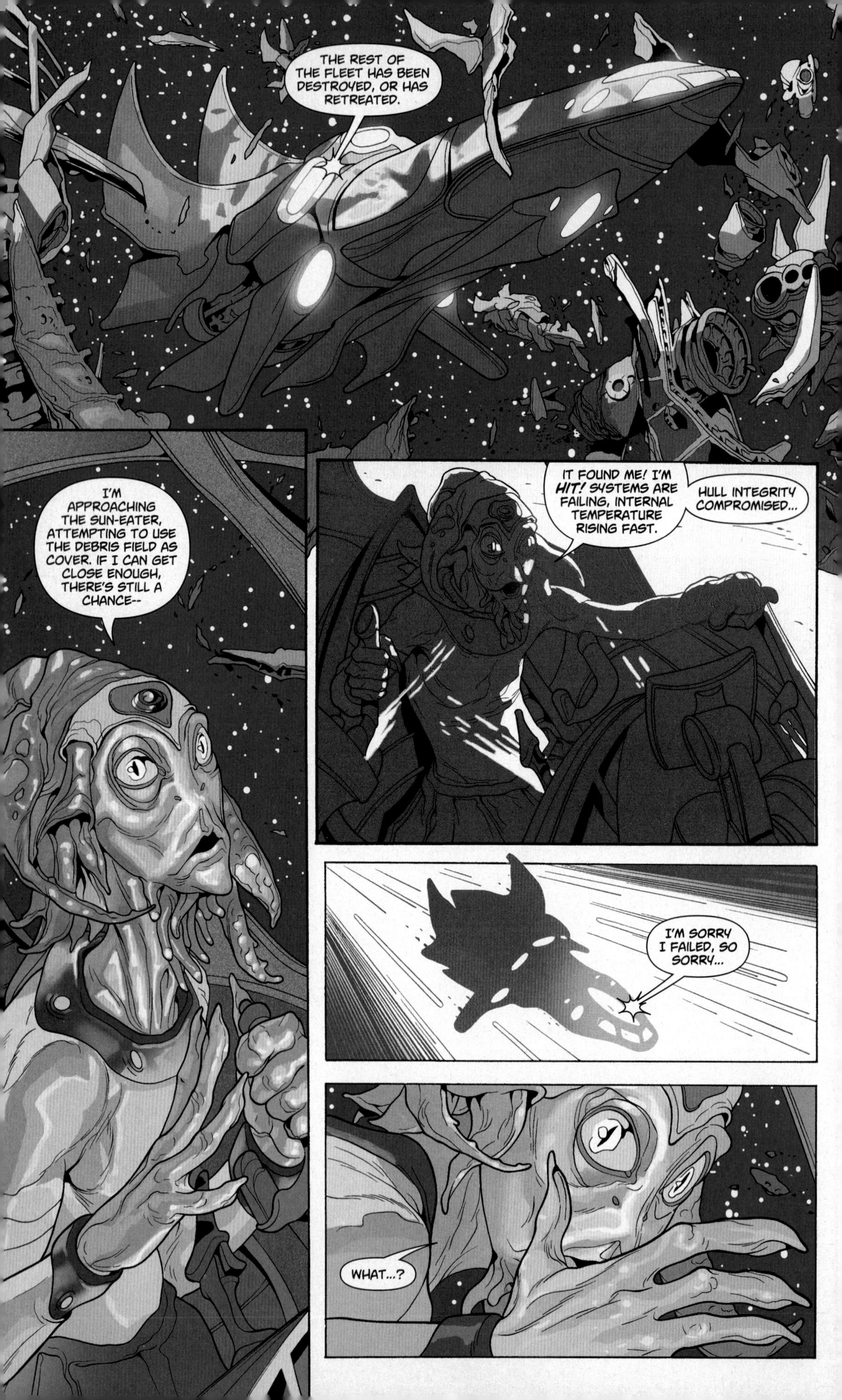
THE REST OF THE FLEET HAS BEEN DESTROYED, OR HAS RETREATED.
I'M APPROACHING THE SUN-EATER, ATTEMPTING TO USE THE DEBRIS FIELD AS COVER. IF I CAN GET CLOSE ENOUGH, THERE'S STILL A CHANCE--
IT FOUND ME! I'M *HIT!* SYSTEMS ARE FAILING, INTERNAL TEMPERATURE RISING FAST.
HULL INTEGRITY COMPROMISED...
I'M SORRY I FAILED, SO SORRY...
WHAT...?

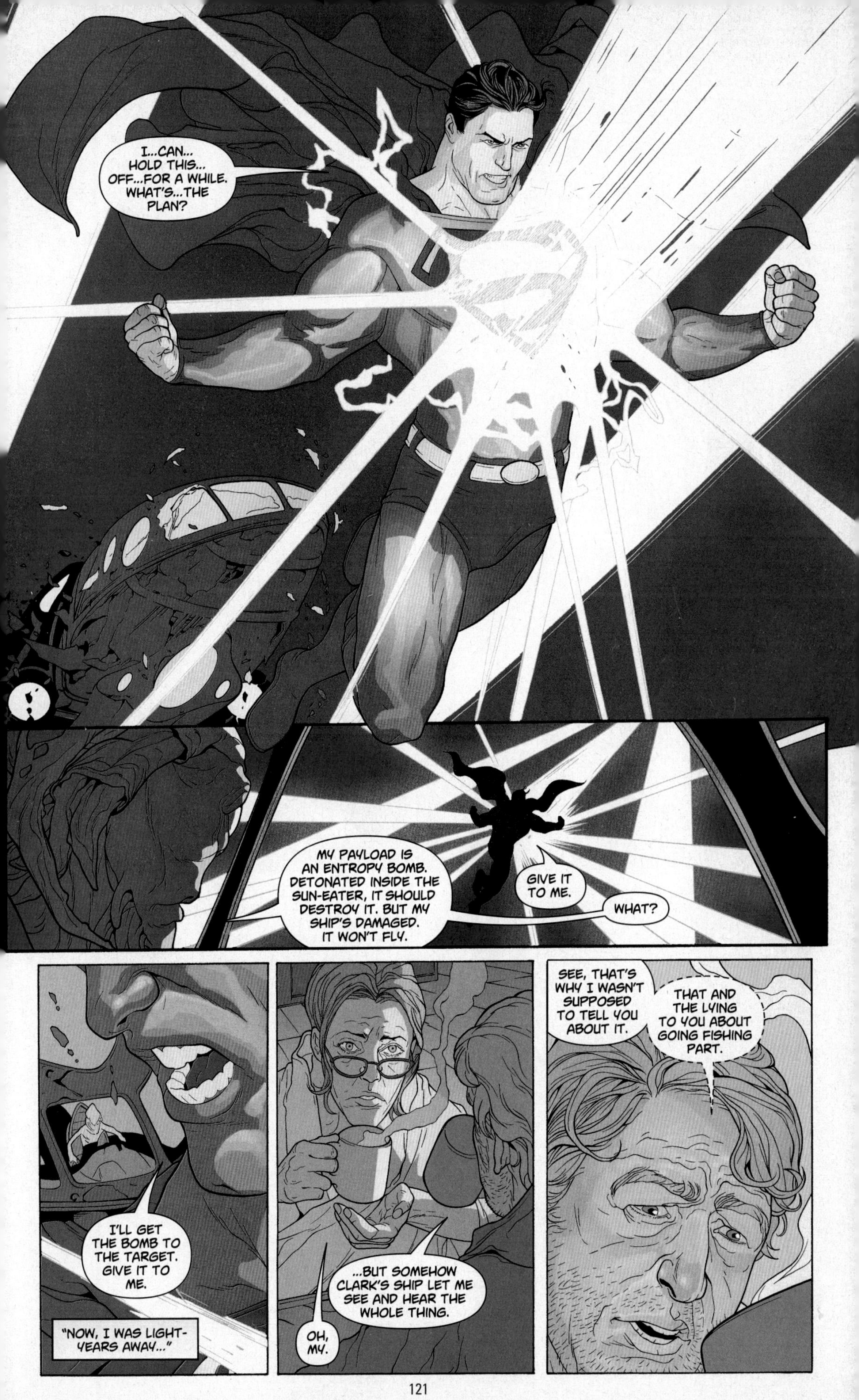
I...CAN... HOLD THIS... OFF...FOR A WHILE. WHAT'S...THE PLAN?
MY PAYLOAD IS AN ENTROPY BOMB. DETONATED INSIDE THE SUN-EATER, IT SHOULD DESTROY IT. BUT MY SHIP'S DAMAGED. IT WON'T FLY.
GIVE IT TO ME.
WHAT?
I'LL GET THE BOMB TO THE TARGET. GIVE IT TO ME.
"NOW, I WAS LIGHT-YEARS AWAY..."
...BUT SOMEHOW CLARK'S SHIP LET ME SEE AND HEAR THE WHOLE THING.
OH, MY.
SEE, THAT'S WHY I WASN'T SUPPOSED TO TELL YOU ABOUT IT.
THAT AND THE LYING TO YOU ABOUT GOING FISHING PART.

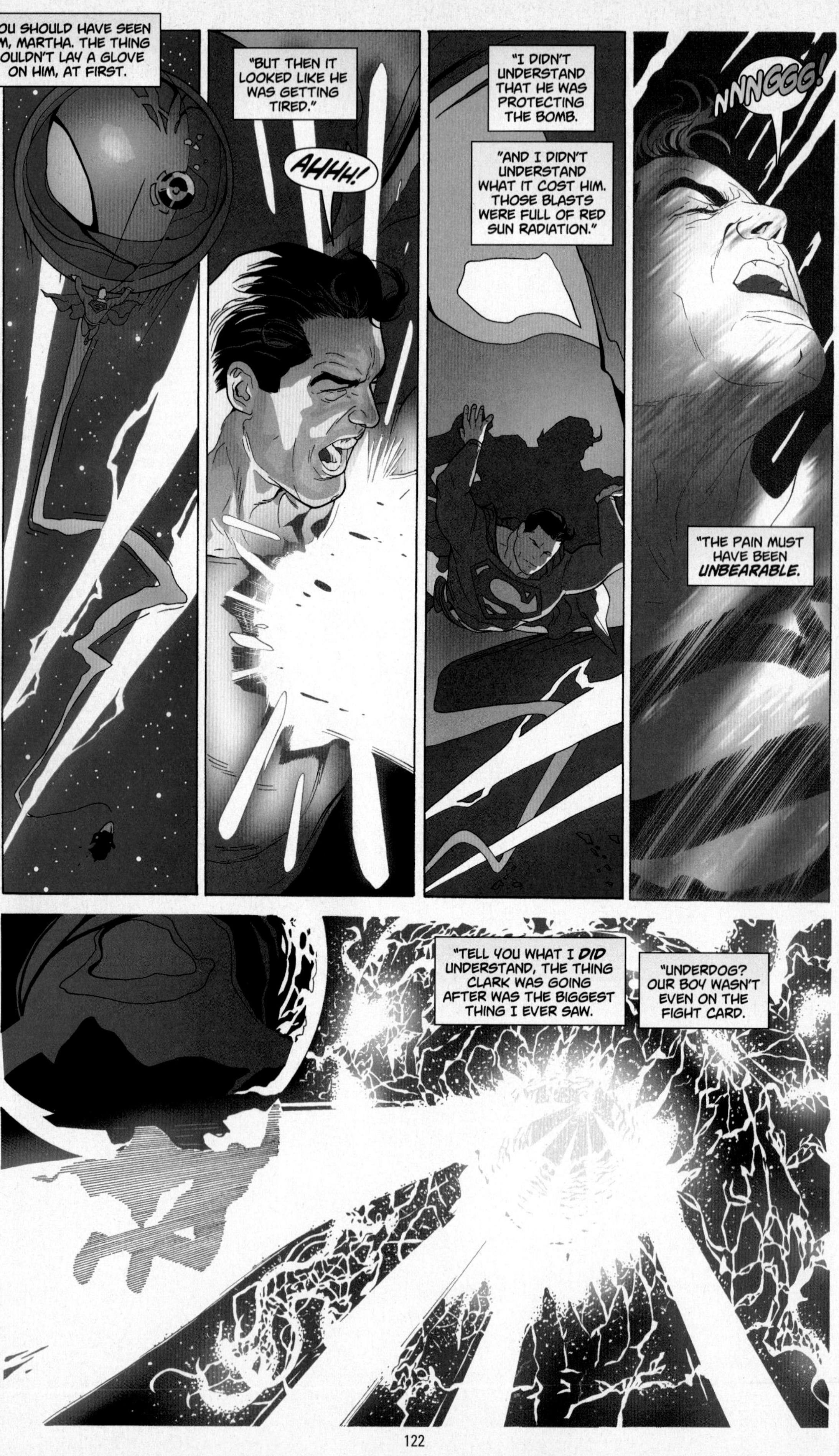
"YOU SHOULD HAVE SEEN HIM, MARTHA. THE THING COULDN'T LAY A GLOVE ON HIM, AT FIRST.
"BUT THEN IT LOOKED LIKE HE WAS GETTING TIRED."
AHHH!
"I DIDN'T UNDERSTAND THAT HE WAS PROTECTING THE BOMB.
"AND I DIDN'T UNDERSTAND WHAT IT COST HIM. THOSE BLASTS WERE FULL OF RED SUN RADIATION."
NNNGGG!
"THE PAIN MUST HAVE BEEN *UNBEARABLE*.
"TELL YOU WHAT I *DID* UNDERSTAND, THE THING CLARK WAS GOING AFTER WAS THE BIGGEST THING I EVER SAW.
"UNDERDOG? OUR BOY WASN'T EVEN ON THE FIGHT CARD.

"BUT SOMEHOW HE DID IT. HE GOT PAST THE RAY BEAMS AND INSIDE THAT THING.

"THE RADIATION INSIDE WAS HORRENDOUS. HIS POWERS WERE EVAPORATING LIKE MORNING DEW.

"BUT HE NEVER QUIT. HE PERSEVERED.

"THE EXPLOSION WAS ABOUT FIFTY TIMES THE SIZE OF KEPLER'S SUPERNOVA.

"THE ELECTROMAGNETIC SHOCK WAVE CAME RUSHING TOWARDS CLARK AT THE SPEED OF LIGHT.

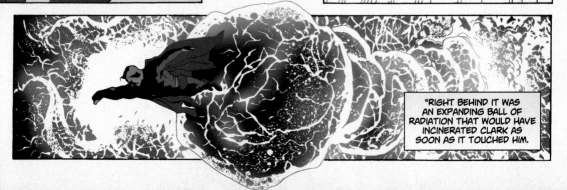

"RIGHT BEHIND IT WAS AN EXPANDING BALL OF RADIATION THAT WOULD HAVE INCINERATED CLARK AS SOON AS IT TOUCHED HIM.

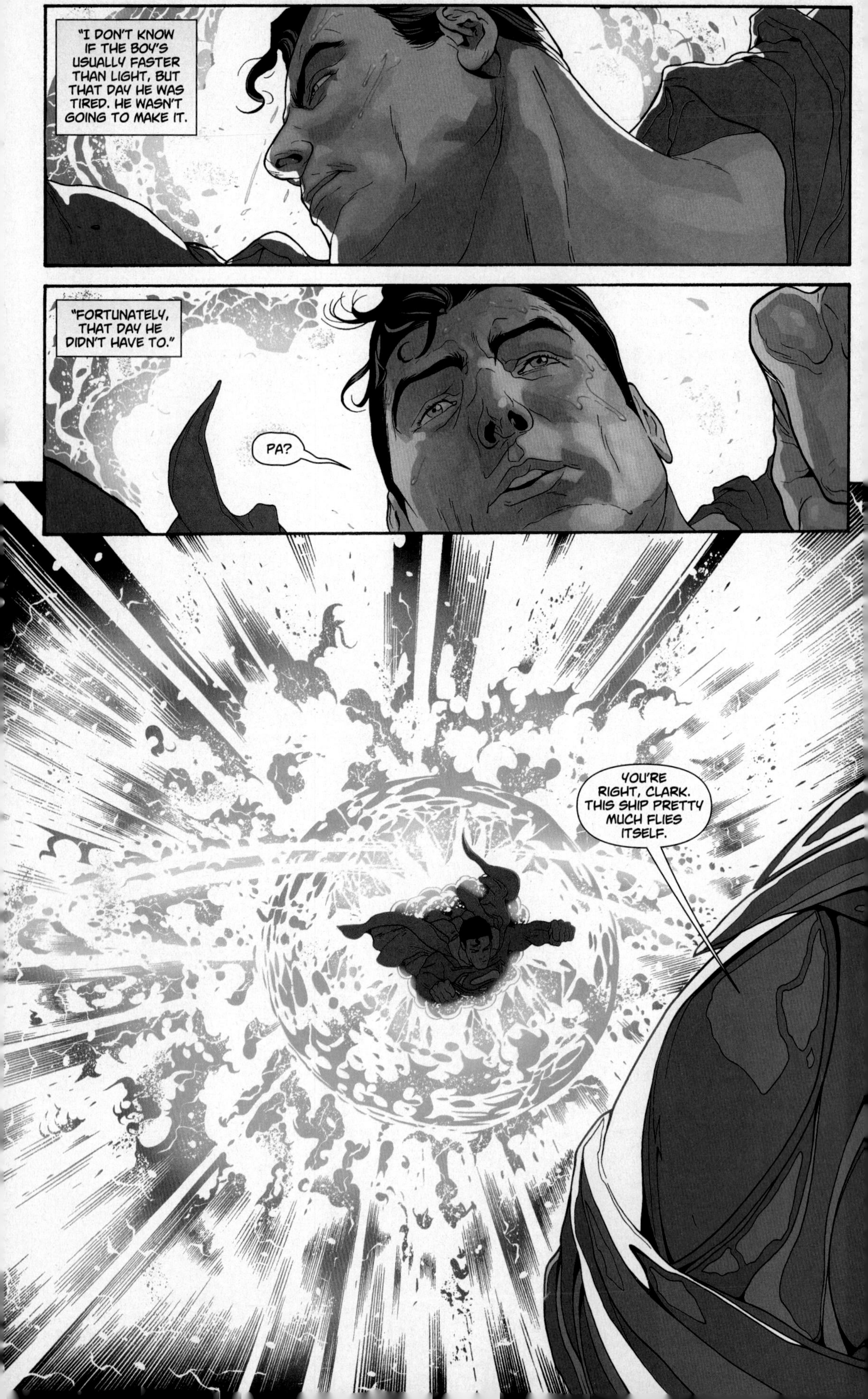
"I DON'T KNOW IF THE BOY'S USUALLY FASTER THAN LIGHT, BUT THAT DAY HE WAS TIRED. HE WASN'T GOING TO MAKE IT.
"FORTUNATELY, THAT DAY HE DIDN'T HAVE TO."
PA?
YOU'RE RIGHT, CLARK. THIS SHIP PRETTY MUCH FLIES ITSELF.

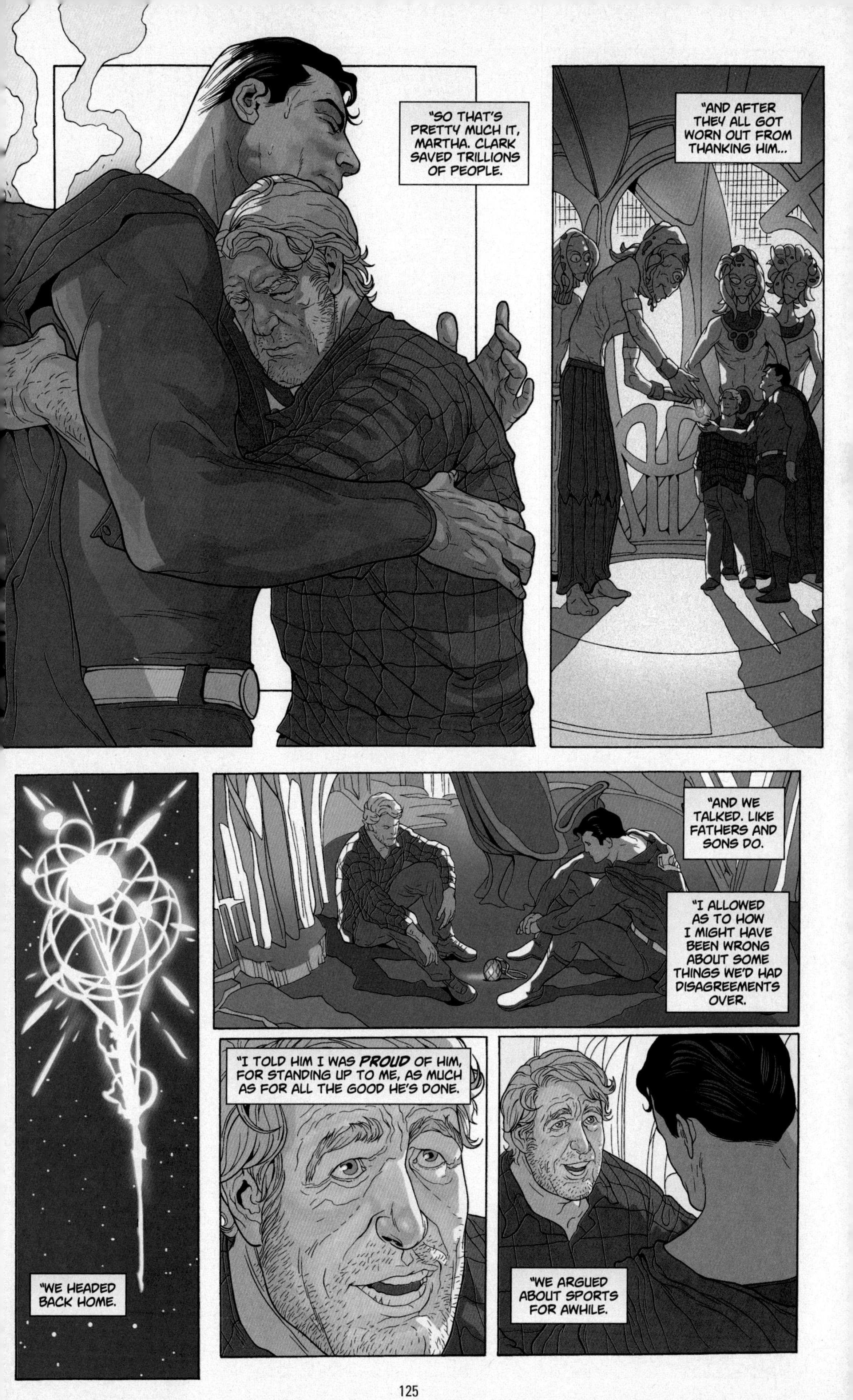
"SO THAT'S PRETTY MUCH IT, MARTHA. CLARK SAVED TRILLIONS OF PEOPLE.
"AND AFTER THEY ALL GOT WORN OUT FROM THANKING HIM...
"WE HEADED BACK HOME.
"AND WE TALKED. LIKE FATHERS AND SONS DO.
"I ALLOWED AS TO HOW I MIGHT HAVE BEEN WRONG ABOUT SOME THINGS WE'D HAD DISAGREEMENTS OVER.
"I TOLD HIM I WAS PROUD OF HIM, FOR STANDING UP TO ME, AS MUCH AS FOR ALL THE GOOD HE'S DONE.
"WE ARGUED ABOUT SPORTS FOR AWHILE.

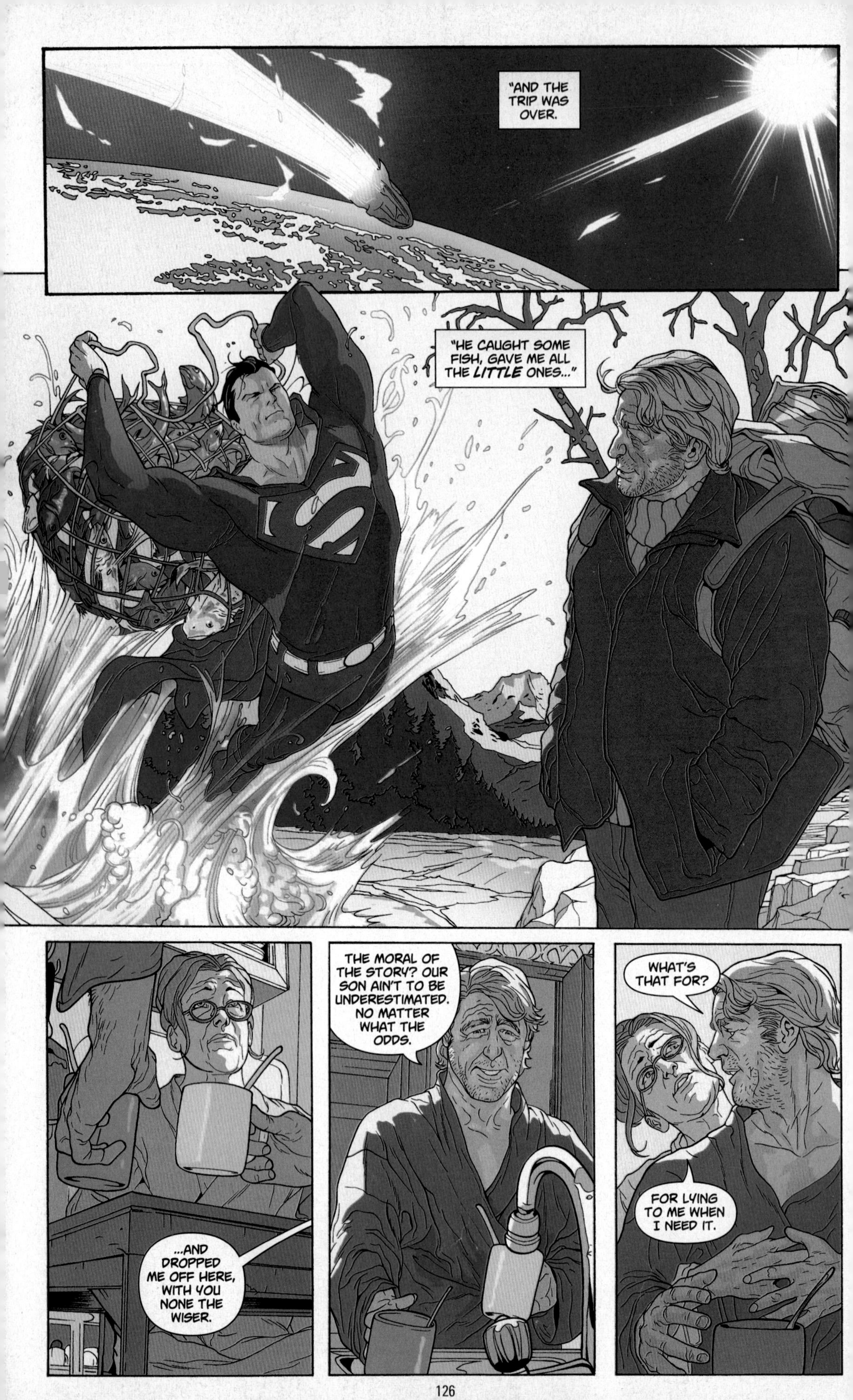
"AND THE TRIP WAS OVER.
"HE CAUGHT SOME FISH, GAVE ME ALL THE *LITTLE* ONES..."
...AND DROPPED ME OFF HERE, WITH YOU NONE THE WISER.
THE MORAL OF THE STORY? OUR SON AIN'T TO BE UNDERESTIMATED. NO MATTER WHAT THE ODDS.
WHAT'S THAT FOR?
FOR LYING TO ME WHEN I NEED IT.

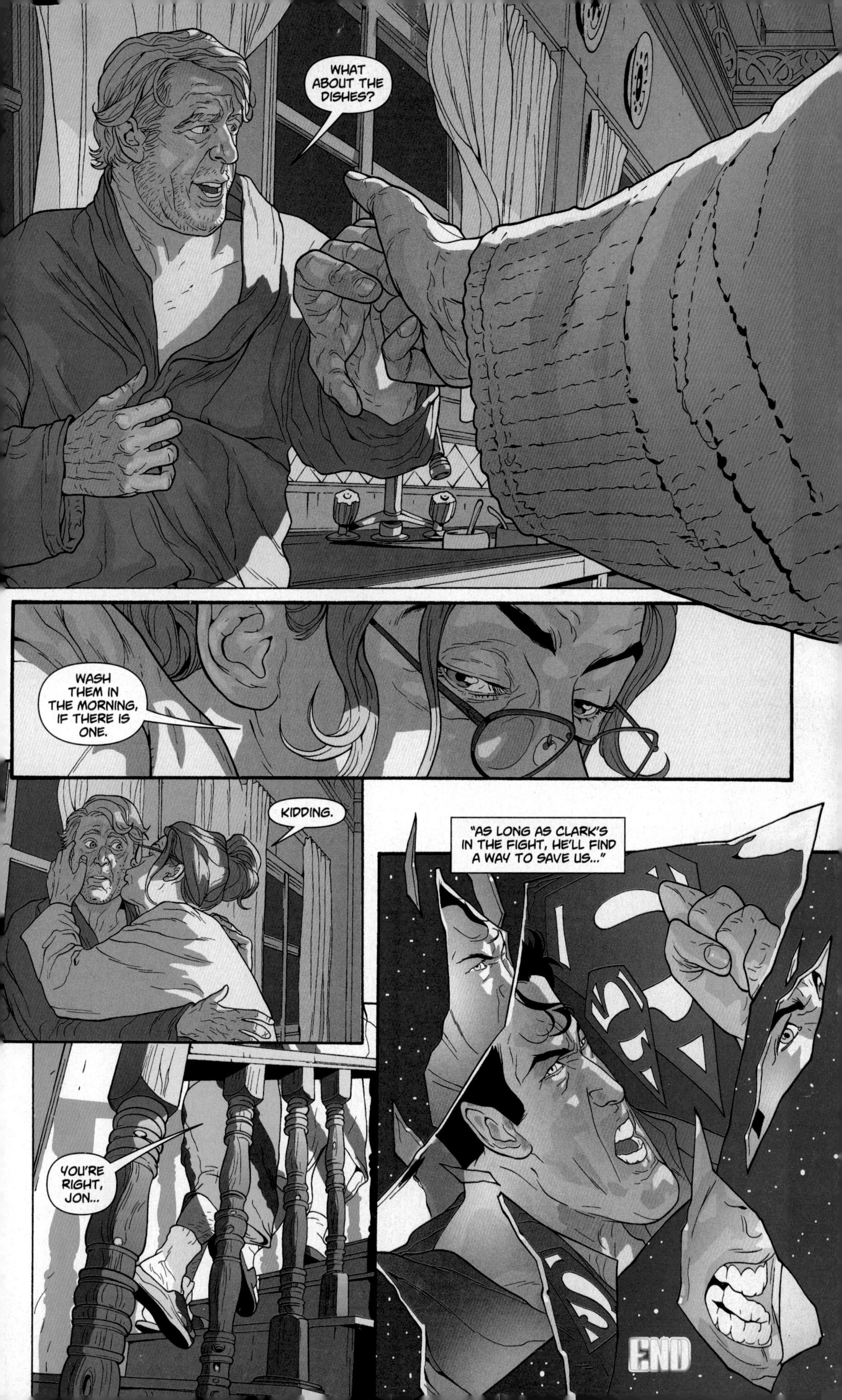
WHAT ABOUT THE DISHES?
WASH THEM IN THE MORNING, IF THERE IS ONE.
KIDDING.
YOU'RE RIGHT, JON...
"AS LONG AS CLARK'S IN THE FIGHT, HE'LL FIND A WAY TO SAVE US..."
END

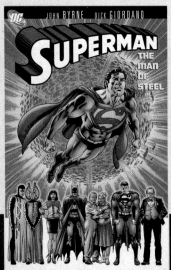